The Short Oxford History of the British Isles

General Editor: Paul Langford

The Eighteenth C

Edited by Paul Langford

The Short Oxford History of the British Isles

General Editor: Paul Langford

The Short Oxford History
of the British Isles

General Editor: Paul Langford

The Eighteenth Century

1688–1815

Edited by Paul Langford

OXFORD
UNIVERSITY PRESS

OXFORD
UNIVERSITY PRESS

Great Clarendon Street, Oxford OX2 6DP

Oxford University Press is a department of the University of Oxford.
It furthers the University's objective of excellence in research, scholarship,
and education by publishing worldwide in

Oxford New York

Auckland Bangkok Buenos Aires Cape Town Chennai
Dar es Salaam Delhi Hong Kong Istanbul Karachi Kolkata
Kuala Lumpur Madrid Melbourne Mexico City Mumbai Nairobi
São Paulo Shanghai Singapore Taipei Tokyo Toronto

with an associated company in Berlin

Oxford is a registered trade mark of Oxford University Press
in the UK and in certain other countries

Published in the United States
by Oxford University Press Inc., New York

British Library Cataloguing in Publication Data

Data available

Library of Congress Cataloging in Publication Data

Data applied for

ISBN 0–19–873131–0 (pbk)
ISBN 0–19–873132–9 (hbk)

10 9 8 7 6 5 4 3 2 1

Typeset in Minion
by RefineCatch Limited, Bungay, Suffolk
Printed in Great Britain by
T. J. International Ltd., Padstow, Cornwall

General Editor's Preface

It is a truism that historical writing is itself culturally determined, reflecting intellectual fashions, political preoccupations, and moral values at the time it is written. In the case of British history this has resulted in a great diversity of perspectives both on the content of what is narrated and the geopolitical framework in which it is placed. In recent times the process of redefinition has positively accelerated under the pressure of contemporary change. Some of it has come from within Britain during a period of recurrent racial tension in England and reviving nationalism in Scotland, Wales, and Northern Ireland. But much of it also comes from beyond. There has been a powerful surge of interest in the politics of national identity in response to the break-up of some of the world's great empires, both colonial and continental. The search for new sovereignties, not least in Europe itself, has contributed to a questioning of long-standing political boundaries. Such shifting of the tectonic plates of history is to be expected but for Britain especially, with what is perceived (not very accurately) to be a long period of relative stability lasting from the late seventeenth century to the mid-twentieth century, it has had a particular resonance.

Much controversy and still more confusion arise from the lack of clarity about the subject matter that figures in insular historiography. Historians of England are often accused of ignoring the history of Britain as a whole, while using the terms as if they are synonymous. Historians of Britain are similarly charged with taking Ireland's inclusion for granted without engaging directly with it. And for those who believe they are writing more specifically the history of Ireland, of Wales, or of Scotland, there is the unending tension between so-called metropolis and periphery, and the dilemmas offered by wider contexts, not only British and Irish but European and indeed extra-European. Some of these difficulties arise from the fluctuating fortunes and changing boundaries of the British state as organized from London. But even if the rulers of what is now called England had never taken an interest in dominion beyond its borders, the economic and cultural relationships between the various parts of the British Isles would still have generated many historiographical problems.

This series is based on the premise that whatever the complexities and ambiguities created by this state of affairs, it makes sense to offer an overview, conducted by leading scholars whose research is on the leading edge of their discipline. That overview extends to the whole of the British Isles. The expression is not uncontroversial, especially to many in Ireland, for whom the very word 'British' implies an unacceptable politics of dominion. Yet there is no other formulation that can encapsulate the shared experience of 'these islands', to use another term much employed in Ireland and increasingly heard in Britain, but rather unhelpful to other inhabitants of the planet.

In short we use the words 'British Isles' solely and simply as a geographical expression. No set agenda is implied. It would indeed be difficult to identify one that could stand scrutiny. What constitutes a concept such as 'British history' or 'four nations history', remains the subject of acute disagreement, and varies much depending on the period under discussion. The editors and contributors of this series have been asked only to convey the findings of the most authoritative scholarship, and to flavour them with their own interpretative originality and distinctiveness. In the process we hope to provide not only a stimulating digest of more than two thousand years of history, but also a sense of the intense vitality that continues to mark historical research into the past of all parts of Britain and Ireland.

Lincoln College   PAUL LANGFORD
Oxford

Contents

List of illustrations

List of contributors

PETER BORSAY is Professor of History at the University of Wales, Lampeter. His publications include *The English Urban Renaissance: Culture and Society in the Provincial Town, 1660–1770* (Oxford, 1989); *The Image of Georgian Bath 1700–2000: Towns, Heritage and History* (Oxford, 2000); as editor, *The Eighteenth-Century Town: A Reader in English Urban History, 1688–1820* (London, 1990); and as co-editor with Gunther Hirschfelder and Ruth-E. Mohrmann, *New Directions in Urban History* (Münster, 2000). He has recently published contributions to the *Cambridge Urban History of Britain*, ii (Cambridge, 2000), edited by Peter Clark, and the Oxford history of *The English Urban Landscape* (Oxford, 2000), edited by Philip Waller, and is currently preparing a history of leisure in Britain since 1500, and editing (with Lindsay Proudfoot) a volume of essays on towns in early modern England and Ireland.

MARTIN DAUNTON, FBA, has been Professor of Economic History in the University of Cambridge and Fellow of Churchill College since 1997; he was previously Astor Professor of British History at University College London. He has written a general survey of the period covered by this chapter, *Progress and Poverty: An Economic and Social History of Britain, 1700–1850* (Oxford, 1995) and is currently completing a companion volume on the period from 1850 to 1939. He edited, with Rick Halpern, *Empire and Others: British Encounters with Indigenous Peoples, 1600–1850* (London, 1999); he has recently published *Trusting Leviathan: The Politics of Taxation in Britain, 1799–1914* (Cambridge, 2001). He has published extensively in the fields of urban history, social policy, and labour relations in nineteenth- and twentieth-century Britain.

MICHAEL DUFFY is the Reader in British History, Head of History, and Director of the Centre for Maritime Historical Studies at the University of Exeter. His books include *The Englishman and the Foreigner* (Cambridge, 1986); *Soldiers, Sugar and Seapower* (Oxford, 1987); and *The Younger Pitt* (London, 2000). From 1991 to 2000 he was editor of *The Mariner's Mirror: The Journal of the Society for Nautical Research*. He has published extensively on British politics, diplomacy, and military and naval policy in the eighteenth and early nineteenth centuries.

DAVID HAYTON is Reader in Modern History in the Queen's University of Belfast, which he joined in 1994 after nearly twenty years on the staff of the History of Parliament Trust, whose volumes on *The House of Commons 1690–1715* will appear in 2002 under his editorship. He has also edited *The Parliamentary Diary of Sir Richard Cocks, 1698–1702* (Oxford, 1996); a volume of Defoe's writings on *Union with Scotland* (Edinburgh, 2000); and, most recently, *The Irish Parliament in the Eighteenth Century* (Edinburgh, 2001). He has published many articles and essays on politics and government in Britain and Ireland in the late seventeenth and early eighteenth centuries, and is co-editor of the journal *Irish Historical Studies*.

DAVID HEMPTON has been the Professor of Modern History in the Queen's University of Belfast since 1993. He is the author of *Methodism and Politics in British Society 1750–1850* (London, 1984); *Religion and Political Culture in Britain and Ireland* (Cambridge, 1996); *The Religion of the People* (London, 1996); and co-author with Myrtle Hill of *Evangelical Protestantism in Ulster Society 1740–1890* (London, 1992). He is a Fellow of the University Professors at Boston University where he is preparing books on the rise of American Methodism and the religious culture of New England. He has published extensively in the field of the social history of religion in Britain, Ireland, and the United States.

JOANNA INNES has been a fellow and tutor at Somerville College, Oxford since 1982. She has published numerous articles on eighteenth and early nineteenth-century social policy in England, some of them within a wider 'British Isles' or European perspective. She has co-edited with Hugh Cunningham, *Charity, Philanthropy and Reform: From the 1690s to 1850* (Basingstoke, 1998), and throughout the 1990s was co-editor of the journal *Past and Present*.

PAUL LANGFORD, FBA, is Rector of Lincoln College, Oxford and Professor of Modern History in the University of Oxford. His principal books are *The New Oxford History of England: A Polite and Commercial People: England 1727–1783* (Oxford, 1989); *Public Life and the Propertied Englishman 1689–1798* (Oxford, 1991); and *Englishness*

Identified: Manners and Character, 1650–1850 (2000). He is General Editor of *The Writings and Speeches of Edmund Burke* and has written extensively on eighteenth-century Britain.

Figure 1 Richard Newton's 'Flight of Scotchmen' of 1796 captures the anxieties of successive generations of Englishmen at the most visible effects of the Anglo-Scottish Union of 1707. In this as in many respects the imperial pride of Britons conflicted with the ethnic jealousy and xenophobia of many Englishmen.

Introduction: time and space

Paul Langford

Posterity and the eighteenth century

Time may be seamless but historians are of necessity snippers and stitchers as they tailor the past. Sometimes they impose their own patterns regardless of pre-existing fashionings. More often they rely on earlier cutters of the cloth. For the scope of this volume there was a considerable number of choices to draw on. There are various 'long' eighteenth centuries, starting in 1660 or 1688 and ending in 1815 or 1832. There are also 'short' eighteenth centuries, from 1702 or 1714 to 1783 or 1789 or 1793.

Regnal years tend to provide the starting, but not finishing points; monarchs mattered more in the sixteen and seventeen hundreds than they have since. Other dates are necessarily more arbitrary but not necessarily less useful. The century qua century is not often used to provide such historiographical 'bookends' though 1700 is close to the beginning of the War of Spanish Succession, and 1800 is close to the Peace of Amiens, both convenient stopping points in international politics and thereby significant in British history. Nonetheless, when it first became normal to characterize something called the eighteenth century, it was accepted more or less as it was defined by the calendar. Such characterizations began to be coined very soon after it ended. The point is not without interest. There was no precedent for treating any earlier hundred-year span in this way.

By the 1820s it had become common to attribute definable features to the age, usually in unflattering terms. So-called reformers were to the fore in this process, sometimes unaware of the extent to which they were perpetuating the ideals they supposedly despised. Their predecessors of the eighteenth century had attacked what they considered the 'new-fangled' corruption of managerial politics. Nineteenth-century reformers attacked the same thing as 'old corruption'. When the 1830s seemingly removed the logjam blocking long desired reforms this tendency was intensified. Each successive triumph of the liberal spirit represented the defeat not only of evil but of an entire century. The struggle of Whig against Tory in this way translated itself into a struggle over periodicity. There were ironies in this. For Whigs, condemning the eighteenth century meant renouncing those of their forebears who had erected that system which modern Whiggism found itself demolishing. For Tories, the defence of the eighteenth century meant defending a regime and a system which their forefathers had once bitterly resented. In each case, of course, it was late eighteenth-century reconfigurations that account for this shift but the convenience of summing up a whole century was such that whole generations of ancestors had to be cast off in this way.

Alongside this treatment of the recent past as England's *ancien régime* went another process. Increasingly, it became plausible to view the eighteenth century as a kind of amiable rogue among historical eras. Reformers of the political or moral kind might view it as fundamentally evil. But for many others it had a lovable eccentricity about it, perhaps too an engaging abandonment to its own hedonism that softened the tendency to condemnation. This version of the eighteenth century was particularly suited to pictorial representation, usually satirical. In one of the eighteenth century's most enduring creations, John Bull, some features continued to have a contemporary plausibility as types of conservatism. Others, such as Oxford dons, country squires, Regency roués, were less enduring but commonly recalled as instances of the politically incorrect eighteenth-century Englishman, rendering the historic memory of the period a kind of gigantic Rowlandson canvas, peopled by amusing 'characters'. Eighteenth-century manners could not be permitted to triumph over nineteenth-century proprieties, but they could be laughed at and even laughed with. This way of viewing an age did not constitute a coherent argument or imply an ideological position, though it did tend to assume that resurrecting such a world was at best impossible and at worst undesirable.

These two trends continued to be marked in the Victorian historiography, and indeed beyond. Both remain recognizable today, and not only at the level of caricature, despite the contrary tendencies of a great body of later scholarship. Easily the most innovative and influential twentieth-century analysis was that of Lewis Namier who brought a fresh perspective to bear as a foreigner who had certainly not been brought up either a little liberal or a little conservative. Namier did not so much provide new answers as ask new questions, treating the eighteenth century not as a battleground for competing ideologies but as a testing ground for a new kind of historical sociology. Parliament was not the theatre of party politics but the arena of individuals and family networks. Whig and Tory were mere names, connection, influence, and management the essence of the political system.

As the title of his initial, and devastating masterpiece, *The Structure of Politics at the Accession of George III* (published in 1929) implied, Namier inserted his historical sociologist's test tube in the mixture of eighteenth-century politics at a more or less fixed point, around 1760. As it happened, this was a time of unusual fluidity and instability. The residuum seemed to consist of little more than the naked self-interest of individuals and the cynical maneouvrings of the aristocratic factions which they composed. Unfortunately, the resulting conclusions work less well for other parts of the period. Nor is it clear that they are wholly convincing even in terms of Namier's own speciality. His ruthless reductionism led him to treat ideas as nothing but the expression of interest. In consequence he has been exposed to two powerful lines of attack. One makes him gratuitously negligent of the issues of principle which featured not only in the discourse of the day but in the minds and behaviour of many whom he studied. Another treats him as a latter-day Tory, in a long line of conservative outsiders for whom a seemingly insular tradition has a peculiar appeal. It is certainly true that the ideas he found most hypocritical were Whig ideas, and the ideologue to whom he took an almost personal dislike was Edmund Burke, the propounder of a Whig politics on whom Whig historians most relied. Moreover, the Tory politicians of the period he examined were effectively independent country gentlemen whose principal ambitions centred on the relatively anodyne politics of family and locality, precisely those whose mental world he portrayed with fidelity and perhaps even affection.

Even so, there is a sense in which the eighteenth century has never been 'un-Namierized'. Nor, considering the master's scholarly rigour and archival enterprise, could it be. Some of the outlying prejudices and underlying assumptions that informed his view of the party struggle have been abandoned, leaving room for renewed debate about the intellectual forces at work in parliamentary politics. But the central achievement, recasting the study of mainstream politics as a systematic analysis of the interests, motivations and aspirations of an entire class, remains unchallenged.

The new historiography

Since the heyday of the 'Namierites' in the 1950s, eighteenth-century history has moved on, and it is the resulting context that provides the historiographical base for much of the discussion in this volume.

'High' politics have featured less in the literature, partly because Namier's school dwelt so heavily on them, partly because historians have found other themes more engrossing. Alternative genres have proliferated. Popular politics and gender politics have both had numerous devotees, and continue to do so. There have also been many studies of local and regional politics. In the case of Scotland, Ireland, and Wales, and even some regions of England, these have uncovered much that previous generations had either ignored or relegated to the realms of historical romance. The study of these 'peripheral' polities has become an engrossing subject in its own right.

Beyond 'metropolis and periphery' alike, but in some ways encompassing the concerns of each, there is the matter of British and Irish engagements with a wider world. At one time the history of the British empire suffered something from the fate of the empire itself. In the 1960s and 1970s 'imperial history' tended to dissolve into con-stituent colonial or ex-colonial parts. In recent years there has been a greater readiness to recognize the importance of imperial policy in a broader sense, not least for its impact on the home countries them-selves. Britain's part in international relations in the traditional sense has suffered a more lasting occlusion. With some notable recent exceptions, historians of the eighteenth century have tended to neglect diplomatic history, even though interest in Britain as a belligerent state has by no means diminished.

Certain themes have driven research through territory sometimes ignored by earlier generations. The immense expansion of commerce, especially overseas commerce, has long been associated with the century that followed the explosive growth of the 1680s. But the social and cultural consequences have rarely been exposed with the zeal that has marked recent historiography. Diverse phenomena have thereby come into new prominence, including the rise of the professions and emergence of new codes of conduct, the development of novel forms of association and expression, the conscious reconfiguration of landscape and townscape, and the remodelling of much political and social theory. All kinds of business, social, and intellectual activity have been scrutinized and found to be influenced by the rampant consumerism that dominated so much of the discourse of the day as well as its economic forms.

Comparative studies placing Britain in a wider context have led to reassessments of its record in a number of fields. England used to feature hardly at all in accounts of the European Enlightenment, though Scotland certainly did. The Scottish contribution has been inspected in ever more detail. England's has been discovered for the first time, sometimes by re-examining strands of thought which were well known in their own right but which had not generally been related to those that existed on the continent. Latitudinarian theology, Real Whig political ideals, and much Rational Dissenting speculation have plausibly been drafted into this cause. But most compelling is the proliferation of all kinds of progressive thought, accessible through new media to new audiences, that suggests the desirability of fitting them into a broader context. Such expansive enquiries can, of course, be plausibly extended to Ireland and Wales, with due allowance for their distinctive cultural trajectories even in an era of growing influence from England in general and London in particular.

It might be supposed that linking the British political tradition with continental developments is less plausible. The evolution of a parliamentary system after 1688 is usually considered a marked divergence from the European pattern of absolute despotism.

Comparative surveys of Europe's nobilities have not succeeded in making the English gentry look very much like its counterparts abroad. On the other hand, a growing emphasis on the power of the British state makes possible some intriguing parallels. As a war-making agency, it more than matched the achievements of other, seemingly more centralized polities. The British system of deficit financing supported mainly by efficient indirect taxation enabled a relatively small country to concentrate its resources alternately and flexibly on military expansion and pacific prosperity. There has also been a notable tendency in recent years to draw together wider developments in the so-called 'public spheres' of Europe as a whole, especially where the development of the press and political associations are concerned. It would be saying a lot, however, to say that such comparisons have revealed more similarities than contrasts.

Some late twentieth-century trends in interpretation perhaps reflect the fashions of their day. In the questioning 1960s and 1970s, a flourishing school of social history identified the tensions created by a rapidly evolving capitalist society. Resulting narratives featured a cynical class of Whig power-mongers, a ferocious penal regime, the triumph of the market economy, an intolerant masculine hegemony, and much else to suggest social injustice and conflict. In the less rebellious 1980s and 1990s, these themes of repression and rebellion gave way to an emphasis on the complacency, conservatism, and loyalism that reigned in supposedly unprivileged as well as propertied society. In some instances victims have been transformed into victors. One of the most striking instances has been the work of revisionist Irish historians who have painted the period, at any rate before the 1790s, as one of relative prosperity and harmony. On the other hand, the same tendency has not been so manifest to the north of the Tweed. Jacobites and Highlanders continue to be treated with pity and a somewhat condescending romanticism as the long-suffering prey of mercenary Whigs both north and south of the border.

One of the most invigorating features of much modern scholarship has been the breaking down of the compartmental barriers that have stood in the way of an integrated and rounded cultural history of the period. The ancient canon beloved of literary historians has given way to more eclectic pursuit of texts and an emphasis on audience, readership, and social context as much as on authorial creativity. Historians of art have joined the rush to contextualize their canvases, prints, and artefacts. The new music history of the eighteenth century also devotes almost as much attention to those who consumed music as those who produced it. The thrust of this readiness to put art firmly in its social context has been to emphasize the unifying as well as innovating consequences of commercialization. If there has been a loss, it is not in terms of the scholarly rigour of cultural history but perhaps in awareness of the complexities of contemporary values. There remained many cultural backwaters, some of them influenced but not necessarily transformed by metropolitan fashions, some, particularly beyond or between the radial lines of communication that fanned out from London across the British Isles, firmly resistant to modernizing tendencies.

In all this reassessment, it is hard to find much that remains of the nineteenth century's deep contempt for the eighteenth. In matters of religion the results are as striking as anywhere. The Victorians were even more withering about the Georgian church than the Georgian state. No doubt their own spiritual climate made such uncompromising condemnation all the easier. In this at least the twentieth century brought a recognition of the challenges that faiths, established or not, must face in an age of mounting scepticism. Modern scholarship has done much to rescue the pastoral reputation and moral seriousness of the clergy and their lay supporters at all levels. This is not to say that attention has been concentrated on spiritual fervour for its own sake. Much of the recent writing about nonconformity, especially in its evangelical guises, has dwelt more on the sociology of dissenting religion than its devotional and pastoral features. The results have been illuminating and not only in England. The recognized importance of the Welsh revival, which preceded by many years the heroic age of industrial nonconformity, has had far-reaching consequences for the reinterpretation of Welsh history. Catholic history has long since ceased to be the domain of devotional sectarianism and increasingly figures in a more sensitive portrayal of the political and social influences that affected Catholic communities in England as well as Ireland.

It is not only long-standing views about religion that have been revisited. The eighteenth century ended, or the nineteenth century began, with two great revolutions, one rooted in Britain, the other deeply affecting it. Each has been the subject of intense debate and considerable revision. The industrial revolution, indeed, has been revised out of existence, with a great battery of statistical analysis employed to diminish the significance of economic growth between 1780 and 1820. This is so radically at odds with the contemporary understanding of the physical, social, and cultural effects of the new manufactures that it requires cautious treatment. What it properly reinforces, however, is the extent to which economic change had occurred in the century (and more) before the 1780s. The political and ideological consequences of the French Revolution in Britain also continue to be hotly debated. In recent years there has been much emphasis on the ways that it reinforced a variety of identities: church and king loyalism, patriotic Britishness, male authoritarianism. On the other hand, the unifying effects of the turmoil of the 1790s can be overdone. In Ireland the hardening of the Protestant Ascendancy and the rise of republican nationalism opened fissures in Irish society which a few years before had appeared to be closing. The Rebellion of 1798 and its bloody aftermath made the union of Britain and Ireland in 1800 by no means a unifying event. In England, Scotland, and Wales there continued a radical tradition which to some extent divided all classes of society and kept alive fears of a republican revolution to match those of the continent.

This mass of historical research and revision is far from cohesive, let alone conclusive. But one line of argument that does unite it is the assumption that the eighteenth century was nothing if not an age of change. Contrasts between the 'reform', 'improvement', and 'transformation' of the nineteenth century and the 'torpor', 'obscurantism', and 'stability' of the eighteenth make nonsense against this background. Even so, it has had less impact on nineteenth-century historians than might have been anticipated, partly perhaps because they do not always read very widely about the eighteenth century, partly because it is convenient in interpreting the changes of the later period to set them against a relatively static earlier one. There remains for many the sense that there was logically some decisive date, 1789, 1800, 1815, 1830, be what it may, at which one world vanished and another, or others, took its place.

Contemporary perspectives: outsiders

Not only is this at odds with what most modern historians of eighteenth-century Britain have argued, it also diverges from much contemporary opinion. Foreign observers of eighteenth-century Britain, who might be thought to be relatively impartial in such matters, generally considered it dynamic and progressive in ways which had implications far beyond the shores of Britain. As the site of an impressive modernity, it had numerous features that occur and recur in the pages that follow, and which also chime with much of the recent historiography rather than the older characterizations of the period. They fall broadly into three categories.

One had to do with the political developments that followed the Revolution of 1688, which deprived not only England and Wales, but also Scotland and Ireland of their hereditary rulers and plunged the islands into strife at home and war abroad. This initially looked like another manifestation of the English capacity for self-destructive lawlessness. But the system that gradually emerged under Walpole came to provide a form of mild but effective government that was much admired by continental visitors for its apparently reassuring combination of monarchical and republican politics. A nation once considered barbarous for its political instability was in the process of acquiring an enviable reputation for mature self-governance.

Simplistic judgements of this kind took little account of the price that was paid for this apparent equilibrium, or of the underlying strains that it concealed. Even so, the management systems that emerged in London, Edinburgh, and Dublin, linked by the network of Whig interests, did achieve a measure of stability, did surmount a prolonged challenge from the dynasty that had been ejected in 1689 and did underpin an impressive re-establishment of British prestige and power, culminating in the humiliation of the Bourbon powers in the Seven Years War. Even later, when the loss of America, and the challenge of the French Revolution, posed new threats to Britain's reputation for effortless supremacy, the resilience of its parliamentary monarchy nonetheless continued to impress.

A second theme of the Anglomaniacs was Britain's status as the outstanding example of a relentlessly entrepreneurial society. Not only did this result in spectacular inroads into the markets of the world, it helped sustain the growing colonial empire that British arms established. Britons became the obvious successors of the Dutch as the traders of the world, but on a scale that far surpassed anything that they had achieved. Nor was pre-eminence in a global economy the only benefit. Foreigners were also impressed by something which seemed unique to Britain: an aristocracy that joined enthusiastically in the making of money and in the process engaged with lowlier men and manners than would have been conceivable for continental nobilities. The resulting accessibility and openness of English society seemed to offer a new template for application elsewhere. In time, when commercialism led to industrialization, the sense of a nation inventing wholly new modes of economic growth and social development (whether it was really progress was more debatable) grew still more marked. And not least there were the cultural values and sensibilities generated by a new political nation of relatively small property-owners who depended on trade or a profession for their wealth. To emulate a nation of shopkeepers was not an attractive prospect for all foreigners, but many had an uncomfortable awareness that future success and perhaps even survival depended upon it.

A third and final cause for congratulation was rooted in foreign, especially French, respect for the apparently innovative character of British thought. On this view Newton and Locke provided the twin pillars of modern thinking and indeed of what came to be called the Enlightenment. The aptly named literary warfare of Ancients and Moderns at the turn of the seventeenth and eighteenth centuries also contributed to somewhat exaggerated continental notions of the freethinking tendencies of the British. Voltaire's celebrated characterization of a nation that encouraged constructive dissent, promoted intellectual innovation, and rewarded talent with power and wealth was a generous assessment but one that remained influential long after his lifetime. The standard portrayal was of an open, tolerant, and forward-looking society that provided a model for the continental reformers right up to the eve of the French Revolution.

Contemporary perspectives: insiders

Among the insiders who inhabited the British Isles, matters were naturally much more complicated. For many self-judgement was in terms of the patriotic benchmarking that was central to so much of the public debate of the period. Even in this relatively straightforward respect the fortunes of peace and war made for conflicting assessments. There were high points such as the battle of Blenheim in 1704, when British leadership humbled the military power of Louis XIV's France, or the Peace of Paris in 1763, when imperial supremacy seemed assured. There were also low points. In 1745 an entire nation quaked before the advance of a troop of Scottish Highlanders that would have aroused derision rather than fear from one of the great continental powers. In 1783 the humiliating loss of the American colonies made Britain's rise seem as comet-like in its waning as in its waxing. And in 1797 the twin horrors of naval mutiny and national insolvency confronted the public with the ultimate threats to national self-respect. The debilitating wars of survival that continued until 1815 did eventually confirm the patriotic self-esteem of Britons. They did not at the time, however, lend credence to a vision of manifest destiny conducting Britannia unrivalled to the leading place among nations.

Nor was there much agreement on the vision of greatness that would have suited national aspirations. Within England alone there were divergent strands of ambition. Before 'Little England' became a political slogan, there was a strong tradition that rejoiced in its substance. In the many and major wars during this period, there were differences between those who took an isolationist stance towards continental Europe and those who regarded British security as dependent on an active part in maintaining the balance of power. Even where overseas expansion was concerned, there were tensions between those for whom territorial annexation was anathema and those for whom commercial enterprise without a colonial empire was fantasy. As for the nation in which all these ambitions were centred, what was it? Most inhabitants of England assumed that it was a kind of Greater England rather than Great Britain. Symbols and signals of Britishness were cheerfully appropriated without much recognition of the equal status of other inhabitants of the British Isles, or even their corporate interests. There were, of course, many in Wales, Scotland, and Ireland who for reasons of material advantage found it convenient to go along with this somewhat one-sided version of national identity. But there were many who did not. The question of the succession was effectively settled by the 1750s but especially in Scotland and Ireland the divisions that marked region, religion, and tribal allegiance continued to make for a highly contested loyalty.

The English were notorious for their arrogance and xenophobia, reflected in their strident propaganda both in peacetime and war-time, the surges of popular sentiment that found targets internal as well as external, and the unpleasant encounters on the streets of London that dismayed so many visitors. Yet triumphalism was not self-evidently the only or even principal mood of the English psyche. Self-deprecation, even self-flagellation, featured just as much in con-temporary discourse, especially when Protestant doctrine, accentu-ated by successive waves of evangelical fervour, took command. The propensity of the English to see themselves as a chosen people was often noted by outsiders. With it there went the less comforting sense of living perpetually under the threat of divine displeasure. Each war, successful or otherwise, was marked by annual 'fasts' or services, held in every church throughout the land, collectively confessing the people's sins and pleading for the Almighty's forgiveness and aid. At times of disaster, such as the loss of Minorca in 1756 and the sur-render at Yorktown in 1781, the nation publicly invited itself to wallow in self-pity. At times of triumph there was usually a grim appreciation of the dangers of tempting Providence.

The rationality that Anglophile observers attributed to the British was not always evident to Britons themselves. Surges of fashionable liberalism such as latitudinarian complacency in the early part of the century and humanitarian sentimentalism in the later part of it drew the fire of much satirical scepticism. Supposedly enlightened attitudes frequently advanced beyond what was tolerable to the unenlightened. At unpredictable intervals superstitions that the polite classes preferred to forget had a disconcerting way of reviving. The near-hysteria that followed a much reported prophecy of the end of the world in 1750 reminded propertied opinion how slender was its hold on public attitudes at large. Hostile reactions to the introduction of the modernizing Gregorian calendar two years after also seemed to demonstrate the limits of rationality below a certain social level. Thirty years later the Gordon Riots of 1780, when popular anti-popery threatened to lay waste London itself, brutally revealed the gulf between the fashionable tolerance of the elite and the entrenched bigotry of its inferiors. Growing faith in the notion of progress is rightly seen as characteristic of much eighteenth-century thought and argument. But it always battled with an older pessimism and frequently suffered humiliating reverses.

Some patriotic themes ran fairly consistently through the public discourse of the period. They often chimed conveniently with the requirements of the post-1688 state as it strengthened its hold on diverse political systems and expanded the influence of Britain beyond British shores. Much the most significant of these was the faith in commerce and commercial growth that worked so effectively at many levels of society to unite private aspirations and public goals. Trade was an eighteenth-century icon, uniting otherwise diverse interests. Whigs praised it to the skies and even the most dyed-in-the-wool Tory squires could not but pay lip service to it. It provided thinkers and writers with a topic of inexhaustible interest. Even those who feared its corrosive effects on private and public morality found themselves having to concede its associated virtues as well as vices. It was indissolubly joined with favourite British values, especially that political liberty for which the English were famous. Liberty and commerce were conventionally twinned in emblematic representations of Britain, the fact that they were often at odds with each other being conveniently forgotten much of the time. Trade brought together the different parts of the three kingdoms far more effectively than anything else could have. It was for trade that the Scots sacrificed their precious parliament in 1707. It was for trade that the Irish made their determined stand against George III's governments in the 1770s, and it was trade that benefited most by union of Britain and Ireland in 1800, though the Irish who negotiated it feared complete immersion in the imperial system and there remained limits on the equalization of duties that it imposed.

Pride in Britain's prowess as the world's leading commercial power at a time when commerce was coming to be seen as the defining mark of modernity was painless when it could be used against French, Spanish, and Dutch rivals. Matters were more complicated when its domestic implications were considered. High society had a reputation for being relatively accessible by continental standards but those directly involved in money-making activities, whether trade, manufacturing, or even the professions suffered from the application of a double standard, being lauded for the boons they conferred on the nation but, in some cases at least, derided for their low origins and manners. There were admittedly exceptions. Merchants in overseas trade, the great bankers, and to some extent the large agricultural capitalists—'gentleman farmers', were on the whole acceptable in genteel society. The same was true of the upper echelons of the law, the church, and the armed forces. Medical practitioners started the century below the salt but in the case of fashionable physicians moved up the table in due course. But provincial merchants and manufacturers found it hard to gain acceptance at all, at any rate before the last decades of the century when there emerged a small and unquestionably super-rich class of industrialists, the Wedgwoods, Boultons, and Arkwrights. Ordinary tradesmen and shopkeepers were unlikely to break through even to the levels of polite society that might be hard to distinguish from them in point of wealth. If anything the economic expansion of the period 1780–1815 made matters worse in this respect as the multiplication of small producers and traders seemed to provide an increased threat to traditional notions of a hierarchical society.

The political consequences of such distinctions were less damaging than they might have been. Men and women of small property tended to be more concerned about the distance separating them from their inferiors than their superiors. These people were just as likely to be supporters of the status quo as critics or rebels. Even so, the most threatening protest movements of the period, such as the Wilkesites in the 1760s, and the radical reformers of the 1790s, depended heavily on this class. It was the class which could have brought about an English Revolution to match the French. The fact that it eventually settled for patriotic loyalism could not be taken for granted. In some places, indeed, it was disinclined to settle for loyalism at all, especially where sectarian discrimination reinforced social snobbery. Protestant dissent of the non-evangelical kind contributed to a perpetual undertow of alienation in the industrial cities of England and, against a somewhat different historical background, in Northern Ireland. Such uncertainties belied the assumption that commercial growth, political harmony, and social ease went naturally together.

There were other tensions that clouded the optimism of the period. Foreigners generally considered that the English lower classes enjoyed a well-being that far exceeded anything their counterparts on the continent could possess. But there was an increasing awareness of the contrast with the peasantries of other parts of the British Isles, especially in Ireland, north and west Wales, and the Highlands of Scotland. This was especially marked in Ireland, where population grew rapidly but where urbanization lagged far behind Britain as a whole. There was also a growing appreciation from the 1770s and 1780s that some of the newer features of the later eighteenth-century economy were highly disruptive. New mining and manufacturing industries generated unregulated and even lawless communities which brought all kinds of social and moral problems to the fore. The mechanization and specialization that marked new employment practices threatened not only the health and well-being of those employed but conventional assumptions about the family's life and economy. Population growth and concentration made cyclical slumps and harvest failures increasingly difficult to mediate or relieve.

Doubts about the sustainability of the economic miracle of industrial revolution were rife long before the crises of the 1830s and 1840s. They are witnessed not least in changing appreciations of the urban growth which was one of the eighteenth century's most obvious features. In mid-century the expansion of towns and cities that benefited by the emergence of an Atlantic economy, London itself, the West Coast ports of Bristol, Liverpool, Whitehaven, and Glasgow, the centres on which developing industries were concentrated, Manchester, Birmingham, Leeds, and Sheffield, was greeted with considerable complacency. By the last quarter of the century there was more emphasis on the problems that such places created. Recognition that urban populations needed new forms of governance as well as new kinds of town planning and social welfare was dawning even if agreed solutions lay in the future.

English propertied opinion itself was in any case far from self-congratulatory in this respect. In no part of the period could it be said that it took a complacent view of that other unpropertied nation which it might exploit, patronize, employ, or even improve, but which it could never take for granted. Relatively few people of substance spent their lives wholly or even primarily in the country-side, and even when they did they were unlikely to view it as the bucolic bliss that figured in the wishing thinking of the poet and the wishful artistry of the landscape painter. Famine was very rare indeed but food shortages were recurrent and always alarming, even during the relatively stable period of good harvests between 1730 and 1750. The social disruption caused by agricultural enclosure and deregula-tion of the grain trade thereafter added further cause for anxiety. Increasing national productivity invariably created losers as well as winners. Sometimes the losers might be entire communities or classes. The process was by no means concentrated in England. By the 1770s and 1780s there was growing concern about the effects of agri-cultural improvement in the Scottish Highlands. Some sentimentally lamented the dislocation of the clan system, threatened not only by the legal and political changes imposed in the aftermath of the Forty-Five, but also by the rapidity with which clan chieftains seemed to be converting themselves from leaders of a people to exploiters of a land. The 'clearances' which commenced towards the end of this period formed part of a pattern that stretched back to the union itself.

In the urban or semi-urban surroundings where so much new wealth was being created and spent, social relations were viewed with still more concern. In the early eighteenth century, when employment was high, population growth slight, and food prices low, much of the attention devoted to the poor was designed to curb their so-called extravagance, especially when it resulted in the destructive gin craze of the 1730s and 1740s. Much too was devoted to improving the dis-cipline and dependability of the workforce, either by ensuring a strict and useful education for the young, or by reforming the morals and manners of the not so young. The Anglican Church, both in England and Ireland, lent institutional weight as well as eloquence to this cause, but it was equally a preoccupation of others, including Methodists and other promoters of evangelical revival as well as self-appointed state economists. By the 1750s, as climatic conditions ceased favouring cereal cultivation and population growth acceler-ated, there was increasing emphasis on the manifold problems cre-ated by an ever larger underclass. Even the most unconcerned and materially-minded worried about the effect of poor rates on their own pockets. The potential political threat posed by a populace trad-itionally attuned to the assertion of its rights and now exposed to seductive new theories of rights added to the strain. By the time Malthus published his disturbing analysis of the dire logic of demographic change in 1798 pessimism about the course of social development was hardly a new phenomenon.

What was novel was a sense that whatever was happening in Britain and Ireland by the time of the Napoleonic Wars was itself new in ways that had implications far beyond the British Isles in space and also beyond the turn of the eighteenth and nineteenth centuries in time. Whether it was for good or ill was naturally debatable. But the notion that a small group of islands off the western shores of Europe had a significant, even defining influence on the future of the world was something that had grown among both insiders and outsiders throughout the previous century so that by the early 1800s it seemed incontestable. Nobody would have said in 1688 as Talleyrand did in 1806 that 'if the English Constitution is destroyed, understand clearly that the civilization of the world will be shaken to its very foundations'.[1]

Insular unities

Construed narrowly, what Talleyrand called the 'English Constitution' might appear to have been but a small portion of the moving picture that makes up the history of more than a century. But like most foreigners and many Englishmen, Talleyrand did not distinguish readily between 'English' and 'British'. Nor did he mean to imply that their contribution to the story of Western civilization was restricted to matters strictly constitutional. It was the belief of many such as he that British achievements in the broadest sense, economic, cultural, and social, were part of what was essentially a political framework. Montesquieu had taught that law and government held the key to understanding the characteristics and prospects of individual societies. In the case of the British Isles the nature of the 'constitution' was particularly important in understanding the eighteenth century. This was true not only because the political

---

[1] *Memoirs of Madame de Rémusat, 1802–1808*, ed. Paul de Rémusat (2 vols.; London, 1880), ii. 160.

developments that began in England in 1688 created a new kind of polity. It was all the more true because that polity expanded to embrace the whole of the British Isles, in effect enabling its inhabitants to see themselves as more than the sum of its parts.

Throughout the period the British Isles were for some political purposes a unit, though it contained many people who preferred not to think of it in that way and many others who did their best to prevent it being so. What bound them was the English monarchy, which by conquest included the so-called principality of Wales and the kingdom of Ireland. By hereditary accident it also included, following the accession of James VI of Scotland to the throne of England in 1603, the kingdom of Scotland. The Revolution of 1688 might easily have dissolved these bonds. That it did not do so was due to war. In Scotland a brief but bloody contest between the followers of William III and James II ensured the triumph of the Protestant crown north of the border on terms similar to those south. In Ireland a longer but still bloodier conflict produced much the same outcome.

The succession was contested for another fifty-five years and throughout that period it would have been possible to envisage the break-up of the three kingdoms. In practice that was unlikely. Successive Jacobite Pretenders paid lip service to the separatist ambitions of some of their supporters but they too aspired to the throne of Great Britain and Ireland as a whole. Charles Edward publicly abrogated the union in 1745 but this was the politics of gesture, and a desperate one at that. So far as Scotland was concerned the union of the crowns was made permanent and reinforced by the union of parliaments through the Act of Union in 1707. In the case of Ireland there was a readiness to argue, especially with the rise of Irish patriotism in the late eighteenth century, that the Irish and English crowns were distinct entities, implying different duties, responsibilities, and loyalties in each kingdom. In practice the fact that the king of England depended on English advisers whether or not he was governing England or Ireland made the distinction somewhat theoretical. It was in any case formally abandoned when the Irish Act of Union took effect in 1801, unifying not only the kingdoms but their legislatures.

Wales had been incorporated in the realm of England long before these parliamentary unions and functioned as an established part of the machinery of government and the workings of parliament. This did not imply that its loyalty could be taken for granted. The Jacobite cause was an appealing one to many Welsh gentry. Moreover Wales had some distinctive judicial and executive institutions with which ministers in London meddled at their peril. But too much can be made of such idiosyncrasies. England itself could hardly be described as a unitary state. The broadly uniform system of parliamentary representation belied the administrative complexities inherited by the Hanoverian monarchy from its predecessors. Edmund Burke remarked that English government resembled a pentarchy in the variety of its separate chains of authority: depending on locality the sovereign figured as King of England, Duke of Cornwall, Duke of Lancaster, Earl of Chester, and Prince of Wales.[2] In any case the regional identities and traditions of England remained very strong, not least in the minds of ministers whose own personal power bases were usually built in the localities. The ambiguity of the word 'country', which signified county or region as readily as the nation as a whole was revealing in this respect.

While the succession remained at issue, during the first half of the period, support for the Hanoverian monarchy had to be thought of as a patchwork of interests and sympathies spread across Britain and Ireland as a whole, interwoven with an equally dispersed pattern of antipathies. One tempting way of picturing the result is to view Whiggism as a kind of metropolitan magnet that represented the interests of the merchants and financiers of London and the magnates of the English heartland. Away from the political centre of the unified kingdoms the magnet lost its force and permitted less loyal elements to flourish. Yet this is not a very helpful way of surveying the political geography of the period. Alienated Tories were numerous in all the major cities and every county of England, regardless of region. In East Anglia, the historic home of a Puritan, Whig tradition that embraced the somewhat unlikely pairing of Oliver Cromwell and Robert Walpole, the Tory gentry contested control of the region throughout the first half of the eighteenth century. In great cities, such as Bristol and London itself, substantial bodies of Tory merchants unsettled successive governments at national as well as municipal level by exploiting the prejudices of an unpredictably mutinous populace. Local factors complicated identities and made

[2] *Writings and Speeches of Edmund Burke*, iii, ed. W. M. Elofson and John A. Woods (Oxford, 1996), p. 497.

remoteness from the centre an unreliable guide to political complexion. In Cumbria and North Wales Whigs were well aware that Hanoverian rule would evaporate overnight in the event of a plausible Jacobite challenge. But in equally distant Northumberland, Pembrokeshire, and Cornwall, Whiggism was a thriving force sustained by both tradition and interest.

Scotland had its own political force fields that not only separated Lowlands from Highlands but rendered generalizations about either insecure. The Irish mix was rendered still more complex by a long history of division and strife that reflected waves of immigration more recent than Scotland had experienced. But in both Scotland and Ireland, there were pockets of intense loyalism, in terms both of geography and class, that were considerably more reliable than what was to be found in parts of England and English society.

In short, governments throughout the period that the Hanoverian regime was establishing itself were forced to take a holistic view of their responsibilities. Whatever the personal prejudices of individual English ministers, their interests extended throughout the British Isles. And later, when the succession had been laid to rest as an issue, strategic priorities continued to dictate an integrated approach to the strengths and weaknesses of the islands as a whole.

Britain's reliance on naval defence as a distinguishing feature of its history has often been noted in terms of the relative insularity that it bestowed on its inhabitants, with a variety of consequences for their political and social character. It does not follow, however, that a maritime country was easy to defend. Every war during this period, with the sole exception of the first three years of the War of American Independence, was a war with at least one first-rate naval power. Famously Britain hardly needed a standing army for the purposes of land warfare in the way that continental powers did. But it lived with the standing nightmare of an unopposed or inadequately opposed descent on its coasts, whether on the invitingly open beaches of Kent and Sussex or the less sensitive but more vulnerable cliffs and crags of Ireland or the Western Isles. The invasion scares of 1744, 1759, 1779, and 1805 posed fearsome threats which were repelled only with difficulty and considerable good fortune. The appearance of William III in Devon in 1688, Charles Edward in the Highlands in 1745, the French Republic's General Humbert in Ireland in 1798 were no less instructive. Even when invasion was not at issue, the coastal depredations of privateers, most famously John Paul Jones during the War of American Independence, were a reminder of the peculiar vulnerability of the united kingdoms. It was this maritime vulnerability that made naval politics the most important of all politics. In retrospect it is easy to see the royal navy of the period as the driving force behind the expansion of empire and commercial power. But in fact its primary purpose lay in home waters.

Ireland was critical to this defensive strategy in more ways than one. Not only was it a potential springboard for an invasion of England. It was also a convenient garrison for an entire army that English opinion was resistant to housing at home and which could be drawn on for all kinds of purposes in war. Above all Irish resources, financial as well as material, were a crucial part of the imperial defence system. When negotiations for commercial union between Britain and Ireland broke down in 1785 it was not because the terms of trade were so controversial, though they were, but because the Westminster and Irish parliaments could not agree on identifying Ireland's share of the imperial defence budget.

It might be supposed that union with Scotland nearly a century before the matching union with Ireland made the former of more consequence to London than the latter. A good case could be made for the opposing contention. In population terms England and Wales were roughly five times the size of Scotland throughout the period, but only twice the size of Ireland. Moreover the dismantling of trade barriers with Scotland in 1707, profoundly though it affected Scots, did not lessen the economic interdependence of England and Ireland. A mixture of protectionism and the magnetic pull of metropolitan commerce meant that Irish trade with Britain grew from barely a half of its total trade in 1700 to around 80 per cent in 1800. From the standpoint of London there was no hierarchy that made Edinburgh more important than Dublin and Scotland more important than Ireland. Particular circumstances decided the outcome of individual episodes or crises but the underlying concern at times of strain was more likely to be with Ireland. Whether England's role in the British Isles is best described as dominion or partnership may be debated. What is not in doubt is that throughout the eighteenth century its rulers did not consider that it could be anything but an active role.

This is not to argue that the peoples over whom they ruled had a view of their own multiple identities that could be relied upon for coherence or consistency. Scots were divided not only by their political differences but by broader cultural rifts. The Highlands had a language of their own and in many instances a religious faith which the new political and economic imperatives of the late eighteenth century did not altogether extinguish. Any possibility of Scotland sustaining its own 'Scots' language was buried by the subjection of educated Scots to an English language whose correctness was determined in London. Yet despite the growing assimilation of the nation to metropolitan manners and mores, there were signs of a cultural counter-revolution that was to engender a powerful new sense of Scottish self-consciousness. The literary revival that began with Ossian and culminated with Burns and Scott provided a platform for the politically muted but in other respects formidable nationalism of the early nineteenth century.

Something of the sort also happened in Wales. The Welsh language proved more resilient than its Irish or Scottish counterparts, no doubt because patterns of migration and commerce disrupted it less. The population of Wales as a whole grew by about 20 per cent in the eighteenth century, which represented significant expansion but at a slower rate than any other part of the three kingdoms. Moreover demographic growth was regionally concentrated in the areas of industrial expansion, first in north-east Wales, then in south Wales. Regional disparities further accentuated ancient distinctions, especially between the north and the south. But as in Scotland, rediscovering or reinventing ancient cultural traditions, as in the revival of Druidism and the poems of Iolo Morganwg, generated sentiments that could in some measure bind together quite different social forces and ethnic inheritances. Wales was politically the least threatening of the 'peripheral presences' but from an English standpoint it did not seem the least distinctive, even alien. On the contrary, the popularity of the Welsh Tour from the early years of George III's reign made Welsh particularism paradoxically the most accessible of all to middle-class English visitors.

Irish identity was inevitably always potentially threatening. If nothing else, an awareness of its history both in Ireland and elsewhere would have made it so. Political and religious divisions did not weaken that threat, but they made it much harder to evolve an Irishness that could unite all, even in the most superficial sense. They also made it impossible to generate the superficial but modestly efficacious national traditions that put the Scots and Welsh in a position to have it both ways, simultaneously glorying in their distinctive national past and joining in a supranational British present. Irishness comprised two (if not three) traditions that made every statement of alleged historical fact or national interest controversial and accordingly either complicit with or subversive of a wider Britishness. Bridging the gap with a kind of cultural sentimentalism that wrapped up diverse legacies proved difficult and ultimately impossible. A common ancestral tongue no longer offered much help in this respect. Thanks more to the disruptive impact of settlement and trade than government policy, the Irish language was increasingly confined to remote pockets of the west coast. And Ireland's stormy history had become hopelessly contestable. Usable myths could rarely be used by all Irishmen.

There was one moment, indeed, when it seemed that an Irish nationalism might be constituted in ways that were more eirenic. The Volunteer Movement of the American War period, and the broader political opportunity that it represented, were supported by very different elements: patriotic Protestants who resented British domination, propertied Roman Catholics who felt marginalized by their faith and welcomed the chance to be part of a new Ireland, and Ulster Presbyterians who seemed ready to bury ancient animosities to secure equal political rights. How secure this coalition might have been rendered will never be known. In the short run, understandably, it concentrated on obtaining recognition of the parliamentary independence of Ireland, which it achieved in 1782, with the inauguration of 'Grattan's Parliament' and a period of relative prosperity and stability. In the longer run it was consumed by the revolutionary holocaust of the 1790s. The politics of ascendancy, rebellion, and sectarian division followed.

It is conventional to assume that the English had the least difficulty in such matters, as they blithely assumed the mantle of Britishness without adjusting it to take account of very much that was not English. Yet England received far more internal immigrants in the course of the eighteenth century than other parts of the three kingdoms, and also far more immigrants from countries outside the British Isles. This was reflected in recurrent surges of hostility somewhat distinct from the kind of patriotic xenophobia that surfaced in wartime, and where foreign visitors were concerned, from time to time on the streets of London. Proposals to naturalize German Protestant immigrants under Queen Anne and Jewish residents under George II, each of which got through parliament, proved controversial and had to be repealed to appease popular sentiment. Seasonal Irish visitors at harvest time in the early eighteenth century and more permanent incomers seeking work on the canals or in the new industries in the late eighteenth century aroused spasmodic hostility. Welsh settlers were used to a degree of abuse, though the 'Garden Girls' from west Wales who found work in English parks and gardens during summer famously preserved their reputation for chastity and honesty, unlike some other visitors. The Scots suffered on a new scale, reflecting their visible presence, particularly in London. The virulence of popular anti-Scottishness in the 1760s when a Scottish prime minister made it easy for opposition politicians to fan the flames, could have had serious consequences for the unity of Britons if it had continued and grown. In the event it gradually subsided to the level at which popular stereotypes could add to the stock of English humour without occasioning ethnic conflict.

Overall England was generally considered a relatively tolerant society both by historic and contemporary standards. London in particular was a city of astonishing cosmopolitanism, as many foreign visitors testified. It is true that the English wholly rejected, or rather ignored the official wisdom that treated them as residents of something called South Britain after the union, but then it is not clear that Scots took pleasure in identifying themselves as North Britons and the Irish certainly did not revise their geography to invent a West Britain, even after the union with Great Britain. The Welsh teasingly recalled their own status as Ancient Britons, the true possessors of 'the British history', a practice treated by most of their neighbours as another example of Welsh whimsicality. Moreover, if it was true that the English were dismayingly prone to use the terms English and British as if they were synonyms, they showed no desire to extinguish the latter in favour of the former. The English self-perception may have been confused and confusing; it did not require formal anglicization of others.

Beyond the British Isles

From a domestic standpoint the unification of the islands, or at least the widespread recognition that they could be treated as a unit, was central to all kinds of activities and preoccupations, affecting every level of society in one way or another. But the external consequences were even more striking. Perceptions are shifting things which depend much on vantage point. But there was one indisputable way in which the inhabitants of the British Isles were bound to appear in a new light as the eighteenth century progressed. This was simply because they were more visible, their presence in the outside world more marked.

Their appearance abroad was not necessarily something of which their rulers could be proud. One effect of the events of 1688–9 was the flight of supporters of the old regime to refuges abroad. English Jacobite refugees were relatively few in number, but of Scots and especially Irish—'the wild geese'—there were far more. They made a considerable impact on various parts of continental Europe, appearing in numerous places as traders whose knowledge of their former homelands could be put to profitable use. Many others served in continental armies, including those which for long periods were pitted against British forces.

This complicated questions of national allegiance. In typical encounters the chances were that the Irish especially were likely to be found fighting on both sides. Perhaps this helped explain the need for English opinion to emphasize the Englishness of the British infantry for much of the period. In the late eighteenth century, however, royal forces drew on new sources of recruitment in the Scottish Highlands and in Catholic Ireland. By the time of the Revolutionary and Napoleonic Wars, His Britannick Majesty could plausibly claim to command a representative 'British' army in a way that would have seemed unconvincing in earlier decades. Growing Scottish identification with the imperial and military objectives of the English crown made this increasingly unproblematic north of the border. In Ireland too, especially after the union of 1801, it was possible for many to bury their ethnic sentiments in allegiance to an imperial monarchy, especially when the enemy was a France that had executed his 'most Christian

Majesty' and pillaged papal Italy. Generalizations about the allegiance of the 'subject' portions of the British Isles tend to break down when the composition of the armed forces is examined.

If British troops were themselves frequent but unpredictable visitors to European lands, more consistent was the steady flow of those whose business interests took them there. There were numerous mercantile colonies on continental littorals, some of which went back centuries and most of which retained a strong sense of their national culture and values over long periods. This was true in the Baltic, on the Atlantic, in the Mediterranean, and the Levant. Aside from this relatively stable presence, there was also the growing contingent of commercial travellers who carried order books for English wares that increasingly displaced older sources of supply throughout the continent. They are a relatively unknown mobile force, except in the letter-books of their employers, yet for those whose communities they travelled through they provided striking evidence of the wealth, power, and distinctiveness of their country. Their apparent prosperity and self-sufficiency made them quite unlike their brethren from other countries, creating social dilemmas for continental noblemen who found it hard to distinguish between aristocratic Britons and their more humble but not necessarily more obsequious inferiors.

The excursions of British noblemen were, of course, the most visible of all. Strictly speaking, by the standards of many continental grandees, they were not necessarily very grand. They did not own enormous estates or command vast servile populations. But for disposable income they outranked all their competitors. Not a little of this income was spent on foreign leisure. The Grand Tour made them perhaps the most influential of all British exports and provided foreigners with much insight into the nature of British society. The wealth they brought with them was too tangible to be ignored but their manners were not always considered agreeable. The English reputation for a certain want of civility was often enhanced by their rowdy behaviour, their insensitivity to continental customs, and their brash assault on older cultures. Italy especially was raided both for its ancient and modern arts and also provided a rich trade in forged old masters and other trash. These early tourists were certainly the big spenders of Europe. Not until the end of the eighteenth century, between the American and French Revolutionary Wars, did the gradual appearance of a lower class of tourists somewhat alter the image of the Englishman as 'milord', but when it did the prevailing sense of an insular, wealthy, and vulgar people remained.

Foreign travel for recreation was hardly new, but was certainly practised by the British on a new scale. Emigration was a basic fact of life throughout the period. It was the English who largely stocked their own Atlantic colonies in the seventeenth century. In the eighteenth century the Scots and Irish came to provide a large proportion of those setting off for colonial territories. Membership of the British political club provided inhabitants of the British Isles with the licence they needed to leave it. Modern historiography often emphasizes the extent to which the emigrants, especially from Ireland and the Scottish Highlands, were forced out by the brutality of their landlords, but it is by no means clear that those who went were the most indigent, or those incapable of making a choice. The Atlantic empire offered opportunities that were often weighed with care. For many Scots and Ulster Scots (but not Irish) what was involved was a kind of joint-stock enterprise involving families and networks of families. In their case the emigration of wives and daughters as well as menfolk made for a powerful and continuing sense of community in their new homes.

Emigration in the eighteenth century was certainly 'economic emigration', but its object was not commonly mere survival. The era of mass involuntary emigration lay in the future. There was one obvious exception. Throughout the period numbers of criminals were exported into indentured labouring or penal servitude. Until the 1770s the American and West Indian colonies acquired most of these forced settlers. After American Independence a Pacific home was found for such expatriates, not in another 'New England', or 'Nova Scotia', but in New South Wales, the first colony named by the crown after its Welsh territories.

The most important of all changes both in terms of the impact that the inhabitants of the British Isles made on the wider world and the impact that the wider world made on them were those that resulted in what is thought of as imperial expansion. The origins of the British empire belonged earlier, but it was the eighteenth century and more particularly the second half of the eighteenth century that proved the formative phase of its modern development. The disaster of losing the thirteen American colonies in 1783 seemed to many to have removed the core of the empire. Yet it did not impede the continued growth of overseas dominion.

In Europe Gibraltar survived the wreckage of the American War. Minorca did not but the acquisition of Malta and the Ionian Islands during the Napoleonic Wars provided still more valuable stepping-stones in the Mediterranean. Hanover was by family descent a part of the British monarchy throughout the period, as much so as Scotland had been between 1603 and 1707. Its severance from Britain in 1837 has made modern Britons unaware of its political and military importance in the eighteenth century. It is not customarily thought of as part of Britain or the British empire yet no other territory of its size had such consistent importance. It made Britain a player in continental politics; whether to its advantage or disadvantage depended on standpoint. Particularly in wartime it was critical in strategic calculations of numerous kinds. Commercially and culturally, it had wide-ranging consequences for the relationship between Britain and Germany. Commitments to this part of the world were not considered insignificant, as the importance of Denmark in the Napoleonic Wars revealed. In 1807 the annexation of the tiny island of Heligoland was not the result of 'a fit of absence of mind'.

In North America itself Canada turned from being a highly problematic enclave of former French subjects to an only slightly less problematic but steadily expanding compound of former American loyalists, old French colonists, and new immigrants from Britain. In the West Indies Britain remained the dominant European power. Dominica, Grenada, and St Vincent had been acquired during the Seven Years War. Trinidad was ceded by Spain, St Lucia and Tobago by France, and Guyana by the Dutch in 1814. The African toeholds multiplied from the old slaving centre on the Gambia to Sierra Leone in 1787 and the Cape of Good Hope in 1806. Toeholds also would have been the appropriate term for Britain's bases in India, at Bombay, Madras, and Calcutta, until the Seven Years War. Thereafter territorial expansion in India brought first Bengal and then large areas of southern and central India under British control, as well as settlements in Ceylon, Mauritius, and Penang on the Malayan coast. And what started as a penal colony at Botany Bay in 1788, with the addition of a settlement at Tasmania in 1803, was later to become a much larger arc of settlement colonies in Australasia.

These gains were made at the expense of diverse parties. Much the greatest was France, the one power with the muscle to break Britain's emergent pre-eminence. In imperial terms the result of more than a century of conflict was bloody but conclusive. In India, in Africa, and in the West Indies, it was Britain that gained the upper hand. France succeeded in enabling the American colonies to cast free from Britain in the War of American Independence but not in establishing a French empire or halting the expansion of the British empire. This state of affairs resulted primarily from the realities and rivalries of European power politics, not from any predatory British thirst for new territories. If it had been otherwise, the Spanish, Portuguese, and Dutch empires would have suffered far more than they did. Dutch losses were significant but not decisive, and British expansion tended to work around the older empires rather than at their territorial expense. Its driver was for the most part commercial hegemony not military ambition.

The exception was partial and came relatively late in the period. In India, remote from Whitehall and subject to local initiatives whether native or imported, there was a growing tendency by the 1790s towards the annexation and incorporation of new territories. Even so, it remains in some ways surprising how little this spirit had figured in the earlier history of British India. The expansion of British dominion, initially in the name of the East India Company and only by degrees recognized as part of the realm of Great Britain, was a gradual, even desultory affair, engendered by wars that had their origin elsewhere in the world. The results were not necessarily more comforting for native Indians, but they belong in long-lasting patterns of political instability in the subcontinent rather than a new, self-consciously self-aggrandizing British imperium. Even Wellesley in the 1790s was hardly an Alexander or a Napoleon, but rather a soldier whose military instincts took precedence over the less clear-cut motives and ambitions of earlier so-called 'imperialists'.

The term 'empire' was not an invention of the eighteenth century, but as a description of Britain's overseas possessions, it was largely its creation, and all the more acceptable after the Scottish and Irish unions which made the British empire a term that could be shared by all the peoples of the British Isles, without conceding precedence to any particular group of one's neighbours. Interestingly, the English themselves did not usually speak of an English empire, perhaps because it did not occur to most of them that there was any conflict of interest or identity between England and Britain. Not that any particular thread of consistent ethnic association would have followed. The English of the empire were not necessarily its most loyal supporters. The American Revolution was led by descendants of New England Puritans and southern Royalists, many of them intensely proud of their English origins, culture, and identity. It is hard to believe that their counterparts in the West Indies would have remained within the empire but for their painful vulnerability to invasion by sea and insurrection by land. Conversely, the loyalists of North America, in the thirteen colonies and then in Canada, were by no means uniformly of English descent but included substantial Scottish and Irish elements. When a settler colony began building in Australia it was ethnically diverse and united more by evident self-interest and dependence on Britain than by a coherent notion of what empire meant. In India and the numerous trading posts around the Atlantic and Pacific worlds which were in some sense of the empire without being formally in it, and where settling was not an avowed object of most of those involved, identities and motives could be even more confused.

At home, of course, the empire was increasingly represented in public and patriotic rhetoric. Whether it was to be considered a good thing remained rather unclear. Conventional wisdom emphasized the value of trading partners more than possessions. Authoritative classical scholarship, not least from the pen of Britain's own Edward Gibbon, portrayed empire as a source of corruption and delinquency for the colonizer rather than the colonized. Such pessimism was reinforced by the experience of the War of American Independence. Perhaps it was only the pressure of some twenty years of bitter and costly warfare between 1793 and 1815 that made imperial identity a valuable rallying point for patriots to distract attention from the uncomfortably contested politics of church and king at home. Even then its survival in the years of peace that followed 1815 was to be quite problematic.

The worldwide impact on alien peoples was nonetheless immense. Some three million African slaves were shipped by the British between 1689 and 1807 when the trade was abolished by act of parliament. This was more than the total shipped by all the other colonial powers, representing a movement of people that far exceeded internal migration within the empire itself. In the mid-eighteenth century West Africa was generating roughly six times the number of other immigrants entering the West Indies and North America. These human imports were intended to provide the labour that was not to be found among the diminishing indigenous inhabitants of the Americas. Whether genocide was the intention is debatable. What is not disputed is that in the English-settled colonies, the natives were liable to be expelled or exterminated. Native Caribs in the West Indies disappeared altogether. American Indians in North America were steadily pushed out to the perimeter. Where the British government took an interest, as it began to in the Ohio Valley in the 1770s and in conquered Canada consistently, conscious attempts were made to provide a measure of protection, but it was to take strong measures to make them effective.

A striking feature of the empire that developed in the course of the eighteenth century was the diversity of peoples that it comprised. Until the time of the American Revolution, it was plausible to regard the empire as an enterprise dominated by White Protestant settlers. The loss of more than two million of these settlers in the American Revolution coincided with the acquisition of dominion over very different kinds of subject. Catholic French Canadians, Hindus and Moslems by the million, and Dutch settlers and African tribesmen at the Cape were all among the twenty-five million subjects of George III by 1815. Viewed as part of such a multi-cultural empire the less Anglo-Saxon portions of the British Isles looked less exotic, though it would not have pleased the inhabitants of Dublin or Edinburgh to be compared with those of Montreal or Calcutta. But the fact was that the English, or British, or even British and Irish, were but a small minority of the population of the empire as a whole.

Such an empire could not be ruled on principles inherited from the past. The old axiom that English colonies needed English laws and institutions was unlikely to be applied where there were few permanent English settlers. In India new forms of government evolved, influenced much by local practice and principles, and still more by the complicated politics of the East India Company as it interacted both with ancient authorities in Asia and the crown in Britain. In effect a new class of British officials was drafted in to run remote lands on principles thought to be appropriate to different cultures. The numbers were not trivial. The East India Company was employing more than 3,000 officers by the end of the eighteenth century, thereby creating the kernel of a new kind of imperial civil service and enriching modestly, or in the early days spectacularly, men of middle class rather than aristocratic origins.

How to govern an empire that was increasingly diverse in character and unpredictable in behaviour was not the only question that came to be debated. The church had long been aware of some other awkward issues presented by empire. One was the spiritual fate that might await pagan subjects of the crown left in ignorance of the prospect of a Christian salvation. Another was the degrading state of negro slaves whose subjection many considered incompatible with Christian values. The foundation of the Society for the Propagation of the Gospel and the Society for the Promotion of Christian Knowledge under Queen Anne represented in part an attempt to grapple with such issues. Evangelical initiatives, including those of John Wesley, followed later in the century. At its end the first great missionary societies were founded. Alien cultures were about to feel the full effects of Western godliness alongside those of commerce and coercion.

Small wonder that Talleyrand saw Napoleon's intended destruction of British power as portentous far beyond the shores of Britain and even Europe. In the following chapters we seek not only to tell a complex and colourful story but to describe and analyse the processes that put the peoples of the British Isles in such a position, as well as the leading personalities that featured in them and the principles, prejudices, or practices that guided them.

Figure 2 Louis Philippe Boitard's 'The Loyal Associators' captures the patriotic anxiety of December 1746, when a Jacobite army was loose in the English Midlands, provoking a campaign for loyalist volunteers. The threat to the Hanoverian succession was finally extinguished in April 1746 at the battle of Culloden.

1

Contested kingdoms, 1688–1756

David Hayton

The realities of the relationship between the three Stuart kingdoms were emphasized by the events of 1688–91: ultimately, events in England determined the political fate of both Scotland and Ireland. After the Glorious Revolution had confirmed the dependence of Scotland and Ireland on their more powerful neighbour, the subsequent chain of events gave this dependence a statutory expression. The Anglo-Scottish union of 1707 created a new constitutional entity, the kingdom of Great Britain, submerging the Scottish estates in a united parliament (while preserving a distinct Scottish ecclesiastical and legal establishment). This new, British, parliament's Declaratory Act of 1720 unilaterally asserted sovereignty over Ireland. Not only were constitutional relationships being reconstructed, in ideological terms the nature of this 'British' state was being redefined. By the mid-eighteenth century some Englishmen (and Welshmen, Scotsmen, and Irishmen for that matter) spoke of belonging to an 'empire', but no longer the English 'empire' which had been proclaimed in the legislation of the reformation parliaments of the sixteenth century, that is to say a sovereign nation state free from foreign jurisdiction. Instead, theirs was a British 'empire' in the modern sense, ruling over diverse countries and peoples from Canada to India; an empire with the united kingdoms of England and Scotland at the core, and in which Ireland occupied an anomalous but decidedly subordinate position.

This chapter closes just before the victories of the Seven Years War greatly expanded Britain's colonial possessions and transformed its position on the world stage. In the half-century after the Glorious Revolution important developments were taking place which moulded the shape of the imperial state and laid the foundations for this expansion. Dynastic uncertainty was ended with the Hanoverian succession and the final defeat of the Jacobites. Scotland and Ireland were pacified, and their troublesome inhabitants subjugated, integrated, or repressed. A new relationship was forged between crown and parliament in England, producing a 'limited' or parliamentary monarchy that proved both stable and effective. The army, navy, and civil administration grew in size and power (albeit not always in efficiency), and a system of public finance was put in place able to sustain high levels of expenditure, while, more generally, English capitalism became stronger through the so-called 'commercial' and 'financial revolutions'. In short, while the power of the monarchy may have declined in this period, the authority and resources of the new British state grew quite remarkably.

Crown, parliaments, and the demands of warfare

In essence, the Glorious Revolution was a *coup d'état* undertaken by an adventurous foreign prince and his mercenary army, supported by local aristocracies, not an uprising of 'the people'. However, in England and Lowland Scotland its outcome was undeniably popular. William's own ambitions centred on preserving his wife's and his own right of succession to the throne, and in securing England's participation in the continental war. But he could argue that he had been invited to intervene in English affairs, admittedly by a small group of bishops and peers, in order to safeguard constitutional liberties. There can be little doubt that the majority of the 'political nation' in England were relieved to see him, even those who did not look beyond their immediate concern with preventing further alterations to the Anglican establishment, and probably did not wish for a change of monarch. After James's convenient flight to France, only a minority in the convention parliament so much as expressed scruples about the form in which the transfer of kingship was to take place. Fear of Catholics, and in particular the Catholic Irish, who were James's strongest and most visible supporters in 1688–9, enhanced popular enthusiasm for the new king and queen.

In Scotland the Revolution began without the Prince of Orange. King James's government simply fell apart, as the leading magnates either opportunistically declared themselves Orangists, or waited upon events in order to make sure they ended up on the right side. Aided by the vigorous anti-popery of the mob, a small group of radicals seized control of the administration in Edinburgh. Outside the capital, effective power passed into the hands of the nobility, who organized their tenantry and dependants into 'volunteer' companies. A powerful Presbyterian reaction across the Lowlands ensured that when the Scottish estates met early in 1689 they not only settled the crown on William and Mary but put into effect a Presbyterian church settlement, moderate by covenanting standards but removing the episcopal hierarchy which had been such a feature of the Stuart kings' attempts to enforce their will upon Scotland. Of course, this Williamite coup was not universally popular. There was considerable opposition in the North, among Highlanders, who were motivated by a combination of dynastic and religious loyalty and localized clan rivalries, and among Episcopalians, once the shape of the religious settlement had become clear. Although the immediate Highland reaction fizzled out, a more substantial armed force was put together by the Jacobite loyalist Graham of Claverhouse, 'Bonnie Dundee', which required a concerted military response from the new regime, and an army sent from England. With Dundee's decisive defeat at Killiecrankie in July 1690, the Revolution was secured, but there remained considerable potential for disaffection in Scotland, among Catholics and Episcopalians, which later Jacobite strategists would exploit.

In Ireland the Revolution was deeply unpopular among the Catholic population, both 'Old English' and 'Old Irish', now scarcely distinguishable components of a united political interest. At their head stood James's lord deputy, Richard Talbot, Lord Tyrconnel, who with a Catholic-officered army held most of the country until his master's arrival in Dublin in the spring of 1689. With only a few exceptions, the Protestant minority declared for William, those in the south and west fleeing to England to avoid reprisals, and leaving only pockets of resistance in Ulster (most famously in the besieged city of Derry), where the resistance of the Protestant squirearchy was stiffened by the support of Scottish Presbyterian settlers. Although there was no repetition of the atrocities of the 1640s, the Irish parliament called by James in Dublin in the summer of 1689 amply confirmed Protestant fears by repealing the Restoration land settlements and confiscating the lands of declared Williamites.

It was in Ireland that the military nature of the Revolution was most glaringly apparent. The 'war of the two kings' involved two full-scale campaigns, which made the fighting in Scotland pale into insignificance (let alone William's bloodless progress across the south of England). William's army, which included Dutch, Danish, and German troops, defeated James's Franco-Irish force at the Boyne in 1690, and again at Aughrim in 1691. The first battle was decisive, in so far as James immediately accepted that his own game was up, and took ship for France. His Irish followers, skilfully led, and given some support by the French, succeeded in prolonging the war for another year. Indeed, at Aughrim in 1691 they came close to victory on the battlefield. Afterwards they retreated to the western ports of Galway and Limerick, and were able to obtain terms of surrender from a regime anxious to return its attention to the continent. Part of the settlement involved the departure from Ireland of the vast majority of the Jacobite troops, including the flower of the Catholic gentry, a haemorrhage that effectively destroyed the Catholic political interest in Ireland for a generation.

However much conservatives tried to hide the brute facts of the Revolution settlement by fudging the constitutional issues, there was no denying that what had happened in 1688–91 had dealt a blow to the principle of hereditary monarchy. The offer of the crowns of England and Ireland to William and Mary by the convention at Westminster disguised the effective deposition of King James under the fiction that he had 'abdicated', and left 'the throne . . . vacant', but the bill of rights explicitly interfered with the hereditary succession in declaring that any Catholic, or anyone married to a Catholic, was excluded from the throne, a provision reinforced in the Act of Settlement of 1701 which ensured that after the heiress presumptive, Mary's sister Anne, the crown would pass to the nearest Protestant heirs, the electoral family in Hanover.

The bill of rights also declared illegal the suspending and

dispensing powers exercised by James II, together with extra-parliamentary taxation, prerogative courts, and the maintenance of a standing army without parliamentary consent. But other key principles—frequent parliaments, free elections, freedom of speech in the House—were only listed as desirable, and there was nothing in law to prevent a repetition of the last four years of King Charles II's reign, when no parliament had been called. The Scottish estates' equivalent of the bill of rights, the claim of right, was even clearer on the constitutional implications of the Revolution, pronouncing that James had 'forfeited the right to the crown' by his violation of 'the fundamental constitution of the kingdom', and, as in England, Catholics were declared incapable of ruling. But the convention in Edinburgh was no more assertive than its Westminster counterpart in establishing parliamentary limitations on the new monarchy. Extra-parliamentary taxation was declared to be illegal but the frequency of meetings of the estates and their freedom from undue royal influence were recommended rather than required.

In Ireland the monarchy was at first in an even stronger position, and parliament even weaker. William and Mary did not convene a parliament in Dublin until 1692, by which time the destiny of the crown of Ireland had already been determined. There was no Irish bill of rights, and the calling of parliament remained entirely at the discretion of the monarch, the only legal restriction being that a parliament ended automatically on the death of the sovereign. Furthermore, the acts passed by the Jacobite parliament of 1689, which included the establishment of legislative independence by the repeal of Poynings' Law, were rendered null and void. In 1692 William need not have held a parliament in Dublin, at least for the immediate future, since the Irish establishment was puny in comparison with the English and the shortfall of the royal hereditary revenue in Ireland required only a small additional subsidy, but ministers thought it politically correct, and in any case there was the (mistaken) expectation that lavish subsidies would be forthcoming from grateful Protestant gentlemen.

Thus, the new king and queen succeeded without the comprehensive constitutional limitations that radical Whigs had envisaged. In practice, however, their need to finance the extensive military commitments demanded by William's continental strategy was greatly to restrict their freedom of manoeuvre, and, at least in England, to shift the balance of power between crown and parliament in favour of the latter. The English parliament was summoned regularly in order to vote subsidies, and in return the crown had to permit scrutiny of its estimates and a close inquiry into accounts by members possessed of a belief in the prevalence of waste and corruption. The system of deficit financing devised in 1693–5 to raise the extraordinary sums necessary to fight a continental war institutionalized the crown's dependence on parliament. The king was able to float public loans on the security of future taxes, and through the issue of government stock, mainly in the Bank of England, which was set up in 1694. He was thus committed to calling parliaments and securing further subsidies in order to service what eventually became the National Debt.

In the Commons, where the major battles over supply were conducted, the court interest could not expect to win easily, despite the votes that could be purchased by offices and pensions. It was essential to employ parliamentary managers to translate this potential influence into majorities. Moreover, MPs had not lost enthusiasm for the preservation of the liberties of the subject. There was a strong 'Country' tradition on the back benches, which manifested itself in measures to guarantee frequent parliaments and frequent elections, to exclude placemen and pensioners from the Commons, to limit the size of the 'standing army' in peacetime, and to prevent royal grants of forfeited property to favourites. Although William III frequently used his veto to block objectionable legislation (the last monarch to do so systematically) he was forced to accept the Triennial Act of 1694, the Disbandment Act of 1699, and resumption of his grants of Irish forfeited estates in 1700. In his reign parliament met every year, and for much longer sessions than under his predecessors. It became, to adapt a phrase coined by a historian of early seventeenth-century England, an institution rather than an event, clarifying its procedures, improving its facilities, and expanding its administrative apparatus.

As far as the monarchy was concerned, the difficulties of parliamentary management were exacerbated by the personal deficiencies of successive sovereigns. William was a foreigner, unfamiliar with English politicians and their ways, who spent a fair amount of his time abroad. His successor, Queen Anne, was a woman of limited intelligence and poor health. With George I, who followed Anne, the throne was once again occupied by a foreign prince, and a partial absentee. Each depended, to varying degrees, on their advisers, 'undertakers' like William's 'minister behind the curtain' Lord Sunderland, or Anne's Lord Treasurers Godolphin and Harley, who acted as intermediaries with the politicians. But not even 'undertakers' could always shield the king or queen from unpleasant political truths, and both William and Anne were obliged on occasion to give way to *force majeure*. This was not exactly a case of politicians 'storming the closet', in the later eighteenth-century usage, so much as a reluctant acceptance of the inevitable. William's preferred option at the start of his reign was a 'mixed ministry' of different parties. Its slow and painful failure was eventually recognized in 1693–4, when he turned to a group of able young Whigs, the so-called Junto, who carried his government through the crucial stages of the Nine Years War. In 1700, against his wishes, he was forced to part with the Junto and take in their opponents, the Tories, many of whom he considered disloyal. Anne, whose personal predilections were the reverse of her predecessor's, kept the Tories in office in 1702, and showed them even greater favour, until she was obliged to re-employ the Junto in 1705–9.

While the position of the crown had weakened, the power of the state had grown. The root cause was England's involvement in two major European wars between 1689 and 1713. After the Third Anglo-Dutch War of 1672–4, Charles II had successfully avoided foreign military entanglements. William, by contrast, was keen that his new kingdom should enter the Nine Years War (1689–97) as a principal; indeed, one of his motives in intervening in English politics had been to add English support to his Grand Alliance against Louis XIV. At first, the results were mixed: his army enjoyed success in Ireland, but suffered discouraging defeats in Flanders, especially at Landen in 1693; while the navy, despite inflicting a significant reverse on the French at La Hogue in 1692, failed to secure mastery of the sea. Eventually, the two sides fought each other to a standstill, and to an enforced peace at Rijswijk in 1697. William regarded this treaty as no more than a temporary truce, and within five years the issue of the succession to the Spanish throne, and Louis XIV's unwillingness to abandon the claims of his grandson, Philip of Anjou, had reignited conflict across Europe. This time, through a succession of spectacular land victories, Queen Anne's captain-general, Marlborough, did establish allied dominance. All at once, England (after 1707, Britain) had become a major military power, and even though successive ministries were unable or unwilling to force the war to a decisive conclusion, and ended by undertaking what were in effect unilateral peace negotiations, the events leading up to the Treaty of Utrecht in 1713 showed that the British were now the arbiters of Europe. Not all Queen Anne's subjects endorsed the strategic priorities adopted by Marlborough and Lord Treasurer Godolphin: there was a strong lobby among Tories for a 'blue-water' policy which would have reduced the commitment to land war in Europe in favour of strengthening naval operations, partly to defend the transatlantic plantations and to protect and promote trading interests. There was an element of political opportunism here, exploiting popular resentment at the cost of the war, but the Tory ministry of 1710–14 showed a commitment to 'blue-water' priorities in concentrating in the Utrecht negotiations on reducing continental commitments and securing commercial concessions, especially from the Spanish in the slave trade.

The system of deficit financing devised in the 1690s to meet the huge costs of warfare reinforced the crown's dependence on parliament, but also brought financial stability, and enabled huge increases in public expenditure. Of course, there were complaints of the high levels of wartime taxation, especially at the time of the great recoinage in 1695–6, when the English government was on the verge of bankruptcy. But the opportunities presented by the public funds also attracted new investors, and gave more of the king's subjects a stake in the continuance of his regime. Higher taxation also required a larger bureaucracy. Here the land tax was less important than the excise, and other indirect taxes, which were collected by professional revenue officers and not by the squires who comprised the county land tax commissions. The excise, though not immune from the damaging effects of patronage and corruption, possessed some of the attributes of a modern bureaucracy: recruitment and promotion by ability, a professional career structure, the absence of sinecures. Much early eighteenth-century administration, especially in Whitehall, was still ramshackle and inefficient by modern standards, but as a whole government was bigger and more efficient than before. Above all, the army had expanded. William was able to put far more men into the field than his predecessors, and the constant danger of Jacobite invasion was used as an argument for the maintenance of a large standing army in peacetime, much of it transferred to the Irish establishment to hide it from libertarian critics at home.

The rise in importance of parliament and the rapid expansion of the state bureaucracy brought more and more Englishmen into active participation in political life. The royal court became less important as the focus for political ambitions, though it still remained a significant employer. It was now possible to make a political career through parliamentary service, where talent, and the capacity for mischief-making, attracted the attention of monarch and ministers, and in government service through patronage. The greater frequency of general elections after the Revolution—ten between 1695 and 1715—involved larger numbers in politics at local level. The overall size of the electorate in England and Wales in this period is impossible to calculate. In most constituencies, we know how many voted, not how many were entitled to vote. One thing is certain however; that the number of Englishmen who cast a vote at some point during the period must have represented a substantial proportion of the adult male population, especially since pollbooks show a rapid turnover in individual constituency electorates. Nor was participation in elections necessarily confined to the voters: thousands more might attend a county poll than were in possession of a 40s. freehold (the English and Welsh county franchise), to witness the event and support candidates, while the choice of borough members was often assisted by the activities of partisan mobs, and the declaration of the result accompanied with ceremony and celebration which gave the event the appearance of street-theatre. In boroughs political infighting became almost continuous, as rival factions fought for control of corporate institutions. A ready market thus opened up for political propaganda—in the form of pamphlets, newspapers, broadsides, squibs, and caricatures—and the print trade rushed to meet it.

In Scotland and Ireland, too, parliaments became much more important. Although in neither kingdom did the scale of public expenditure begin to compare with that in England, the capacity of the crown to 'live of its own' was correspondingly weak, and defensive and strategic imperatives meant that parliamentary subsidies were needed. Order had to be maintained, against restive Highlanders and potentially disaffected Irish Catholics, and each kingdom had a role to play in the Williamite war effort, Scotland providing troops and Ireland a domestic 'holding area' for regiments waiting to be transported to a theatre of war overseas.

After 1689 the Scottish estates met more regularly than before, and enjoyed greater control over their own proceedings with the abolition of the Lords of the Articles, the committee, nominated by the crown, which had previously controlled the agenda for business. The constitutional independence of the Scottish parliament, particularly over the question of the succession to the throne, made parliamentary management a high priority for William's Scottish ministers, magnates who at this stage remained entirely independent of the ministry in England.

The Irish parliament had much less initiative, and in the last resort legislation could be passed for Ireland at Westminster. But on the whole English governments tried to avoid doing this. They were wary of using the English parliament to tax Ireland. Thus, although the debts of the Irish administration were a drop in the ocean of English public finance, they had to be met by Irish parliamentary subsidies. Management of the Dublin parliament was the responsibility of the viceroy, appointed from England, who negotiated with local political figures to secure a majority in the House of Commons, where fiscal matters were decided. The first parliamentary session after the Revolution, in 1692, proved a disaster and was dissolved without a grant of supply. The subsequent history of the Irish parliament was punctuated by failures and irregular subsidies: after a restoration of management in 1695 there was another period without parliaments between 1698 and 1703, and at the end of Anne's reign another disaster in 1713, which resulted in two years without a subsidy and the beginnings of an Irish national debt. Thereafter, a pattern was established whereby parliament met every two years and granted only so much 'additional' taxation as would keep the government in being until its members met again.

In both Scotland and Ireland parliamentary management proved a tiresome business. In Scotland the difficulties lay in the structure of politics, and particularly in the dominance of magnate interests over all three estates (aristocracy, lesser barons, and burghs). As in England, the court was not strong enough on its own to be able to guarantee a majority. The ministry in Edinburgh could only subsist with the support of noblemen like the dukes of Argyll, Atholl, Hamilton, or Queensberry. But these 'great men' were consumed by personal ambition and rivalries. It seemed as if they would only cooperate when in opposition. Various experiments in the construction of a Scottish administration around other, lesser political interests, foundered on the hostility of the magnates. For a time, the crown found a successful Scottish 'undertaker' in the person of the second duke of Queensberry, but magnate rivalries, uncertain political direction from Whitehall, and an underlying resentment at the inequalities inherent in the 'union of the crowns' reduced even Queensberry to exasperation. There was also the danger that the Scottish parliamentary opposition, exploiting patriotic sentiments and residual Jacobite enthusiasm, would attempt a separate settlement of the succession. An incorporating union came to be seen as the only safe expedient, simultaneously solving two problems: the insecurity of the Protestant succession, and Protestantism itself; and the chronic weaknesses in Scottish political management. It was sold to public opinion in 1707 as a measure that would bring economic benefits to both kingdoms, but the essential motivation was political, and as such it was generally successful, at least in parliamentary terms. The small minority of Scottish MPs and representative peers was effectively submerged at Westminster. There were teething troubles, most notably in 1713 when the Scottish contingent in both Houses, enraged by the extension of the malt tax to Scotland, pressed for the repeal of the union. But this desperate motion was easily defeated by the English parties.

Although Ireland should have been easier to manage, the ministers in Dublin suffered a succession of embarrassments, even after the belated parliamentary settlement of 1695. The problems in Ireland were not structural, as in Scotland, but lay in the weakness of particular viceroys, the tendency for Irish factions to intrigue in England, and the sporadic ebullition of patriotic rage against English interference in Irish affairs. The first serious outbreak occurred in the late 1690s, with a series of offensive actions taken at Westminster. The English House of Lords reasserted its disputed appellate jurisdiction over Irish cases; then the Woollen Act of 1699 banned Irish cloth exports; finally, Westminster cancelled King William's grants of Irish forfeited estates. Each incident was viewed in Ireland as an attack on national interests: the autonomy of the Dublin parliament; the markets for Irish manufactures; and, most sensitively, rights of landownership. One Irish response was William Molyneux's *Case of*

Ireland ... stated (1698), which put the argument for legislative independence. Another, even more alarming in some respects, was the 'national remonstrance' organized in 1701 against the Resumption Act, consisting of a coordinated campaign of county addresses. Many otherwise rational English politicians came to believe that Irish Protestants were aiming at independence. Sittings of the Irish parliament were suspended, for fear of the lengths to which Irish MPs might be led by patriotic zeal. By 1703, however, the exigencies of public finance made it impossible to avoid an Irish parliament any longer, and then the successful outcome of this session showed that the violence of Irish Protestant patriotism had been a mirage. In any case, Irish politics had by this time been transformed by the appearance of very different political issues, as Protestants became divided, just as Englishmen were, into 'Tories' and 'Whigs'.

The rage of party

The 'damned business of party', as Swift once called it, dominated English and Welsh politics from the Revolution to the Hanoverian succession and beyond. The members of both Houses of Parliament at Westminster, the voters in the constituencies, and the extended 'political nation' of the unenfranchised, were split along party lines. Those who defied categorization, neutrals, eccentrics, and turncoats, were objects of curiosity or suspicion. Classifying individuals by party became a compulsive pastime: we can find contemporary lists of clergymen, naval officers, even stockholders in the public funds, each marked to distinguish Tories from Whigs.

In Anne's reign, the crisis of party fever, the infection spread north of the Tweed and across the Irish Sea. From Edinburgh to Dingwall, Coleraine to Youghal, self-styled 'Whigs' battled with self-styled 'Tories' for ascendancy. In some cases, what was happening was the adoption of cant names by local factions in order to dress up traditional rivalries. When the members of the clan Mackenzie tussled with the Rosses and Munros for political control of Ross-shire, they knew that they stood a better chance of obtaining support at Westminster if they could portray themselves as Tory victims of Whig oppression. The parties in Scotland and Ireland were not wholly artificial constructions, however. Admittedly, Tories and Whigs appeared on the Celtic fringes much later than they had done in England, enjoyed a much briefer history there, and failed to develop very elaborate ideologies. Yet party politics in Scotland and Ireland did reflect real divisions within Scottish and Irish society. Indeed, the very titles 'Tory' and 'Whig' had originated in Ireland and Scotland, respectively, 'Tory' meaning a rebellious Irish Catholic, 'Whig' (short for 'Whiggamore') a rebellious Scottish Presbyterian.

The Tory and Whig parties had first appeared in England during the Exclusion Crisis. They held opposing views on the nature of the monarchy and its relationship with parliament, and on the political position of the established church and the constitutional rights of Protestant Dissenters. Under Charles II the first Tories had been the party of 'church and crown', distinguished by loyalty to the monarchy in the hereditary line, and an equally powerful determination to uphold the privileges of the Church of England and the Anglican Ascendancy in government. Whigs had been the defenders of the liberty of the subject, anxious to restrict the powers of the monarchy, and to remodel the succession in order to exclude a Catholic king. To the same general purpose, Whigs strove for the political emancipation of Protestant Dissenters, as a step towards unity among Protestants against the threat of popery and 'arbitrary government' at home and abroad.

The events of James II's reign, and the Glorious Revolution, placed the Tories in a cruel dilemma, which most resolved by choosing the maintenance of the established church over divine hereditary right. Thereafter they concentrated on their mission as 'the Church party', united in their devotion to the Anglican establishment and hatred of Dissent. Their attitude to the crown was ambivalent. In general Tories were at least embarrassed and sceptical about the Revolution and the parliamentary settlement of the succession. A minority were nonjurors (refusing on principle to swear the oaths to the new monarchs) or outright Jacobites. Many more felt a sentimental attachment to Jacobitism, or at least alienation from the *arriviste* courts of William III and the Georges. In their resentment they now took on the attitudes of a 'Country' opposition: suspicious of ministers, scenting 'corruption' everywhere, and determined to resist any expansion of executive power.

The Whigs, naturally enough, had embraced the Revolution as a defence of Protestantism and liberty, though only a few radicals were willing to maintain an extreme view of 1688 as a vindication of the right of resistance and of the origin of monarchical authority as elective in 'the people'. Most integrated themselves into the Williamite government, adopting characteristically ministerial attitudes in justifying the extension of royal power as a necessary evil, a safeguard against the power of the French and the treachery of Jacobites. They also came to be identified with the interventionist foreign policy that involved England in expensive continental warfare in the 1690s and 1700s. This enabled the Tories to complete the reinvention of themselves as the more conservative of the parties in foreign affairs. Swift's classic pamphlet, *The Conduct of the Allies* (1712), written in support of the Tory ministry's peace policy, attacked war-profiteers and the 'moneyed interest' in general, on behalf of the downtrodden country gentlemen and the 'honest merchants'.

In Scotland and Ireland Tories and Whigs were not divided by such a range of issues. For one thing, they did not differ over war strategy; nor was the antipathy between 'Court and Country' incorporated into party politics, for every opposition faction, whether Whig or Tory, adopted the rhetoric of 'Country', or, as they put it 'patriotic', outrage. The issue of the succession was of considerable importance in Scotland but not in Ireland, where there were few, if any, Jacobites, since the very existence of the Protestant landed elite depended on the maintenance of the Williamite settlement. In Scotland, the exiled Stuarts enjoyed substantial support, and the core of the Scottish 'Tory' interest that emerged after 1708 may be found in the 'cavaliers' who nurtured hopes of a Jacobite restoration. But even here the issue of the succession would not by itself have been enough to form the basis of a two-party system. Although there were irreconcilable cavaliers among the Scottish Tories, and downright revolution-men among the Whigs, between these two extremes lay a broad middle ground, inhabited by Tories who were willing to accept the Hanoverian succession, and Whigs with selective amnesia over the claim of right.

Instead, what really divided the two parties in Scotland and Ireland, especially at local level, was religion. In Scotland the Whigs were the party of the Kirk, the Tories the party of 'prelacy', and the issues which provoked the greatest passion were the demand for toleration for the episcopalian remnant, and for the preservation of surviving lay rights of nomination to parish livings, which enabled Episcopalian lairds to provide for ministers of their own kidney. In Ireland too, public policy on ecclesiastical issues was the prime source of division between Tories and Whigs. Here the religious divisions that plagued English society, between churchmen, Dissenters, and papists, were presented in a peculiarly acute form. The small minority of Church of Ireland Protestants felt themselves threatened on both sides, by the native Catholics, vastly more numerous and assumed to nurture a visceral hatred for the Protestant religion, and by the concentrated 'Scotch colony' of Ulster Presbyterians. Recent experience reinforced memories and myths of 1641, to keep alive the fear of 'popery', even for those Protestants who realized that the outcome of the war had meant that the Catholic interest was effectively disabled. Observation of the 'Presbyterian revolution' in Scotland had also heightened anxiety about the intentions of the Scots in Ulster, and a huge influx of immigrants from Ayrshire and Galloway during the 'lean years' of the 1690s transformed the religious demography of Ulster, and made many Anglicans fear for the continuance of their establishment, if not in Ireland as a whole, at least in the northern province. Those who paid more attention to the threat from popery argued for an eirenic approach to Dissent, in the hope of fostering Protestant unity. Those more fearful of a Presbyterian coup, or at least a secession, took the contrary view.

After an initial skirmish over toleration, ending in the failure of the Whig viceroy Capel in 1695 to obtain a Toleration Act, the conflict between the parties in Ireland focused on the issue of Presbyterians' access to political power. A 'sacramental test' was inserted by Tory privy councillors in England into the 1704 Irish Popery Bill, and the unsuccessful efforts made by Whig ministries to secure its repeal in the Irish parliament elevated the test into a symbol of Anglican Ascendancy. The clear majority against repeal may perhaps be taken as evidence that there was more theatricality than substance to party conflict in Ireland. In fact, most Irish MPs were in favour of keeping up the test, with only a handful of Whigs calling for its removal, and there was a similar consensus in support of penal laws against Catholics. The political nation as a whole, it could be argued, were 'church Tories but state Whigs'. However, this did not prevent bitter disputes between Tories and Whigs in parliament and in the constituencies, the breaking of friendships and the creation of lasting enmities even within the same family.

In England and Ireland the rise of 'party' made it difficult for the crown to manage parliament. Loyalty to a faction, or to an ideology, could override loyalty to the sovereign, at least in parliamentary terms, so that the monarch's freedom to choose ministers could be seriously compromised. 'Moderate' ministries were not impossible: Lord Treasurer Godolphin maintained an uneasy coalition of moderates and placemen between 1704 and 1708. But such frail plants could only survive in exceptional political circumstances, when party forces in the Commons were in equilibrium. The arch-'moderate' Robert Harley was reminded of this truth in 1710/11. Returning to power at the head of a predominantly Tory administration, after a general election which had produced a massive Tory majority, he found it impossible to retain in office even a favoured few 'moderate' Whigs. The history of Harley's ministry also illustrates another danger posed by the 'rage of party', the tendency of Tory and Whig extremists to advocate violent measures against their opponents: witch-hunts after corruption, the impeachment of enemies, the passage of legislation (in the case of the Tories, against Protestant Dissenters) which, though satisfying in party terms, damaged the social fabric of the country.

In Ireland too, the rise of party cramped the freedom of manoeuvre enjoyed by the viceroy. Thus, the Whig Lord Wharton, on his arrival in Ireland in 1709, found himself deserted by the former Tory parliamentary managers in Dublin, and obliged to rely on a set of Irish Whig politicians whose ability to secure an adequate subsidy was not clear. Two years later, when the Tory Ormond succeeded Wharton, these same Whigs prepared to oppose the new ministry long before they were removed from office. Viceroys who attempted coalition ministries were asking for trouble. The moderate Whig, Lord Pembroke, got away with it in 1707, because of the peculiar political situation in England, which inclined both Irish parties to support him, but the duke of Shrewsbury's ham-fisted efforts at moderation in 1713 cost him Tory as well as Whig support and made it impossible to secure a supply.

At local level, across the British Isles, party politics were also disruptive of political and social order. Press campaigns and popular demonstrations accentuated the divisions within society, especially sectarian divisions, and aroused the passions of the populace. The ideal of a harmonious local community, in which the gentlemen met in advance to settle the parliamentary representation, survived as a convention of political discourse, but in practice was subverted or ignored. The impressive decorum of county elections, once a scene of order and the expression of hierarchical values, vanished amid displays of party rancour: in 1705 the Tory candidates in Cheshire were chased by an angry crowd through the streets of Chester, while in Norfolk in 1710 the young Robert Walpole was pelted with dirt by Tory voters. The larger and more popular boroughs witnessed routine displays of physical violence: pitched battles between club-wielding thugs in such notorious troublespots as Coventry and Westminster, and even in Ireland, in the Dublin election of 1713, when troops fired on Tory rioters and a man was killed.

Parliamentary elections were not the only occasions of disorder. Municipal politics were badly affected: borough corporations divided and local government brought to a standstill. There could be violence here too, and not just the innocuous slapstick that saw aldermen wrestling for occupation of the mayoral pew in Devizes, but serious fighting, which left bodies on the streets. The Sacheverell impeachment of 1710 ignited anti-Dissenter riots in London and elsewhere, in which chapels were attacked and pulled down. In Ulster in 1714 'church mobs' nailed up the doors of meeting houses, and in the north of Scotland Presbyterian ministers and elders were 'rabbled' when they attempted to enter into parishes which had formerly been served by Episcopalian clergy.

Some historians have nevertheless sought to argue the paradox that, while superficially disruptive, the 'rage of party' actually served as a force for social stability. Tories and Whigs, they remind us, were competing with each other for power within the existing political system, not seeking to overturn that system. Moreover, the poor were being drawn into sectarian or partisan conflicts, rather than asserting economic grievances against the propertied. Thus, the urban radicalism of the 1680s and early 1690s lost its social dimension. The Whig populists who had previously challenged aldermanic oligarchy in London, Bristol, and other towns were now replaced by Tories, stirring up the emotions of the 'commonality' against Dissenters and foreigners in ways that left social hierarchy unchallenged. Even the Jacobite riots of 1715 and 1722, although they gave vent to scurrilous and subversive criticism of the king and the court, did so in the name of another monarch, not of republicanism. Indeed, the regime to which the Jacobite rioters harked back was in many respects more reactionary than the one against which they protested. There is certainly some weight in these arguments, but a risk in overstating them. The rage of party produced more than manifestations of different varieties of conservatism. There were acts of violence against persons and property, and expressions of popular hatred against men of wealth, merchants and financiers, albeit plutocrats distinguished by their foreign ancestry and religious nonconformity. Moreover, there seems little to choose between rampant sectarian animosities, on the one hand, and bread riots and agrarian disturbances, on the other, as signs of social instability. In Scotland, moreover, the logical extension of party conflict was civil war, in the wake of the Jacobite rising of 1715, and again in 1719 and 1745. These rebellions threatened the existence of the state as well as the ruling dynasty, because Scottish Jacobites tended also to be committed anti-unionists, for whom a separation from England was as important as the replacement of German George by the Stuart Pretender. It is in Ireland, perhaps, because of the peculiar circumstances of the Protestant propertied elite, that 'party politics' can best be presented as a force for political stability. Admittedly it accentuated the divisions within the Protestant population, between Anglican and Dissenter. However this focusing on internal divisions, over which there was in any case a degree of consensus among the gentry, diverted attention away from the potentially more disruptive problems of Anglo-Irish relations.

'Party' politics first began to disappear where they had most recently arrived: on the periphery of the British state, in Ireland and Scotland. The more acute implications of the succession issue for Irishmen meant that Jacobitism there was confined to a few English imports, bishops and government officials like the Tory Lord Chancellor in 1714, Sir Constantine Phipps, and the callow youths of Trinity College, Dublin, who (when drink had been taken) routinely defaced the equestrian statue of King William erected in College Green. Tories had already suffered losses in the Irish general election of 1713, at a time when the party was still in the ascendant in England. In the aftermath of the Hanoverian succession the process of attenuation speeded up, and the Irish general election of 1715 saw very heavy defeats. The more timid, or pragmatic, of the Irish Tories quickly sought to recast themselves as Whigs, and within one parliamentary session in Dublin, in 1715–16, the Tory interest in Ireland was reduced to a rump of 30–40 MPs in a House of over 300. Henceforth, parliamentary politics in Ireland was fought out between rival groups of Whigs. In Scotland the Tories' downfall was even more dramatic. Again, a drift towards 'Whiggism' had been detectable in the election of 1713, in so far as it was ever possible to define Scottish politics in party terms. In fact, many of the 'Whig' gains in 1713 were attributable to a revival in the Argyll interest. The duke of Argyll was the most powerful single magnate in Scotland, and ever since 1712, when he had severed his ties to administration, had identified himself with the Whigs. As in Ireland, Tories in Scotland did poorly in the 1715 election. The Scottish parliamentary contingent was now divided between different Whig factions, headed on the one hand by Argyll and on the other by a coalition of lesser magnates known as the Squadrone. A few of the more supple Tories discovered, or rediscovered, lost Whig credentials. Those who did not found themselves excluded from power and then from parliament. A substantial section of the party was already sufficiently alienated from the Hanoverian regime to take up the Jacobite cause in 1715. Needless to say, this was a political disaster for the Tory interest in Scotland, which was permanently tarred with the brush of Jacobitism.

In England Toryism did not collapse in the same way. True, the Tories lost ground significantly at the 1715 general election, but in pocket boroughs rather than in counties and popular urban constituencies. While the 'coronation riots' in 1714, and popular expressions of Jacobite sentiment during the rebellion of 1715, revealed a degree of alienation among ordinary people at the accession of a German king and the political triumph of the Whigs, Tory MPs were more circumspect. Although a few, including the former secretary of state, Bolingbroke, either fled to the Pretender, or dabbled in Jacobite intrigue by correspondence, hardly any prominent members of the party were willing or able to participate in the Fifteen. Despite indecisive and divided leadership, the party thus maintained a significant presence throughout the parliament of 1715–22. Moreover, the new regime showed itself unexpectedly vulnerable. Its oligarchic and authoritarian tendencies, highlighted in the passage in 1716 of the Septennial Act (lengthening the intervals between general elections), encouraged 'Country' Whig opposition. Moreover, both the court and the ministry were soon divided: George I quarrelled with his son, the Prince of Wales, who became a focus for political opposition to government; and then the Whig ministers quarrelled with each other, leading to the so-called Whig Schism of 1717, when Lord Townshend and his brother-in-law Robert Walpole left the cabinet. In response, the two chief ministers, Stanhope and Sunderland, embarked on a high-risk political strategy designed to reunite the Whig party behind government, appealing to radical Whigs and discontented Scottish members, by attacking the Anglican establishment. The Occasional Conformity and Schism Acts were repealed, and there were plans to remove the sacramental test in Ireland and to reform the English universities. Ultimately, this ambitious programme ran aground with the failure of the Peerage Bill in 1719, a measure intended to restrict the powers of the Prince of Wales, when he eventually became King George II, by limiting the crown's prerogative in the creation of peers. The ministry's defeat over the Peerage Bill was a massive blow to its self-confidence, and a year later a second disaster struck, as an era of feverish financial speculation came to a climax with the bursting of the South Sea Bubble, which not only appeared to endanger the public credit but threatened to engulf the court in scandal.

One aspect of government in which Tory opposition and the sniping of renegade Whigs had relatively little effect was Stanhope's conduct of foreign policy. Here there was considerable potential for discontent. British ministers had not lost the taste for strutting on the diplomatic stage; Stanhope in particular saw himself as a major European statesman. Nor indeed was it possible for Britain to abdicate from the position of responsibility in international affairs which Marlborough's victories had secured. Moreover, the accession of a Hanoverian monarch, with a strong personal stake in the maintenance of peace in northern Europe, not only made isolationism impossible, but created a potential conflict of interests between England and Hanover, and opened the way for opposition criticism that England's welfare was being sacrificed to the needs of the electorate. It was Stanhope's achievement to avoid these pitfalls, largely through a remarkable reversal of alliances. At the core of his diplomatic schemes was a rapprochement with the French, who in 1718 were induced to join Britain, the United Provinces, and the Empire in the Quadruple Alliance. The neutralizing of France allowed Stanhope to force the Spanish, probably Britain's keenest colonial rivals, to enter the alliance two years later, after a brief and successful naval war, and the defeat of a Spanish-supported Jacobite invasion of Scotland. Stanhope was somewhat less successful in his efforts to restrict Russian, Prussian, and Swedish power in northern Germany, which the king and his Hanoverian advisers regarded as a threat to the electorate, though the Treaty of Nystad in 1721 did bring some stability to Baltic diplomacy. Essentially, the entente with France permitted British ministers to preserve both English and Hanoverian interests for the next two decades without resorting to arms, with all the unpleasant consequences, in relation to recruitment and taxation, that would inevitably have followed.

After a reconciliation in the royal family and the reunification of the Whig party in 1720, the ministry recovered its poise, and the Whig Ascendancy was not only restored but extended. Having ridden out the storm over the South Sea Bubble, ministers went on the offensive. With the exposure of the Atterbury Plot in 1722, which appeared to implicate many leading Tories in Jacobite intrigue, Tory morale slumped and there was in effect a retreat into the political wilderness. This did not mean the end of party politics. There continued to be a recognizable Tory party in the Westminster parliament, sustained by surviving Tory interests in the English and Welsh constituencies. But the Tories were no longer able to compete for power on their own, and were obliged to work in parliament in alliance with dissident Whigs, as a 'Country party' or 'patriot' alliance. At their lowest point, during the 1727–34 parliament, they were almost inert. While party sentiment was still of importance in some constituencies and on some issues, notably questions between Church and Dissent, it was no longer the major source of political conflict, or the principal form of political discourse.

The Walpolean ascendancy

The period between 1720 and 1725 saw political settlement in all three kingdoms. At Westminster the establishment and reinforcement of a ministry under Robert Walpole; in Scotland the resolution of the struggle for pre-eminence between the Argathelian (Argyll) and Squadrone factions; in Ireland the emergence of a stable system of parliamentary management under a single 'undertaker'. The political settlement of Scotland and Ireland, involving the delegation of responsibility for management to local magnate interests, represented in part a belated recognition of the limitations of viceregal government. It was also a natural consequence of the establishment of a stable ministry in England.

After the general election of 1722, the Whigs enjoyed a comfortable majority in both Houses of the British parliament. The bulk of the Tories were quiescent; their leaders, even if inclined to volubility, were isolated and, ever since the Atterbury affair, vulnerable to innuendoes concerning their Jacobite associations. Party loyalty, and the operation of the patronage network, kept the Whigs in line. As prime minister, Walpole was quite secure. First, he could rely on continuing support from the throne. George I always remembered with gratitude his prime minister's achievement in defusing the South Sea crisis. Then, after a very brief period of difficulty following the succession of George II, Walpole was able to restore his reputation at court through his close friendship with Queen Caroline. Second, those able or willing to challenge him from within the administration were eased out of office one by one: William Pulteney, probably his only serious rival as a House of Commons performer, went in 1725; Lord Townshend in 1730. Carteret, the ambitious secretary of state, had already been exiled to Dublin castle as a reluctant viceroy. Third, he developed the techniques of parliamentary management pioneered by his predecessors (in particular Robert Harley). In the Commons Walpole led from the front, a natural parliamentarian with superb gifts as a debater (rather than an orator) and 'man of business', assisted by a coterie of bright young men, waspish wits like the young Lord Hervey and Thomas Winnington, and apprentice statesmen of the calibre of the future prime minister Henry Pelham and Lord Chancellor Philip Yorke, whose presumption irritated older parliamentary hands but whose ability and energy, when directed by their masterly mentor, ensured success in debates and divisions. In the Upper House he relied on a troop of 'poor lords' and pensioners, Scottish representative peers, and compliant careerist bishops, to do his work for him.

Such problems as Walpole did encounter in both Houses of Parliament were largely self-inflicted. Mindful of the disasters suffered by the Junto in Anne's reign, he was careful enough on religious questions not to raise the hackles of churchmen, and in general plotted a steady course between the demands of dissenting agitators and radical Whig anticlericals, on the one hand, and the outrage of High Church reactionaries, on the other. Until the closing stages of his premiership he was also able to avoid the dangers of involvement in military conflicts overseas, which had similarly weakened the Whig ministries of his youth. He was less successful in steering clear of scandals over governmental corruption, which inflamed the sensibilities not only of the opposition, but of the 'independent country gentlemen'. The report of the gaols committee in 1730, which disclosed a culture of graft and cruelty in the Fleet, followed soon afterwards by the exposure of profiteering by ministerial Whigs in the sale of confiscated Jacobite estates and in dealing in the stock of the Charitable Corporation, alienated many pious and patriotic Country Whigs and lowered the reputation of government significantly, just at the point, in 1733, when Walpole's political judgement for once deserted him and he introduced his ill-fated excise scheme.

In the event, the excise crisis was a turning point that failed to turn. Walpole lost the excise bill, but maintained his authority over the House of Commons. The aim of the project was to extend the scope of the existing excises, partly in order to get rid of the land tax, whose unpopularity Tory propagandists had exploited so devastatingly in Anne's reign. From this initiative, Walpole expected political gains in advance of the next general election in 1734. The effect on public opinion was, however, quite the reverse. Commercial interests, headed by the City of London, petitioned against the scheme on economic grounds. The parliamentary opposition took up the libertarian issue, arguing that the extension of the tax would necessitate the creation of an army of new officials, with powers of search and confiscation, and in any case that Walpole's real intention was to introduce a general excise, which would entirely overbalance the constitution by placing too much power in the hands of the executive. Discontent at the dubious moral basis of the 'Robinocracy', as Walpole's government was now derisively nicknamed, came to a head in a parliamentary and press campaign against the excise, which made good use of the imminence of the next general election, as constituency 'instructions' were issued to many MPs threatening them with ejection if they voted in favour of the bill. Desertions in Commons and Lords brought about the defeat of the excise scheme.

As a result Walpole lost face, and the parliamentary opposition gained some impetus, but the prime minister recovered his position through the harsh disciplining of recalcitrant placemen, and in the 1734 election the overall government majority in the Commons, although reduced, was still nearly 100 seats.

The excise crisis not only demonstrated that Walpole could not take parliament for granted. It signalled that some important changes were taking place in English political culture. With the parliamentary eclipse of the Tories, the tension between the established church and Protestant Dissent was no longer at the centre of public attention. Equally, the (essentially artificial) opposition of land and money, which had sustained Tory propaganda at the end of the War of the Spanish Succession, ceased to be a theme of critics of the Walpolean regime. Instead, it was the prevailing culture of corruption within the ministry, the overweening power exercised by Walpole himself, and his contrasting failure to protect or promote the real, commercial and colonial, interests of the kingdom, that constituted the constant refrain of opposition pamphlets and journals. The honest merchant, or as Bolingbroke's eponymous journal defined him, the 'Craftsman', became for political purposes the embodiment of public virtue, set against the corruption of power. The increasingly urban character of the campaigns against Walpole's administration reflected the fact that in practical terms the dynamic of opposition to the Whig regime was provided by radical figures in civic politics, in London especially, where Toryism had long since been redefined as resistance to aldermanic Whig oligarchy. The Country 'patriotism' espoused by Tories in Walpole's youth, cautious of becoming embroiled in foreign wars for fear of the high taxation involved, and the consequent expansion of executive power, had been transmuted by the late 1730s into an aggressive, expansionist, imperial 'patriotism', which no longer saw courtiers as selfish warmongers but as corruptly pusillanimous in defence of British interests.

The Walpolean settlement of Scotland involved little more than a recognition of the realities of Scottish politics. The Jacobite military challenge having failed in 1715, and even more ignominiously in 1719, partisans of the exiled Stuarts, like George Lockhart of Carnwath, made their peace with the Hanoverian state, and, even if they did not entirely abandon dreams of restoring 'James VIII', at least made little effort to turn them into reality. The real source of anxiety for ministers lay in the power-struggle between the Argyll connection, headed by the imperious second duke and his more tactful and dextrous younger brother, Lord Islay, and the Squadrone. The Argathelians suffered for a time after 1717 because of the duke's friendship with the Prince of Wales. Argyll was stripped of his offices, and intrigued with Walpole and Townshend during the Whig Schism. But although the Scottish ministry was now dominated by the Squadrone, Islay still retained his place as justice general. Thus, both factions were comprehended within government, even if at daggers drawn, and after 1720 Argyll and Islay were able to capitalize on their friendship with Walpole, and the tactical misjudgement committed by the Squadrone leader, Roxburghe, in making common cause with Walpole's rivals within the cabinet, notably Lord Carteret. Roxburghe found his own position as Scottish Secretary steadily undermined, and Argyll's steadily advanced, until the Scottish government's failure to preserve public order at the time of the Shawfield riots in Glasgow in 1725 (an outbreak of popular hostility against the malt duty) gave Walpole the pretext he needed to purge the Squadrone and replace Roxburghe with Argyll as principal Scottish manager.

There was a similar story in Ireland, though without any military prologue. Insurrectionary Jacobitism had long ceased to be a factor there, so completely had the Catholic interest been crushed by the Williamite victories of 1690–1 and the subsequent confiscations. During the Fifteen, the Nineteen, and as late as the Forty-Five, Catholic Ireland lay still. As in Scotland, problems arose from uncertain parliamentary management. The materials for a settled system were to hand, in the volume of patronage available to the crown, and the presence of several Irish politicians fit for the role of parliamentary 'undertakers'. What was needed was a clear and consistent approach to strategy, from Whitehall and Dublin castle. This was, however, easier said than done. The party conflicts of Anne's reign had had a disorienting effect, and it took time for the smoke to clear after the Hanoverian succession and the new contours of Irish politics to become visible. The collapse of the Tory interest left an overwhelming Whig majority in parliament, but the Irish Whigs were divided, between the followers of the Lord Chancellor, Alan Brodrick, and the Speaker, William Conolly. Not only was it difficult for successive viceroys to decide which of the two was the more powerful or more reliable; there were additional complications engendered by the Whig

Schism in England and the intrigues of both Brodrick and Conolly with prominent English politicians.

Matters came to a head in the Irish parliament of 1719, which granted an adequate supply but snubbed the advances made by the viceroy, the duke of Bolton, for a repeal of the sacramental test, a pet project of the Stanhope–Sunderland ministry. At the same time, the long-running dispute between the Irish and British House of Lords, over the appellate jurisdiction in Irish causes, reached a new level of bitterness, with the imprisonment of several Irish judges for giving an opinion on the British side. This was a critical moment. Stanhope and Sunderland seemed determined not to call another Irish parliament again, and to opt for a form of direct rule. The Declaratory Act, passed at Westminster in January 1720, asserted not only the right of the British House of Lords to hear causes on appeal from Ireland, but also the right of the Westminster parliament to legislate on Irish affairs, a power long assumed in England but rarely invoked. Why this second clause was added is a mystery, but it may have been in preparation for the use of the British parliament in some way as an instrument of Irish policy.

The crisis of 1719/20 was defused by the ministerial reconstruction in England, and the reintegration of the Walpole/Townshend faction into government. And in fact the aftermath of the Declaratory Act again showed up the limits of Irish Protestant 'patriotism' and the fundamental stability of Anglo-Irish relations. When parliament met again in Dublin nothing was said against the Act, and the overheated opinions of resident English bishops and office-holders, who had reported that Irish Protestants were ready to rise up in arms in defence of their parliament, were revealed as fantasy.

However, the underlying problems remained, and it required another crisis in Anglo-Irish relations before they were resolved. This time the *casus belli* was economic. The grant of a patent in 1723 to the Birmingham ironmaster William Wood, to produce copper coinage for Ireland, raised an outcry in the Dublin press, and violent popular demonstrations. So strong was the tide of opposition that neither of the 'two great men', Brodrick or Conolly, could or would stand against it. The involvement of George I's mistress, the duchess of Kendal, as original recipient of the patent, made the issue explosive, and Walpole decided that at all costs it had to be defused. In a tactical master stroke, he despatched to Dublin castle his ministerial rival

Carteret, suspected of intriguing with Brodrick and other Irish politicians, with instructions to settle the dispute. Carteret's solution involved recommending a withdrawal of the patent, which Walpole accepted with a bad grace, but more important in the long term was his decision to break with Brodrick and throw the weight of viceregal influence behind Conolly. This marked the beginning of what Irish historians understand as the 'undertaker system', the contracting out of Irish parliamentary management to local politicians. It was not a new idea, and one can find proto-undertakers as early as the mid-1690s. What was different in 1725 was the clear endorsement of a single 'undertaker'.

From a British perspective, the long period of Walpolean Ascendancy, from c.1725 to the sudden fall of the prime minister in 1742, seems to have been most effective in Scotland and Ireland, where after the crises of the mid-1720s a settled system of political management was established, relying on the loyalty of local political magnates. Walpole's 'Scottish system' survived until the brothers, Argyll and Islay, quarrelled among themselves and Argyll resigned from government in 1739. The Irish 'undertaker system' survived a period of uncertainty following the death of Conolly in 1729 and was reincarnated in 1733 in the person of his ultimate successor, Henry Boyle.

There were other developments tending towards a growth in political stability in Scotland and Ireland in this period, which went deeper than successful parliamentary management. The social tensions that had produced war in 1689, and rebellion in 1715 and 1719, were receding. Jacobitism appeared to be on the decline in Scotland, while the Catholic interest in Ireland lay prostrate. Furthermore, the large and restless Presbyterian community in Ulster, which in Anne's reign had appeared so formidable, was weakened by divisions over the imposition of theological orthodoxy, and by successive waves of emigration to the American plantations. The potential for disruption remained, of course. Neither of the established churches, in Scotland or Ireland, had succeeded in eradicating nonconformity. In Scotland Highland Catholicism survived the educational efforts of the Scottish Society for Promoting Christian Knowledge. Similarly in Ireland the penal laws had ensured conformity among the landed classes, but had not eradicated Catholicism or Presbyterianism as such. The process of acculturation or absorption was only half-complete, and in the process had superimposed a new layer of grievances. In Ireland the denial of civic and political rights to Catholics under the penal laws added to the historic burden of land confiscation. In Scotland the Argathelian Ascendancy over government in Edinburgh was manifest locally in a northward expansion of clan Campbell into the territory of its traditional Highland enemies.

But for those Scotsmen and Irishmen who were firmly inside, rather than on the fringes of, the Hanoverian state, the new system of governance had a great deal to offer. For the political classes, government patronage was effectively channelled through the Argathelian regime in Edinburgh, and the 'undertakers' in Dublin. It was true that in Ireland some of the plums, in both church and state, were reserved for Englishmen, but at the lower levels, and especially in the army, and in the expanding revenue service, Irish Protestants predominated. In other ways too, government was becoming more responsive to Scottish and Irish needs. Scotland's participation in the united parliament was not particularly advantageous: Scottish legislative business seems to have suffered from competition with English vested interests, while the Scottish members, few in number, erratic in attendance, and generally subservient to administration, enjoyed little influence. But there were other institutions available to the Scots in which business might be done, and vested interests satisfied. The Convention of Royal Burghs still functioned, and new boards and commissions were established to foster economic development, and incidentally to provide further resources of patronage. In Ireland the subordination of the Dublin parliament to the imperial government and the imperial legislature remained largely a matter of theory. Westminster MPs rarely if ever legislated for Ireland, and the privy council in London was restrained in its interference in the legislative process. Of course, the Irish parliament itself was less effective as a legislator than its British counterpart, meeting less often and taking longer to get things done, but by mid-century it was developing methods of assisting local economic development, by appropriations and grants of revenue, which satisfied some of the demands of the county elites. Most important, perhaps, in both Scotland and Ireland economic growth began to be perceptible from the 1730s onwards, particularly in the south-west of Scotland and in the north-east of Ireland, which eased social and political tensions.

We must be careful, however, not to exaggerate the degree of assimilation even among the loyalist elements in Hanoverian Britain. There was some overlap between the different landed elites as the result of intermarriage, and the inheritance of property, in particular the holding of large tracts of Irish lands by absentee English land-lords. There were also a few cases of Irish settler families returning to establish themselves in England, most notably the different branches of the Boyle family, Lords Burlington (in Yorkshire and Middlesex) and Orrery (in Somerset). Such connections were far more typical of the Irish, and for that matter the Welsh, than they were of the Scots. And just as it would be premature to talk of the development in this period of a transnational 'British' landed elite, so the degree of polit-ical or official intermixing was relatively small. Scottish politicians looked for advancement in Scotland, Irishmen in Ireland. Irishmen mixed with Englishmen in army regiments, since the Irish and English military establishments were to all intents and purposes the same, but Scottish regiments were proudly exclusive.

Nor was theory much in advance of practice. In the immediate aftermath of the Anglo-Scottish union ideas of 'Britishness' were aired, as representing an umbrella national identity which could pro-vide a focus of allegiance for the newly created state. Contemporary scholarship furnished the materials from which a shared ethnicity and heritage could have been fashioned. The notion of the common descent of Celts and Goths, which theologians took from Scripture, and antiquarians, both the serious-minded and the mountebank, deduced from their study of ring-forts and stone-circles, could have comprehended the Celtic peoples of Wales and Scotland (and even Ireland) in a common Britishness. Moreover, in this period concepts of national identity among the different inhabitants of the British Isles were by no means hard and fast. The Welsh gentry, for example, among whom one may detect both a process of Anglicization and a growing interest in Welsh culture and antiquities, saw themselves as 'Britons', 'Cambrians', and sometimes 'Englishmen'; the Irish Prot-estant gentry were in their own words both 'English' and 'Irish'. All this suggests a promising context for reconstructions of national identity. Yet, apart from a handful of Scottish virtuosi, the scholars whose work tended towards suggesting a communal ethnicity and identity did not write with political ends in view. Nor were English ministers and politicians really very much interested in the project of developing a common sense of national identity. Some political writers did use the word 'British', especially in connection with the crown's expanding overseas empire, but this connoted an essentially Whiggish understanding, emphasizing the importance of a pan-Protestant alliance against popery and Jacobitism, and thus was as much internationalist in scope as it was national.

Without any pressure for integration from the centre, the social and cultural elites of Ireland and Scotland returned to, or redeveloped, notions of a separate national identity. In Scotland this was politically unimportant: the interest in national history shown by the 'moderate literati' of the Presbyterian Church who formed the intellectual elite of mid-eighteenth-century Edinburgh, and the popularization by James Macpherson of an invented Gaelic bardic tradition under the name of the supposed poet 'Ossian', had no visible consequences for the regime. Anti-union patriotism had long since been absorbed into Jacobitism: it had given some inspiration to the Fifteen, but its role in the Forty-Five is much less clear. In Ireland, on the other hand, the development of 'patriotic' notions among the Protestant political nation did from time to time threaten unpleasant consequences for government, in the agitations of the parliamentary opposition against English 'misrule'. But these outbursts of 'patriotism' were stimulated by economic grievances rather than 'patriotic' sentiments as such, and in practice would probably have been unaffected by the diffusion of a sense of 'British' identity.

The end of the 'Robinocracy' and its consequences

The fall of Walpole in 1742 was a high political event, though significantly it was in parliament rather than at court that the blow was struck. Walpole lost office because he lost the confidence of the House of Commons, not because he lost the confidence of the king, nor because of any shift in 'public opinion'. Admittedly, his decline was accelerated by popular reaction to the failures of foreign policy which marked his closing years in power. After he had been pushed at long last into declaring war on Spain, which opposition press and English overseas trading interests had long demanded, Walpole's conduct of the war at sea attracted criticism. The stirring victory at

Porto Bello in 1739 was not followed up, and the British Lion cut a dismal figure in the public prints. Diplomatic imperatives, and George II's determination to defend his Hanoverian electorate, then drew Walpole into precisely the kind of situation Whig politicians had sought to avoid since the Peace of Utrecht, namely another major European land war, the War of the Austrian Succession. The disintegration of his foreign policy accentuated Walpole's own loss of confidence and control in 1741–2. He also suffered from the recrudescence of a dynastic 'reversionary interest' in the person of Frederick, Prince of Wales, who in true Hanoverian style quarrelled with his father and set himself up as a focus for opposition; and from the temporary breakdown in Scottish management consequent upon the split between the brothers Argyll and Islay, and Argyll's estrangement from government.

The end of the 'Robinocracy' was greeted with rejoicing in some quarters, but in the long run it seems to have made relatively little difference to English government. Not only did Whigs remain in office, these were for the most part the 'Old Corps' of Walpolean Whigs who had governed under the great man himself, and were now led by Henry Pelham and his brother the duke of Newcastle. It took the Pelhams a little time to establish themselves. Their hesitancy in committing British resources wholeheartedly to the war encouraged George II to turn to others who were more supportive of his Hanoverian interests, and to re-employ Carteret and other former Whig critics of Walpole alongside the Old Corps. Further military difficulties, and spiralling expenditure, brought to a head the differences within this uneasy coalition, and in 1744 the Pelhams were able to present the king with an ultimatum, and enforce Carteret's dismissal. A brief period of ministerial instability ensued, in which Tories were induced to participate with the Pelhams in a 'broad-bottom' administration, before the king attempted to intrude Carteret again, this time alongside another long-term critic of the Walpole Ascendancy, William Pulteney. By 1746, however, the Pelhams had once more re-established their authority in cabinet, and completed their triumph by securing a peace settlement.

The end result of four years of ministerial manoeuvring after Walpole's fall was thus the reinstatement in power of his principal lieutenants, who set themselves to follow broadly similar policies, in which low taxation and the maintenance of credit took precedence over diplomatic adventurism. Those who had expected the Robinocracy to fall with Walpole himself experienced a crushing disappointment. The eagerness with which former 'patriots' like Pulteney snatched at the opportunity to advance themselves added to the general sense of disillusionment and, indeed, may have prompted some of the more determined or radical critics of government to abandon traditional 'patriot' politics and turn towards ideas of parliamentary reform.

In Scotland and Ireland the fall of Walpole and the establishment of the Pelham administration had almost no impact. The death of the second duke of Argyll in 1743 left Islay, who had succeeded as third duke, without a serious rival as the government's de facto viceroy for Scotland. The seeds of future problems were detectable, in the personal animosity between the new duke of Argyll and Newcastle, but Henry Pelham was able effectively to restrain his brother's desire to peg back Argyll and lessen the ministry's dependence on a single Scottish manager. Alternatives were available from within the Argyll interest—Lord Deskford, the Lord Advocate Robert Dundas of Arniston, even the duke's faithful political fixer Lord Milton—but these creatures of the Argylls needed to be prompted and assisted before they would strike out for themselves. In Ireland, too, it was a case of business as usual: the same viceroy, Devonshire, at least to begin with, and the same 'undertaker', Henry Boyle. The only cloud on the horizon as far as Boyle was concerned had antedated Walpole's fall: the emergence of the Ponsonby family as rivals within the Irish administration.

In broader terms the 1740s witnessed the copperfastening of George II's rule over England and Scotland with the defeat of the Jacobite invasion of 1745. This was largely a Highland movement, although its initial success in Scotland (partly attributable to military incompetence on the Hanoverian side) had encouraged recruits from the Lowlands and raised for the last time the hopes not merely of Stuart loyalists but also of patriotic opponents of the Union. Having occupied Edinburgh and proclaimed James VII king of Scotland, Prince Charles Edward was able to advance south as far as the English Midlands, without serious opposition but at the same time without the additional recruits which the north of England had supplied to the Fifteen. English and Welsh gentlemen who had been happy to drink to the 'king over the water' while he or his representatives remained there, found various pretexts for not making good their promises. Their inactivity looked ever more prescient as 'Bonnie Prince Charlie' retreated from Derby, further and further until the remnant of his army was cut to pieces at Culloden and the duke of Cumberland's redcoats began to sweep the Highlands clear of rebels. The calamitous end to this episode has sometimes overshadowed the remarkable success of the Jacobites in reaching Derby in the first place, but in turn admiration for Charles Edward's initial successes should not blind us to the fact that, taken overall, and in comparison with the Glorious Revolution, the events of 1745–6 were evidence of a sharp decline in the extent of Stuart loyalism on the peripheries of the British state.

This period concludes therefore, with a confirmation of the changes to the British political systems wrought by the Glorious Revolution and its immediate aftermath. The balance of power between crown and parliament had shifted significantly towards the latter: George II was not able to choose his ministers, either to keep Walpole in 1742 or to employ Carteret in 1744, against the wishes of a majority of the members of the House of Commons. The core of the British state, and more particularly the south of England, the most commercially developed and the most Protestant region, and the most over-represented in the Westminster parliament, had consolidated its economic and political dominance over the archipelago. Disruptive elements in outlying regions had been suppressed.

At the same time new forces were perceptible which would threaten, and eventually undermine, this stable order. The emergence of Great Britain as a great power in Europe, and the expansion in British overseas commerce had brought new problems for government, the most important being the necessity of conciliating trading interests, which were better organized and better focused as political lobbyists. Disillusionment with the traditional politics of opposition, led by country gentlemen in pursuit of an old-fashioned concept of public virtue, would stimulate calls for parliamentary reform. Above all, 'public opinion' had swollen in importance. The growth of the press, particularly the provincial newspaper press, in the first half of the eighteenth century, and not just in England but in Ireland and Scotland too, disseminated information and opinions to a much wider audience. 'Popularity' was almost an objective in itself for some politicians; certainly William Pitt in England and Henry Boyle in

Ireland (during the so-called 'Money Bill crisis' of 1753–6), each appealed to the tribunal of public opinion when frustrated in parliament. Of course it is easy to exaggerate the extent to which the views of 'the people' mattered in mid-eighteenth-century politics. In fact, general elections were much less frequent after 1716 than they had been before the passage of the Septennial Act, and in many boroughs the franchise had become more exclusive since 1689, through decisions of the House of Commons on disputed elections. Public opinion may have been an object of attention, but it played very little part in the political decisions of the 1750s: neither the so-called 'diplomatic revolution', when Britain reversed its European alliances to pave the way for the Seven Years War; nor the settlement of the Money Bill dispute in Ireland in which Boyle, having appealed to public opinion against government, then concluded a deal with the Lord Lieutenant in defiance of public opinion. Nevertheless, these extra-parliamentary campaigns of English and Irish politicians were harbingers of a different style of politics, and of the different problems which imperial success would bring.

Representation of the Heiva at Otaheite

Figure 3 Daniel Dodd's depiction of the women of Tahiti confronting their European visitors as engraved for the *Journal* (1781) of Cook's last voyage. The great explorations were undertaken in the cause of science and enlightenment but for the public at home their interest lay in the exotic and, not infrequently, erotic.

2

Enlightenment and faith

David Hempton

Once upon a time, interpretations of the religious and intellectual history of the British Isles from the Glorious Revolution to the end of the Napoleonic Wars were based upon a straightforward set of interlocking propositions. The Church of England was regarded as a spiritually moribund, but exceptionally privileged establishment, with even less glorious episcopal outposts in Ireland, Wales, and Scotland. Old Dissent, with its roots deep in the seventeenth century and beyond, was seen as a tradition in which Calvinism inexorably surrendered to Unitarianism, piety to rationality, and political acquiescence to uncompromising resistance. Methodism was perceived as a peculiarly English species of counter-enlightenment enthusiasm designed to convert, delude, and, ultimately, subjugate the masses. Roman Catholicism in Britain and Ireland was thought to be languishing, punitively so in Ireland, under penal legislation, one beneficial consequence of which was an era of relative religious peace sandwiched between the vigorous and often destabilizing anti-Catholicism of the seventeenth and nineteenth centuries. Above all, the eighteenth century was regarded as an age of Enlightenment in which faith and superstition gradually gave way to reason, revelation to natural theology, and intolerance to tolerance. Enlightenment was thus a relatively tidy concept applied to the ideas of those who frequented salons and learned academies, and who then contributed individually and collectively to compendiums of triumphant new learning. The ideas generated during the Enlightenment were regarded as international in scope, universal in application, and progressive in direction. Enlightenment was regarded as having a specific chronology, a relatively unified body of ideas, and a new emphasis on the use of reason in understanding and improving the human condition.

The clarity of these propositions was matched by the geographical specificity of regions of enquiry. The British Isles were regarded as being exceptional within Europe, and even within the British archipelago each of the three kingdoms was treated as having a more or less autonomous religious history. Autonomous, but not equal, for the chief focus of attention was England, and more specifically its established church, either its genius or its nemesis. Most pervasive of all was the assumption, both explicit and implicit, that religion, however defined, was a less important feature of eighteenth-century life than before, as the British Isles and continental Europe emerged from their seventeenth-century wars of religion to concentrate upon state building, commerce, and improvement.

Not many of the above propositions have emerged unscathed from the critical scrutiny of the past twenty years. In particular, our understanding of the Enlightenment has been dramatically changed by those who have sought to expand its purview from learned coteries to much broader national, social, and cultural contexts. The old, relatively unified picture of the Enlightenment has thus given way to a more fragmented emphasis on process, context, and consumption. Certainly, Enlightenment ideas require proper social and economic contexts, if for no other reason than ideas and books were marketable commodities in the growth of commercial economies in the eighteenth century. Definitions of Enlightenment, therefore, if they are to be attempted at all, need to be flexible enough to embrace both the traditional emphases on the ideas generated by Newton, Locke, and the great Scottish moral philosophers, and movements such as Freemasonry, Methodism, mesmerism, and millenarianism, which were once, but no longer, regarded as unambiguously counter-enlightenment. Similar ambiguities and unresolved tensions are to be found in eighteenth-century preoccupations with the exotic. Strange encounters on colonial fringes before and during the Seven Years War excited the imagination, as did Captain Cook's voyages, the Journals of which became best-sellers. Indeed, the eighteenth century's preoccupation with difference, including its far from consistent reflections on racial and gender differences, is one of its most central features. Genre paintings of the British Caribbean islands, for example, display an exotic and erotic fascination with European, African, and Carib women. On the one hand, they reveal the existence of rigid European racial, social, and gender classifications, while on the other they explore through clothes, nudity, and physiognomy the consequences of new cultural encounters in tropical landscapes, including a voyeuristic fascination with women of mixed race.

Time, space, and religion

Where then to begin with sketching in the topographical features of an appropriate map of faith and Enlightenment in the eighteenth century? One place to start in the construction of a new mental picture is with the mapping of the ultimate boundaries of time, space, and religion, all of which underwent significant modifications in the eighteenth century. Conceptions of the beginning and end of all things, the territory that for centuries religion had marked out as its own, had to adjust to some fresh data. For most of the eighteenth century, the biblical narratives conditioned views about the history and destiny of the world. Indeed, pictorial representations of the equally unknowable deep past and millennial future shared many of the same characteristics. Both focused on the sequential and purposeful aspects of God's creative energy. Both viewed the beginning and the end of time more from a cosmic than a terrestrial perspective. Both presented the history of time, from its beginning to its consummation, as a divinely created stage upon which the drama of human redemption and punishment was played out. Both were suffused with sacred imagery borrowed mostly from the books of Genesis and Revelation. Indeed, up until the end of the seventeenth century Europeans had little conception of the past that was not rooted in the creation narratives and little concept of the future and of progress, except salvation history. However, the growing persuasiveness of the idea that human history was of much shorter duration than prehuman history presented serious imaginative problems for natural philosophers and illustrators alike. There were two dimensions to the problem. First, the steady drip of fossil discoveries began to show that the same creatures as traversed both biblical and modern landscapes did not populate the deep past. Unfortunately however, they were the only landscapes that painters and illustrators were in the habit of imagining. Fossils helped unlock the imagination. Indeed, the modern fascination with exotic, primeval creatures had its origins deep within the fossil collections of the late eighteenth and early nineteenth centuries, many of which were gathered in Britain by clergymen. Moreover, the sale of fossils, as with books, was a thriving commercial enterprise. Even more revolutionary in its implications, was the notion that perhaps it was better to uncover the deep past not by the common method of travelling backwards from modern times, a kind of natural philosopher's version of Whig history, but by travelling forwards from the deep past itself. Moreover, travelling geographically in space was seen by eighteenth-century explorers as travelling back in time. When travellers encountered exotic 'others' in their explorations, they thought they were witnessing the condition of their own ancestors when they lived in a pre-civilized state. In this way, space calibrated time. Unsurprisingly, therefore, the study of anthropology and prehistory were born together.

The realization that nature too had a sequential history, as distinct from a set of divinely created epochs, was one of the great intellectual shifts of the eighteenth century, and it laid the foundations for the more sophisticated evolutionary theories of the nineteenth century. The fact that the most telling advances were made in Britain, arguably the one European country where there was no great hostility between religion and science, is surely no accident. The reason for beginning with beginnings is not only for its intrinsic interest, but also for what it reveals about the thought structures of the eighteenth century itself. Although its views of the deep past and the future were undergoing profound modification, including in some quarters a repudiation of the fearsome belief in hell and eternal punishment, its imaginative frameworks remained essentially religious. Scholars who have detected the same pattern in government, politics, and economics have vigorously argued a similar case. Whatever else may be said about the eighteenth century, its public and private discourse was saturated in religion, even among those who resented it.

Moving from the conceptualization of time to the mapping of space, some of the new work on the Enlightenment has not only emphasized the importance of the geography of Enlightenment ideas, that is the local spaces and analytic sites in which they were conceived and debated, but also the geographical conceptions of the world that emerged from travellers' encounters with the new world. Indeed, the origins of modern geography as an empirical science have been traced to the processes of systematic observation, classification, and comparison carried out by the naturalists and illustrators who accompanied voyagers like James Cook. Mapping new lands, understanding different civilizations, especially those around the Pacific Rim, and posing new questions about the nature of human societies with religions very different from those of Europe, threw up problems and generated debates. Moreover, the nature of the debates about foreign places and their differences of culture and religion were partly shaped by the characteristics of the regions and geographical spaces in which the debates took place. But more than that, eighteenth-century encounters with geographical and social 'others' helped cement the Enlightenment, or the set of processes to which we affix the label, as thoroughly and self-consciously Eurocentric. For example, eighteenth-century Britons may have been intrigued and even enamoured with tales of Polynesian civilizations, but when it came to making charts and maps of 'religion, population and civilization' such as that constructed by James Wyld in 1815, the European nations were always placed on top and accorded the status of the most civilized. From that perspective, it could be argued that Enlightenment ideas helped lay the foundations for the export of commerce, Christianity, and civilization, which underpinned the rise of the British empire in the eighteenth century.

Enlightenment ideas, when rooted in the social and political spaces where they found expression, were as much about the exercise of power and control over nature and the world as they were about liberating minds from the tyranny of religious dogma. Human reason and self-interest were never discrete categories. Yet the most tangible result of an increasing interest in non-European cultures was the foundation of the great Protestant missionary societies at the turn of the century. Evangelicalism, exoticism, millennialism, and cultural imperialism all came together in an unprecedented explosion of voluntary societies including: the Baptist Missionary Society (1792), the London Missionary Society (1795), the Church Missionary Society (1799), and the Methodist Missionary Society (1813). Never before in British religious history were so many people involved, through raising money, sending missionaries, and disseminating 'missionary intelligence', in spreading Protestant Christianity beyond the borders of Europe. The unlikely fusion of evangelical zeal and the Enlightenment's fascination with the exotic dramatically brought to an end a century of British religious insularity.

An awareness of the complex issues involved in the rise of foreign missions should act as a warning against glib formulations of the relationship between Enlightenment and religion. In the traditional story the high priority ascribed to rational thought in the eighteenth century is regarded as part of a revolt against religion in general and against its association with bigotry, intolerance, and superstition in particular. But in reality the Enlightenment threw up a wide variety of responses to religion, from the advanced scepticism of some of the French-speaking thinkers to attempts to bolster orthodox belief by demonstrating its essential rationality, which was a more typical pattern in the British Isles. Even within the British Isles there was considerable variation in the religious priorities of thought originating in London, Edinburgh, and Dublin, reflecting the different political and religious conditions of the three kingdoms. In England, J. G. A. Pocock and others have referred to the notion of a 'conservative Enlightenment', which had as its central feature a determination to safeguard the painful gains of the seventeenth century, most notably the achievement of a mixed constitution, the survival of the Anglican establishment, the supremacy of law, the security of property, and the achievement of a limited measure of religious toleration. Thus, one interpretation of the English Enlightenment is to see it as a movement to protect a civilized society from the ravages of religious enthusiasm, superstition, and intolerance thought to have emanated principally from the respective religious capitals of Rome and Geneva. Presented in that light, the English Enlightenment could be regarded as a distinctively English fusion of conservation and modernization operating within an ordered providence, polite discourse, and the rhetoric of improvement.

However, eighteenth-century England was not without its religious spats. The Trinitarian controversy, opened up within Church and Dissent with the publication in 1712 of Samuel Clarke's *The Scripture-Doctrine of the Trinity*, rumbled on for the rest of the century and became the organizing principle for much of the subsequent discourse about the relationship between church, state, and society.

At stake in these disputes were not only complex metaphysical disagreements about the divine substance, most of which had been rehearsed centuries before, but also the respective weight that was to be given to Scripture, tradition, and human reason in formulating theological arguments. Clarke's work was therefore noteworthy as much for its *method* of reasoning as for its conclusion. At issue was not only theological, but also political orthodoxy. The famous debate between Clarke and Leibnitz, for example, during which they articulated their respective views about God, nature, the vacuum, metaphysics, and the nature of space and time, was in reality as much about seeking out resources for political ideology as it was about science and nature.

Although the English church had been rocked by the Deist controversy that lasted for some fifty years after the Glorious Revolution, there was a widespread consensus by mid-century that the Deists effectively had been answered by the combined orthodox onslaught of Berkeley and Butler, Waterland and Warburton, who had appealed both to reason and revelation in their defence of orthodoxy. For the rest of the century, the chief threat to the intellectual and ecclesiastical Ascendancy of Anglican enlightened conservatism came from the rational Dissenters. There are still unresolved debates about whether dissenting radicalism emanated principally from theological heterodoxy, the curriculum of the dissenting academies, an autonomous ecclesiastical polity, or from a sense of political and social exclusion in an age of revolutionary change across the world, but there is no doubting the contribution of rational Dissenters to reforming impulses throughout the eighteenth century. Although the Anglican Tories of Queen Anne's parliaments tried to restrict the political influence of Dissenters through the passage of the Occasional Conformity Act (1711) and the Schism Act (1714), Dissenters soon found practical ways around the legislation, and were further liberated by the passage of almost annual Indemnity Acts from the late 1720s. The Test and Corporation Acts nevertheless remained on the statute books as tangible reminders of the lack of civil equality enjoyed by Dissenters. Energetic attempts to repeal the hated acts in the 1730s under the leadership of the newly formed Protestant Dissenting Deputies came to nothing. Later in the century, Dissenters began to sense a more tolerant attitude towards those outside the Anglican establishment, which was reflected in the passage of Savile's

Relief Act of 1778, benefiting Roman Catholics, and in the Dissenter's Relief Act of 1779, which relieved dissenting ministers and school-teachers from subscribing to the Thirty-Nine Articles. Mild concessions like these were one thing, but as events were to prove, the achievement of full political and civil equality was quite another.

Nevertheless, with a secure base among the mercantile elite in England's great cities, rational Dissenters had links with most of the reforming movements of the late eighteenth century, including access to the Whig political elite. What they wanted was religious liberty and parliamentary reform, not an end to existing hierarchies or social inequality. They were as frightened of the atheistic, democratic, and demagogic impulses of the extreme fringes of English reform movements as any moderate Anglican. The limits of dissenting radicalism, even of its most famous exponents such as Priestley, Price, and Lindsay, are therefore as revealing as its extent. Take law as an example. Given the legal disabilities of eighteenth-century Dissenters it is not surprising that some dissenting congregations, most notably Theophilus Lindsay's in Essex Street in London, had a dense concentration of lawyers, or that the social dimensions of law were of particular interest to dissenting intellectuals like Joseph Priestley. In 1769 Priestley professed himself outraged by the sections relating to religious Dissent in Blackstone's magisterial, if unmistakably Anglican and property-centred, *Commentaries on the Laws of England*. But the remarkable feature of this public disagreement is how quickly the two combatants found a *modus vivendi* based upon a shared admiration for each other and for the centrality of the law in English life. There is a parallel here with E. P. Thompson's immensely influential *Whigs and Hunters* with its portrayal of a simultaneous admiration for the history of English common law and contempt for some new statutes and their brutal enforcement under the Hanoverian Whigs.

The impression is often given in books about Anglican and dissenting political theology in the eighteenth century, that the debates were either a substitute for, or a deflection from, more conventional religious piety, but that is not how it was seen at the time. Within Dissent, sermons on public affairs were kept mainly for public occasions and anniversaries, the rest of the time what was enjoined on listeners was chiefly a practical piety informed by reverence, moral excellence, and a sense of duty. In the main, heterodox theology was not embraced by Dissenters as a way of evading Christian disciplines, as some nineteenth-century evangelicals perversely thought, but as a way of protecting them from the corrosive influences of enthusiasm and fanciful notions. Whatever the intention, the result was the steady decline of the old dissenting interest in England in the second half of the eighteenth century before it was revived and energized by the very evangelical enthusiasm it had for so long feared. When growth came, it came not to the predominantly middle class and this-worldly Unitarians and Quakers, but to the largely working-class evangelical Nonconformists who were otherworldly and more ignorant.

Some of the same tensions and intellectual influences that dominated religious life in England also found expression in Scotland and Ireland, but the contexts were different and so too were the emphases within enlightened thought. As with England, the shape of the Scottish Enlightenment cannot be understood without a grasp of the distinctive nature of Scottish institutions and culture in the years after the Act of Union. Although Scotland did not exist as a sovereign state after 1707, it retained many of its distinctive institutions and cultural traditions including a Presbyterian established church, its own legal system, its own schools and universities, and even its own spoken languages, which thrived in some parts of the country. The Scottish Enlightenment brought forth talent of truly international significance, spanning three generations from Francis Hutcheson, born in the 1690s, through Adam Smith, David Hume, Thomas Reid, and William Robertson, who were born in the 1710s and 1720s, and culminating in the work of James Beattie and John Millar, who were born after 1735.

The scope and depth of the Scottish Enlightenment defies easy compression, but it was distinctively Scottish in essence as well as international in scope. Unusually among the thinkers of the European Enlightenment, most of the Scottish literati worked in institutions, were not alienated intellectuals, did not run state bureaucracies, and did not wish for the overthrow of the existing order in any political sense. They were mainly professional men who made their most significant contributions in the fields of political economy, jurisprudence, natural science, anthropology, and moral philosophy, especially the common sense tradition that made such a deep impact on the American colonies. The Scottish Enlightenment requires a proper social context so that the productions of its· stellar elite should not be isolated from the wider cultural life of Scotland and

Edinburgh, its capital city. Religion is a good example. The Moderates who came to dominate the Church of Scotland by 1760 tried to inculcate a rational and urbane form of Presbyterianism some distance removed from Knox's hard Calvinism and Hume's arch scepticism. They emphasized public virtue, ethical obligations, social improvement, religious tolerance, and freedom of expression. Their ideas were rooted in civic humanism, classical republicanism, and moderate Whig constitutionalism. Above all, they wanted their church and their society to be models of urbanity and virtue, a Presbyterian 'godly commonwealth' of a more enlightened kind than Knox's sterner sixteenth-century vision.

Largely a creation of the migration of Lowland Scots, the Presbyterian dissenting community in Ireland experienced similar tensions between old orthodox Calvinism and 'New Light' influences. 'New Light' intellectuals gathered around Francis Hutcheson's dissenting academy in Dublin in the 1720s and both influenced and were influenced by the Scottish Enlightenment through their close links with the Scottish universities where many Irish Presbyterian ministers were trained. Central to 'New Light' thought was a more optimistic view of human nature than was to be found in orthodox Calvinism. Their emphasis on human rationality, benevolence, natural law, and religious toleration made them unwilling to subscribe to the Westminster Confession, which they regarded as a mere product of its time and place. Moreover, enforced subscription to a human formulation seemed to be an offence against voluntary commitment, which they saw as the best guarantor of religious and civic virtue. The resultant subscription controversies rocked Irish Presbyterianism throughout the eighteenth and early nineteenth centuries, but they also had the effect of keeping alive a vigorous debate about the essence of Irish Presbyterianism that sustained a surprisingly rich intellectual tradition. A central component of that tradition, and, given its Irish situation, its most contested feature, was its enthusiasm for a wide range of religious toleration. What was worked out in the relatively calm atmospheres of Irish dissenting academies and Scottish universities could not easily stand up to the social and political turbulence of the 1790s, when Irish Presbyterians faced hard choices about how much religious toleration and political emancipation should be extended to Roman Catholics. Revolutionary violence in France, bitter social disturbances in the Irish countryside, and the

United Irish risings of 1798 divided and then chastened Irish Presbyterians. The 'New Light' tradition of Presbyterian liberalism was far from extinguished by the events of the 1790s, but its optimistic view of human nature had suffered a rude shock from which other traditions, more conservative and evangelical, stood to benefit in the nineteenth century.

Enlightenment in Ireland was not confined to its Presbyterian Dissenters. Nevertheless, despite a much greater penetration of French books and ideas than one might expect, the Enlightenment was not a distinctive phase in the history of Irish culture in anything like the same way as it was in Scotland. Although the cult of improvement made an impact on Dublin's civic culture, and an era of landlord prosperity facilitated a rage of country house building that brought Ireland into the milieu of European architectural and landscape design, the intellectual culture thrown up by the so-called Ascendancy was of a characteristically Irish kind. Acute social observation, linguistic dexterity, quizzical argumentation, and a sense of ambiguity and irony, far more than a distinctive moral philosophy, mark the literary output of the great Irish writers: Swift, Berkeley, Burke, Goldsmith, and Sheridan. In that sense, they betray their largely middle class and Anglican origins (though Burke's mother and wife were Catholics). Uneasily poised between resentment of and dependence upon England, between contempt and compassion for Irish peasant culture, and between a preoccupation with the uniqueness and universality of Irish problems, the characteristic output of the Irish literati is not devotional piety or moral philosophy, but social and political observations of the most biting and satirical kind. In essence, they are the concerns of a relatively homogeneous and provincial colonial elite exploring the inner contradictions of its own position. There could be no clearer example of the importance of process and context in the evaluation of the thought and literary output of the eighteenth century. The respective intellectual cultures of London, Edinburgh, Dublin, and even Manchester and Birmingham thus reflected both wider currents in European thought, and, more particularly, the preoccupations of the social spaces they inhabited.

Established churches and the rise of pluralism

The public social spaces most familiar to eighteenth-century Europeans were the ecclesiastical parishes, church buildings, and graveyards of the various established churches. Generally speaking, European states relied upon established churches as the chief devices for christianizing their native populations. That pattern was particularly evident in the Protestant established churches of Britain and Ireland, for unlike their European Catholic counterparts, there were no viable alternatives. The absence of anything like the Catholic religious orders, on the one hand, and the lack of substantial investment in the British national churches, on the other, left the established churches particularly vulnerable to increased demands or expectations. For much of the eighteenth century that was not a significant problem, for established churches were not so much expected to do things as to be things. They were an integral part of the theory and practice of governing, and they were expected to baptize, catechize, confirm, ordain, pastor, bury, celebrate, and educate. Within certain limits, however, the social salience of established churches depended less upon their performance of religious duties than upon their perceived centrality to the religious life of the nation, broadly conceived. The two concepts are not unrelated, but they were not as closely related in the eighteenth century as later evangelical, utilitarian, Nonconformist, and radical critics alleged. Hence, until relatively recently, much of the historiography of the established churches in all parts of the British Isles has been critical of their moral, pastoral, and structural deficiencies, but has been less insightful in understanding their function within the framework of eighteenth-century conditions. Much of recent scholarship, while not denying the existence of abuses and anomalies, has presented a more optimistic picture of these churches as relatively benign, if rather ramshackle, institutions doing a reasonable job within the parameters of contemporary expectations. Even the Irish and Welsh churches, for so long regarded as the sharp edge of Episcopalian malpractice, now have sophisticated modern defences of their achievements. What put established churches under increasing pressure in the second half of the eighteenth century, however, were new circumstances. These circumstances included rapid population growth, the virtual collapse of ecclesiastical coercion, the erosion of deference, the rise of new religious alternatives, and a subtle intellectual shift, itself the product of the Enlightenment, that meant that churches could avoid neither religious competition nor utilitarian audit.

Just as the impact of the Enlightenment was played out in different ways in different parts of the British Isles, the same is true of the fate of religious establishments. In England, the Toleration Act of 1689 seriously undermined the legal basis for the enforcement of religious uniformity and moral discipline. Although the church courts did not wither away as quickly as once was assumed, the combined effects of a decline in Puritan morality and the expansion of the population and the economy contributed to their steady decline. By the end of the eighteenth century, many churchmen were more disposed to use persuasion than coercion, and more inclined to work for diocesan reform and renewal than to rest on existing privileges. It is true that the French Revolution and the phenomenal spread of itinerant preaching in England during French wars reawakened old neuroses about the fate of Church and State, but the attempt to restrain itinerant preaching failed miserably in 1811, and it was quickly followed by an extension of religious toleration in 1812. The decline of its coercive power was not necessarily a disadvantage to the Church of England, which had generally valued parochial loyalty to the Book of Common Prayer's rites and ordinances more highly than the fruits of inquisitorial zeal, but it did point up a subtler shift in the relations between church and people in the eighteenth century. Attendance at church services, participation in catechizing, and the practice of communion all became more dependent on the inclination of parishioners than on the insistence of the clergy. This alteration in the balance of power between the producers and consumers of Anglicanism was perhaps the most important consequence of a century of increased religious toleration.

The picture of the Church of England that has emerged from the large number of local studies and printed visitation returns of the past two decades is of an institution reasonably well adjusted to the prevailing social and political conditions of the eighteenth century, at least up to the 1770s when those conditions rapidly began to change. The church had some legal powers and privileges, but was not unduly inquisitorial or persecuting. It was supported by property owners, and was in turn preoccupied, indeed almost obsessed, by the defence and enhancement of its own properties including tithes, parsonages, and pew rents. Its clergy, in the main, were neither piously devoted nor scandalously negligent, but were generally dutiful if rather unambitious pastors. Although pluralism and non-residence were rife, few parishes were pastorally neglected and few pluralists were consumed by greed. Its parish churches, much more than its clergy, were focal points of a genuinely popular Anglicanism, which valued tradition, community rituals, and religious harmony. The church's performance of its basic duties of administering the rites of passage, conducting services, and catechizing the people was, by and large, more impressive than was once thought.

By the 1760s, therefore, it seemed that the church had successfully weathered a century of intense religious conflict. Some of the Old Dissenting denominations were palpably waning; the Deists had been refuted; the Whig proscription of Tory office-holders was a thing of the past; the old High Church party was on the verge of a remarkable intellectual and ecclesiastical revival; the growing evangelical movement within the church was pastorally innovative, but scarcely ecclesiastically radical; the perceived threat from Roman Catholicism was much diminished after the failure of the Jacobite uprising; Methodism seemed nothing more than a ginger-group of empty-headed enthusiasts; church parties were on the whole more united on essentials than divided on peripherals; in terms of property, the church had profited enormously from the enclosure movement and the general prosperity of the British economy; in terms of ideas, the Church of England was regarded as supplying the ideological underpinning of the fairest and most enlightened constitution in Europe. All was subsumed under a Protestant providentialism that viewed the English church as a divinely blessed via media between the excesses of Rome and Geneva. England's successful wars against the French, its growing overseas empire, its social stability and its mercantile hegemony were all interpreted as the blessings of a beneficent providence on a Protestant people. It was in the 1760s that Robert Hay Drummond, Archbishop of York, concentrated his energies on the transformation of Bishopthorne palace into a mansion fit for a prince of the church, added his weight to the campaign for the appointment of bishops for the American church and told his evangelical clergy that inculcating the morality of Socrates would do more good than 'canting about the new birth'. The palace survived, the American church found itself on the wrong side of a political and social revolution, and the rise of evangelical religion in Yorkshire, both within and outside the church, proved unstoppable. In short, by the 1760s the superficial appearance of the Church of England could hardly have been more attractive, but appearances were deceptive.

The church's much-vaunted connection with the state was more impressive in theory than in practice. During the eighteenth century the successive pet plans of bishops and archbishops such as Wake, Gibson, and Secker were all entertained and then ignored by their political masters, a trend that became ever more alarming to churchmen in the early nineteenth century. The meagre resources of Queen Anne's Bounty could not adequately address the internal structural problems of the church, which seriously hampered its pastoral efficiency. More seriously, the church's claim to be the church of the English nation suffered under the stresses and strains accompanying the American and French Revolutions, and the wars they generated. By the end of the eighteenth century, rising population, the spectacular growth of Methodism and Roman Catholicism, political disaffection in town and country, and the establishmentarian neurosis of the church itself all combined to give fresh credence to the old slogan, 'the Church in Danger'. Although in the nineteenth century, the church, sometimes aided by the state, displayed remarkable powers of survival, reform, and renewal, it never again emerged as the uncontested church of the English.

Understanding the fate of Anglicanism outside England poses special problems, for in both Ireland and Wales the churches were later disestablished, essentially for failing to attract enough support within their host populations to satisfy utilitarian calculations or to mitigate old cultural animosities. Once lack of success is defined by a terminal destination, especially a destination arrived at by a long history of bitter conflict, historians are inclined to concentrate on looking for the seeds of subsequent decline. The conventional picture of Anglicanism in Wales, therefore, is of a church of spectacular weaknesses and abuses, fully deserving of its disastrous fate in the nineteenth century, when evangelical nonconformity swept over the country like a tidal wave. That the Welsh church was indeed riddled with defects, most of them occasioned by crippling administrative and financial problems inherited from the sixteenth and seventeenth centuries, is not in dispute. Some of the most quotable cases of ecclesiastical absenteeism, corruption, and neglect in the entire eighteenth century are to be found in Wales. But such quotations draw attention away from other salient features of Welsh Anglicanism. The northern dioceses of Bangor and St Asaph were better off and attracted more ecclesiastical talent, sometimes of an unusually high order, than the southern dioceses of St David's and Llandaff. Moreover, for all its perceived weaknesses, the established church was not faced by rapidly growing alternatives. In Wales there were significant and energetic pockets of Roman Catholicism and, more commonly, Dissent, but together they ministered probably to less than 10 per cent of the population before 1780. Most impressively of all, the Welsh church, aided by a remarkable commitment to elementary education and to the dissemination of religious literature in Welsh, succeeded in nurturing a strong popular devotion to Protestant Christianity cloaked chiefly in Anglican garb. Seen from that perspective, the striking gains made by Methodism later in the century were as much a result of pre-existing Anglican devotion as they were of Anglican pastoral neglect. Enthusiastic Anglicans like Griffith Jones helped nurture the first generation of Methodist revivalists such as Howel Harris, Daniel Rowland, and the hymnologist William Williams (Pantycelyn), who made their most striking early gains in those parts of south Wales most neglected by the pastoral machinery of the established church. Similarly, Jones's hugely successful circulating schools, designed to instruct Welsh children in the vernacular, not only helped rejuvenate popular Anglican devotion in many Welsh parishes, but also brought into being a rough popular literacy upon which Methodist preaching thrived. Methodism thus traded on both the negative and positive poles of Anglican spirituality. Put another way, Methodism enthusiastically satisfied the religious expectations that the established church helped raise but could never properly fulfil.

If the Welsh church has suffered from a bad historical press, it is as nothing compared to that endured by the episcopal established church in Ireland. The conventional picture of the Church of Ireland is of a minority religious establishment imposed ineffectually from above and buttressed by a draconian set of penal laws against Catholics and the sacramental test against Presbyterians. Such a foundation, it is alleged, militated against the prosecution of the church's pastoral mission. Criticized for preferring to rely upon coercion and political influence among the elite rather than pastoral efficiency among the many, the Irish church had the appearance of an upper-class sect seeking to impose itself on an unwilling nation. Given the less advanced state of historical research on the Irish church in comparison with the Church of England, it is difficult to make bold statements about its condition in the eighteenth century, but it is clear that the Irish church was not as bad as it was painted. Once the point is conceded that the Irish church, whatever the stated aspirations of some of its more extreme High Churchmen, was not in reality a national establishment at all, but rather a church with a limited constituency, then its apparent lack of resources, manpower, and national coverage become less critical. Shrill calls for internal reform from the likes of William King, Archbishop of Dublin, and the disappointed expectations of newly arrived English clergymen, both of whom had a vested interest in exposing deficiencies, should not detract from the achievements of a church which in truth was embarked upon an unachievable mission.

The Irish church was neither fabulously wealthy nor, by eighteenth-century standards, unusually ineffectual in its pastoral conduct; it was simply a rather threadbare established church creaking under the weight of unrealistic expectations, not unlike many of its European counterparts. Its main strength, partly owing to its patronage connections with the Church of England, was in supplying a religion ideally suited to the Irish landed classes. Its main weakness as an established church was that its rituals, symbols, and celebrations could not operate as socially binding mechanisms on anything like the same terms as in England, for the victories it celebrated were interpreted as defeats by the majority Roman Catholic population it could neither convert nor coerce. The Church of Ireland was not without its reforming movements in the eighteenth century, most notably its commitment to elementary education in the early part of the century and its surprisingly vigorous evangelical movement centred from the 1780s on Dublin, but it was hard for it to escape the logic of its own history as a church imposed from above and without. The Act of Union in 1800, far from helping to secure its position, merely reduced the influence of its bishops, brought it within the sphere of an increasingly unfriendly utilitarian audit and rendered it the softest target of all the established churches in the British Isles.

Arguably the most successful of the established churches, at least in terms of popular allegiance, the exercise of moral discipline, and the weakness of alternatives, was the Presbyterian Church of Scotland. Although the Act of Union of 1707 delivered favourable terms, the church still had to work hard to clear out Episcopal ministers from its parishes, redeem the Highlands from Catholicism and Episcopalianism, and impose the Kirk's discipline on a rapidly changing society. Its Achilles heel was the issue of church patronage, which agitated the church relentlessly for a hundred and fifty years, resulting eventually in the creation of a Presbyterian dissenting population almost twice as large as that of the church itself. The apparently simple question at issue in the bitter patronage disputes of the eighteenth century was who had the rightful authority to appoint ministers to parishes. But the issue was addled by serious disagreements about the proper role of the church in Scottish society, social conflicts amounting almost to primitive class-consciousness in the Scottish countryside, and the brokering of political power both within Scotland and between England and Scotland. The genesis of the conflict was the Patronage Act of 1712, passed in contravention of the Act of Union of 1707 by an English Tory government, which left church patronage in the hands of the crown and the aristocracy. For some time after 1712, patrons were slow to exercise their right of presentation in the face of popular hostility, but the situation changed in the second quarter of the eighteenth century when Walpole's Scottish agents used patronage as a device to encourage political loyalty, social stability, and religious moderation. Given the relatively open and democratic nature of the Kirk's ecclesiastical structure, patronage disputes had both local salience and national resonance. The predictable consequence was a string of Presbyterian secessions, not essentially over doctrine, but over different styles of Presbyterianism. The rise of religious pluralism in Scotland, albeit on a rather modest scale before 1800, was therefore a predominantly Presbyterian phenomenon.

Helping to feed secessionist impulses was the growing influence of evangelical religion, which burst into spectacular prominence in the Cambuslang revivals of 1742. It seemed like the old enthusiasm of the long communion seasons, the 'holy fairs' of Ulster-Scots culture, were to be reinvigorated by the new evangelical preaching of George Whitefield and others. The Cambuslang conversion narratives not only show the susceptibility of young women and men to new, transatlantic forms of religious revivalism, but also pay tribute to the slow, patient efforts of the Scottish Kirk in laying foundations of biblical literacy through catechisms, Bible reading, and parish instruction. Cambuslang proved not to be the dawn of a new millennial age of 'vital religion' in Scotland, as its perpetrators had hoped, but it did further persuade intelligent Scottish moderates like William Robertson that the Scottish church was in danger of capitulating to a ragbag of evangelical enthusiasts, narrow-minded secessionists, and extreme Calvinists. The rise of the Scottish Moderate party to prominence in the General Assembly of the church was as much a product of fear of the alternatives as it was a systematic application of Enlightenment concepts to the life of the Scottish church.

Concentration upon patronage disputes, revivalistic zeal, and the nuances of ecclesiastical politics can sometimes deflect attention away from the profound impact of Scottish Presbyterianism on Scottish life and culture. Perhaps more than anywhere else in the British Isles, the Scottish established church was a vital instrument of civil, moral, and judicial authority that affected the lives and behaviour of most of the Scottish people. Church courts there were able to conduct a more sustained campaign against fornication and other moral 'evils' than anywhere else in the British Isles. Conventional religious observance as measured by attendance at church and communion was probably not very high, but there was general acceptance of the Kirk's centrality to the life of the local community, at least until the end of the eighteenth century, when rapid social and economic transformation created new pressures and social divisions.

Popular religion

The emphasis so far on the structure of Enlightenment thought and the function of established churches reveals more about the intellectual priorities and ecclesiastical policies of social elites than about the religious beliefs and practices of ordinary people. Vexing questions such as how far down the social scale did Enlightenment ideas actually penetrate, or what was the structure of popular religious belief, are difficult to answer, given the paucity of evidence and the provisional state of research upon the subject. Local studies from around the British Isles have drawn attention to both the extent and the limits of the religious influence of established churches over their parishioners. Their almost universal control over the rites of passage, their surprisingly high levels of commitment to catechizing, and their centrality to the ritualistic and celebratory rhythms of life in the countryside all testify to their significance. Eighteenth-century parishes, regardless of the state of their pastoral supervision, celebrated important events in national history such as Guy Fawkes Day, Oak Apple Day, the martyrdom of Charles I, and the accession of the reigning monarch. They were also at the heart of a much wider range of celebrations associated with the Christian and agrarian calendars, the precise balance of which varied according to inherited local custom from parish to parish. But even these statements fail to convey the central importance of religious rites and customs in early modern Britain. Partly legitimized by the Book of Common Prayer and the Books of Homilies, and partly guided by ancient custom, parochial rituals helped shape the mental frameworks of rural dwellers. For example, the annual Rogation week celebrations following the fifth Sunday after Easter were designed to emphasize the beneficence of God as provider of all good things and as regulator of the social order. The custom of perambulating the parish was not only designed to inculcate a sense of spatial boundaries, but was also a way of reinforcing a primitive social consensus about the ownership and utilization of land. Often associated with degrees of bawdiness and drunkenness, the purpose of these perambulations was to reinforce the mental maps of parishioners, including the boundaries of territory, the legitimacy of the social order, the management of change (associated with enclosures), the resolution of conflict, and the right of access to rudimentary welfare provision. Even the aural culture of parishes with their rough music and customary bell ringing was inexorably linked to parochial celebrations of one kind or another. They were supplemented also by manorial processions, the chief purpose of which was to secure property rights from any unwelcome encroachments. The celebratory mapping of boundaries among common people was a practice of ancient provenance, but it has curious parallels with the more sophisticated cartographic productions of 'enlightened' geographers.

Public displays of parochial religiosity, however mixed up with other economic and social frameworks, are useful to the historian not only for what they reveal about the centrality of religion in village custom, but also for what they suggest about the internal belief structure of quite humble people. It is wise to state at the outset that any analysis of popular belief and practice in the early modern period has to acknowledge the complexity of the subject, shifts over time and from place to place, and the inadequacy of essentially Enlightenment distinctions between religion and superstition and the sacred and the profane. Except for great tracts of the Irish countryside, which were relatively unaffected by either the Reformation or the Counter-Reformation, the great mass of the population of eighteenth-century Britain accepted Protestant Christianity in some sense. But in what sense? Despite substantial efforts to transmit Christian doctrine through catechisms, sermons, liturgies, and manifold forms of cheap literature, the beliefs of the bulk of the population were characterized more by providentialism and Pelagianism than by a detailed appreciation of Christian theology. Compliance with the rites of the church mattered more than subscription to propositions of faith. Similarly, there was on the whole no great tension between accepting basic Christian formularies and utilizing a whole set of other devices to manage nature and assuage anxiety. Social function is therefore as important as form and content. Indeed, it could be argued that the very rational and scientific methods promoted by the Enlightenment to validate knowledge are more of a hindrance than a help in understanding the popular religiosity of its own century. Some of the most stimulating attempts to uncover that religiosity have drawn attention to the prevalence and longevity of a relatively integrated system of alternative beliefs only marginally penetrated by orthodox Christianity. These beliefs were grounded in memory, experience, and observation rather than verbal instruction or religious revelation. They were designed to help the individual cope with perceived natural and supernatural adversity. While some elite thinkers thought this belief system was bunkum and others paternalized it as an exotic form of folk religion, both undervalued its inner coherence, insight, and utility in the lives of the rural poor. The kind of popular fusion of religion and nature being described here was once regarded as having been rendered obsolete by the Reformation, and then extinct by the Enlightenment, but there is now formidable evidence to the contrary. The continuity of popular beliefs and practices, albeit with their different characteristics throughout the British Isles, is a far more striking feature of the eighteenth century than the apparent penetration of 'rational' religion from above.

Although much of the evidence points to higher levels of Pelagianism and syncretism in popular belief and practice than the clergy were pleased to accept, it would be a mistake to think of the eighteenth century as a century of relatively benign and placid indifference. Such work as exists on religious identities in the eighteenth century points to the existence of strongly held views based upon interpretations of past events in the life of the nation and on stereotypical conceptions about religious 'others'. Such patterns were not only ubiquitous among Anglicans, Roman Catholics, and Dissenters in Ireland, but were also surprisingly strong in other parts of the British Isles where religious stereotypes were often informed by memories of the religious turmoil of the mid-seventeenth century. Hence, Anglicans were regarded by some as authoritarian persecutors, Presbyterians as regicidal fanatics, Roman Catholics as conspiratorial traitors, Methodists as deluded enthusiasts, and Jews as malevolent disturbers of Church and State. Stereotypes were constructed from selective memories and were reinforced by rhymes and slogans. They were most often pressed into service at times of perceived national threat and crisis such as the aftermath of the Glorious Revolution, the Jacobite rebellions, the American Revolution and the dissenting campaigns of the 1780s for the repeal of the Test and Corporation Acts. Militant displays of anti-Catholicism, which were once thought to be in abeyance in the more tolerant landscape of the eighteenth century, were surprisingly luxuriant throughout the British Isles culminating in the grim violence of the Gordon rioters in 1780. A similar tale could be told of the anti-Methodist disturbances of the 1740s and 1750s. Even allowing for an amount of orchestration from above, anti-Methodist rioting was, on occasions, a genuinely popular phenomenon, proving that religious stereotyping and sectarian violence could proceed from below as well as from above. Therefore, religious identity was instrumental in the construction of communal loyalties in eighteenth-century Britain and Ireland, regardless of the level of piety and devotion, or even in the complete absence of both.

Catholics and enthusiasts

The biggest religious losers in the age of Enlightenment in Europe are often thought to have been the Roman Catholic Church and the supposedly irrational religious enthusiasts, yet in the British Isles no religious traditions made stronger headway in the eighteenth century. In particular, the rise of Methodism from an inconsequential religious society within the Church of England to, by 1815, the fastest growing religious movement in the North Atlantic world, seems to cut across the grain of a century of increasing religious rationality. Explanations of the rise of Methodism, therefore, often portray it as explicitly a movement of counter-enlightenment or, equally commonly, as an appropriately vulgar religion *of* and *for* the poor in an age of rapid demographic growth and economic change. Elements of each of those explanations may well be necessary components of a complete picture, but they are insufficient. Any satisfying account of the rise and spread of Methodism has to address two distinct but linked questions: What was there in the general political and religious climate of Britain in the 1730s that led to the evangelical religious conversions of the disparate leaders of the movement, especially the Wesley brothers, and why was Methodism able to spread so rapidly thereafter?

The first question is the more difficult and a full explanation would have to take account of such factors as the general sense of malaise affecting European Protestantism in the early eighteenth century, the anxiety generated by Deism, the sense of foreboding attendant upon the decline of the church's powers of compulsion after the Toleration Act, the malaise of High Church spirituality (out of which Methodism was spawned), and the sense of acute disillusionment with Walpole and his ecclesiastical policies. The writings of many of the early evangelical protagonists in England and Wales betray an acute sense of *anxiety* about the state of religion in national life, from the top to the bottom of the social pyramid. Anxieties were cross-fertilized and animated by the remarkable speed and volume of religious communications in the early eighteenth century. A triangular trade in religious ideas and personnel linked continental Europe (especially the pietist centres of Halle and Herrnhut), Britain (especially Oxford and London), and the American colonies (especially Savannah in

Georgia). Contacts were made through societies such as the SPG and the SPCK and were facilitated by the arrival in London of German Lutherans sometimes associated with the periphery of the Hanoverian court. Particularly significant was the Fetter Lane Society in London, which acted as a meeting point for German visitors, Welsh and English evangelists, some French Prophets, and not a few London artisans. There was much egotistical jockeying for power and influence in this religious pollen factory, which was often rocked by doctrinal, ecclesiological, and political disagreements, but there were also remarkable displays of religious enthusiasm. It was here that John Wesley further developed his contacts, first made in Georgia, with the Moravians, which brought him face to face with a heart-warming variety of European pietism with roots deep in classical Lutheranism and Reformation spirituality. There came a parting of the ways in 1740 over Moravian 'stillness', which Wesley repudiated as naked antinomianism, and over Wesley's early views on Christian perfection, which the Moravians regarded as a dangerous delusion, but not before Anglican High Church spirituality had been energized by Lutheran pietism.

What turned the spiritual stirrings of the late 1730s among a small coterie into a widespread movement was Wesley's fusion of outdoor preaching, itinerant evangelism, and connectional organization. He had a particular talent for taking over the pioneering work of others and shaping it around his own sense of organizational priorities. Growth, on the whole, came more through careful institutionalization than by extravagant revivals. Cottage meetings and religious societies offered a sense of friendship and fellowship, a powerful combination of individual assurance and community discipline. Methodism also benefited from operating in a legal twilight zone between Church and Dissent. As a movement of religious societies within the Church of England, Methodism depended upon Anglican services, catechisms, liturgies, sacraments and buildings, but it also required a separate organization outside episcopal and parochial control. Wesley refused to accept the dissenting logic of some of his organizational innovations and he only conceded to the Toleration Act's provisions for the licensing of preachers and buildings under duress. Licences were eventually obtained, not as emblems of a new-found status, but as tactical devices to safeguard life and property.

Methodism's steady growth in the British Isles before Wesley's death in 1791, when there were around 100,000 members of societies and some 250,000 adherents, and, in common with the rest of evangelical nonconformity, its remarkable expansion thereafter, requires some explanation. In general, Methodism grew where the population grew, and it benefited both from the seeds sown by the Church of England and from its pastoral shortcomings. Methodism was more likely to thrive in open than in closed villages, and was more vibrant in settlements of between 500 and 5,000 people than in larger towns and cities. The growth of industry and manufacturing helped free workers from Anglican paternalism, while the superior flexibility of the Methodist system enabled it to exploit new opportunities more successfully than the Church of England, particularly in large or dispersed parishes. Once Methodism became established in a given area, the Church of England found it difficult to reclaim lost ground. The spoils went to those who were in first. In terms of occupational structure, Methodism attracted both the self-improving artisanry of the industrial villages and the small farmers and agricultural labourers of the countryside. The majority of Methodist members were women, and the majority of converts of both sexes were predominantly young, relatively uneducated, and from some sort of religious background. The reasons given for religious conversion vary between fear, guilt, and anxiety at one pole to the attractiveness of the Methodist message and its sense of community at the other. What sustained the longevity of commitment among its laity, however, was not so much fear of death and hell, what one historian memorably called 'the promiscuity of Methodist theology', as assurance of sins forgiven and the benefits of participation in the life of the chapel as an extended family of the faithful. Whether one looks at the corpus of Methodist hymnody or at the sermons and journals of the itinerant and lay preachers, there is an invitational and celebratory dimension to the Methodist message that adds up to more than simply 'fleeing the wrath to come'.

The number of Methodists in Britain at the end of the eighteenth century was roughly equal to the number of Roman Catholics. In fact, these religious traditions were often bracketed together by hostile eighteenth-century writers who saw them as representing the unenlightened and unacceptable margins of British religion. Compared as enthusiasts, accused of Jacobitism and political disaffection, and considered equally guilty of trading on the popular superstitions of the gullible, Methodism and Roman Catholicism were regarded as threats to the Protestantism, providentialism, and prosperity of an enlightened state. Comparisons could be pressed even further. Both grew steadily in the eighteenth century, though Methodism obviously from a lower base, and both grew much more quickly after 1770 when the religious pluralism sanctioned by the Toleration Act of 1689 became a dramatic social reality. From that perspective, the evolution of the British state from one with a traditional emphasis on confessional conformity to a more modern state embracing religious pluralism, voluntarism, and toleration, owes more to the supposedly unenlightened outsiders than to their more urbane and celebrated critics. It is well not to be too sentimental about this, however, for consequences are not always intended. For most of the late eighteenth and nineteenth centuries, Methodists and Catholics were as much at each other's throats, as they were unlikely partners in the erosion of the social foundations of a confessional state.

The geographical distribution of Roman Catholicism in the British Isles was dramatically uneven. Although the English Catholic community was growing, it was by 1780 still confined to its regions of traditional strength in Lancashire, the north-east, and parts of the West Midlands. In Scotland and Wales, Catholicism had been effectively shunted to the margins. It had been pushed out to the Highlands and islands of the north of Scotland, where Catholic peasants were subjected to clearances and evictions, and to parts of Monmouthshire, where anti-Catholicism was surprisingly virulent throughout the eighteenth century. But the great centre of Catholic strength lay in Ireland, where between three-quarters and four-fifths of the population were Catholics. The penal laws under which Catholics suffered, and in the shadow of which historians have struggled to offer a realistic assessment of eighteenth-century Irish Catholicism, represented an attempt more to erode the social, political, and economic significance of Catholicism than a commitment to serious religious persecution. Enacted over four decades according to contingencies, the penal laws aimed at control, not extinction, and they were more significant in creating a climate of resentment among Catholics than in altering the social structure of eighteenth-century Ireland. Their main targets were the Catholic aristocracy and gentry, whose proportion of landownership continued to fall throughout the eighteenth century. But the penal laws did not prevent the emergence of Catholic mercantile and tenant farmer classes, which provided the social foundations for both ecclesiastical reform and the agitation of political causes in the later eighteenth and the nineteenth century.

Although the Catholic Church in eighteenth-century Ireland tried to build on earlier Counter-Reformation achievements by further extending a system of diocesan and parochial control, its efforts were limited by internal weaknesses, lack of resources, and the persistent survival of popular 'superstitions' that were sometimes mediated, but never eliminated, by the priests. The progress of a more sacramental, catechetical, and mass-centred Catholicism was faster among urban dwellers and among social elites than among the peasants of the south and west of the country, whose Catholicism was of a very different kind from what the church intended. At no point in the eighteenth century was regular mass attendance at a parish church the norm for the majority of Catholics living in Ireland. It was from such stock that the Irish migrations to Britain, which steadily gathered pace from the 1790s, were drawn.

Naturally the arrival of large numbers of Catholic Irish into the growing cities of industrializing Britain altered the shape of the indigenous Catholic community, but that community was already undergoing profound changes. Concentrated in the parts of the country experiencing the most rapid economic and social change, the English Catholic community became steadily more urban and more clerical long before Irish immigration further reinforced the trend. Far from underlining the commonly accepted notion of antipathy between Catholicism and capitalist economic development, local studies of late eighteenth-century Catholicism have presented a different picture. In Lancashire, for example, Catholics were at the centre of the mining, metallurgical, and cotton-spinning industries. The old Catholic borough of Wigan, which by 1767 had the largest Catholic population outside of London and Liverpool, was a dynamic centre of industrial development driven by Catholics that in turn sucked in Catholic workers from the surrounding countryside. It is a statistical fact that around 1818 the combined numbers of Irish-born Catholics outstripped the numbers of native English Catholics in the four Lancashire industrial towns of Preston, Wigan, Liverpool, and Manchester, but the dramatic impact of the Irish migration should not detract from the remarkable changes that took place within the English Catholic community between 1770 and 1815.

Religious traditions that profit, rather than suffer from, social and demographic changes, must also have an accompanying religious zeal to enable them to seize new opportunities. In that respect, eighteenth-century Catholicism was a remarkably sturdy plant. Sustained by a rich tradition of rites and rituals, a missionary organization (albeit not without its internal squabbles), and an impressive sense of devotion exemplified in Challoner's much reprinted *Garden of the Soul* (1740), the church was far from moribund. The spatial boundaries of its old geographical heartlands had survived the vicissitudes of penal laws, civil wars, political turmoil, Jacobite rebellions, and economic transformation. They stood as rocks weathered by the sea. In many cases, the old Hundreds, which had been the centres of survivalist strength in 1600, remained so two centuries later. When the Catholic community began to grow in the later eighteenth century, it expanded first from its traditional areas of strength and then into new urban landscapes. The additional impetus provided by Irish migrants, French émigrés, and a general shift to a more reformist political outlook enabled the Roman Catholic Church in Britain to build rough communities of working-class religiosity in the cities. Described by one historian as cultures of 'belligerent fidelity', they were often derided, but not underestimated, by representatives of other religious traditions.

Conclusion

The apparently opposite poles of Enlightenment and enthusiasm, within which much of the discourse on eighteenth-century religion has been located, were in reality more like the magnetic poles of a fast-spinning solenoid than fixed opposites. It is now commonplace, for example, to see someone like John Wesley as simultaneously a man of enthusiasm and as a creature of the Enlightenment. He struck some contemporaries as astonishingly credulous, yet his doctrines of assurance and religious experience owed more to John Locke than to anyone else. In his repudiation of the limited atonement of Calvinism, in his advocacy of religious toleration and slavery abolition, and in the construction of his quirky doctrine of Christian perfection, the apogee of human optimism, Wesley, it could be argued, was a true man of the Enlightenment. Of course there is another side to the story, but the same could be said of any number of figures with better rationalist credentials than Wesley. Isaac Newton, for example, was as much interested in showing how human reason and proper scientific methods could unlock the prophetical codes of the biblical books of Daniel and Revelation as he was in his more celebrated scientific investigations. Newton's millenarian enthusiasm, based upon the deeply held notion that human history was orchestrated by God, was matched later in the century by the millennial speculations of the high priest of rational Dissent, Joseph Priestley. Priestley's public enthusiasm for the conversion and restoration of the Jews to Palestine as the event necessary to usher in the millennium ensured that his writings circulated with other restorationists with fewer enlightened credentials, such as Lord George Gordon and Richard Brothers. In the circulating literature of the radical underworld of late eighteenth-century London, the gap between the writings of scholarly Dissenters like Priestley and the rougher ranters and prophetical enthusiasts was a good deal narrower than was once thought. A similar argument could be made for Freemasonry. It was both a product of the New-tonian Enlightenment and a bizarre creation of a secret world of rituals, oaths, and ceremonies, which, if they had been constructed by a church and had not had such a sprinkling of elite participants, would have been regarded as unpardonable excesses of enthusiasm.

The point of all this is not merely to suggest that the eighteenth century contained both Enlightenment rationalism and religious enthusiasm, but that the two apparent polarities frequently informed and defined one another. Just as the scientific revolution stressed the central role of experiment and experience in the pursuit of natural knowledge, religious enthusiasts likewise stressed religious experience and experimental religion. In this way Newtonianism could be put to cultural use for religious and other purposes. It is now recognized that the brutally mechanical philosophy that many followers of Newton pursued, and which some historians of science now cele-brate, was not shared by Newton himself. Similarly, John Wesley, Jonathan Edwards, and many other eighteenth-century religious 'enthusiasts' did not share the repudiation of scientific enquiry sub-sequently advocated by some religious fundamentalists. In short, the traditionally separated out categories of science and religious enthusiasm were in the eighteenth century as mutually invasive as Newton's own scientific and prophetical modes of enquiry. One is simply admired more than the other by posterity.

Figure 4 John Bacon's monument to the prison reformer John Howard in St Paul's Cathedral, 1795. Howard was the first national hero to be commemorated in this way in St Paul's.

3

Governing diverse societies

Joanna Innes

Ruling classes

The basis of internal government throughout the British Isles was the allocation of power to local elites: landowners in the countryside, trading and professional elites in the towns (sometimes with some share of power for local gentry too)—and below them, at the level of the manor or parish, small landowners, tenants, or ratepaying householders. One effect of this arrangement was that the character of government in the localities varied, even when formal institutions were the same, as social structures, social relations, and political and religious cultures varied.

Formal institutions of government in the three kingdoms, though differing in certain respects, did in fact have a great deal in common. This was no doubt in part because they drew upon a common European stock of institutional forms—thus, boroughs or urban corporations had long flourished, with local variations, throughout Europe. Other common features derived from England's long history of influence, shading into dominance, over neighbouring realms—thus, in the course of several centuries, Ireland and Scotland had been shired (divided into counties) and equipped with sheriffs, on the English model.

In England, from the later middle ages, justices of the peace rose to ascendancy as county authorities, marginalizing sheriffs. The differing ways in which this development was echoed elsewhere provide an example of the differences that distinguished arrangements in the different kingdoms. Irish arrangements often echoed English ones closely, and in this case, Irish justices too attained ascendancy and marginalized sheriffs (though Irish justices enjoyed less independent financial power than their English counterparts). Scotland's longer sustained independence, distinct legal tradition, and the special character of its Highland region helped to determine that its echoing of English example was both more lagged and more partial: justices of the peace appeared more belatedly (in some regions not until the early eighteenth century), and always had a smaller share of power.

Throughout the three kingdoms, county justices held power by virtue of centrally issued commissions of the peace—issued afresh with each new reign, and open to more or less radical tinkering in between as central authorities saw fit. We know more about the characteristics of those appointed in England and Wales than elsewhere. The ideal-type justice was a local landowner of some substance: peer, esquire, or at least gentleman. In 1732 a statute set a property-owning minimum at an (in the circumstances) relatively modest level: the would-be justice had to hold property by freehold, copyhold, or a lease for lives worth £100 a year. In practice, late seventeenth and early eighteenth-century governments were only secondarily concerned with the propertied status of appointees, and rather more concerned about their political reliability. Under William and Anne, as the balance of power between parties shifted back and forth, the composition of commissions shifted accordingly; under Walpole, Whig dominance was sustained. The property requirement represented a *reaction* against what was said to be central government's plumbing of social depths to find politically reliable men. Only as party tensions subsided was a less partisan approach adopted; only when the young George III declared an end to party conflict did commissions become in effect a simple roster of local men of substance. At the accession of Anne in 1702, almost 4,000 men were appointed to commissions of the peace in England and Wales—on average, about 75 per county, although in practice of course there was substantial variation, from Rutland's 14 to Yorkshire's 223. In 1761, that total was more than doubled.

Appointing a man to the commission was only the first step towards getting him to act. Many, though perhaps gratified by the symbolic recognition, never went through the further formalities required before they were entitled to exercise the powers of a justice.

Intelligibly if frustratingly, men were least eager to serve where the workload promised to be heaviest: in rural industrial regions, where gentry might be relatively few in relation to a large if scattered rural industrial population, or in urban areas where, in the absence of a corporation, governmental responsibilities fell to centrally appointed justices: thus in the city of Westminster, Birmingham, Manchester, or, in the early nineteenth century, the boom town of Merthyr Tydfil. In these regions especially, willingness to act might compensate for lack of status in earning a man a place on the bench. Hence the notorious prevalence of 'trading justices' in eighteenth-century Westminster: men said to be as willing to trade in justice as in commodities. From the 1790s on, the favoured expedient in such urban regions became the appointment of 'stipendiary magistrates'. The ordinary magistrate, like all local government officers, served without pay; by contrast, the stipendiary—often a barrister by training—commanded a salary.

In general, such were the burdens of office that active justices were most likely to emerge from among those sufficiently far down the ranks of the propertied for the cost in time and trouble to be counterbalanced by an expected gain in status. Most counties had at least some major landowners prepared to bear their share of magisterial duties, but the active bench as a whole was unlikely to represent the cream of county society, more likely to be a mixed bag. In the more industrial counties, the trend over time was in favour of admitting manufacturers who met the property qualification. In the west country, where the dominant type was the merchant-manufacturer, they had been brought on to the bench by the middle of the century; in Yorkshire, where industrial structures were somewhat different, not until the century's end. Clergy, not admitted in large numbers in the early eighteenth century, multiplied later, perhaps in part because their number included some of the most zealously active men.

English and Welsh justices were required to take oaths of allegiance and supremacy, also Anglican communion at least once a year. Partly because religious conformity was a prerequisite for most forms of office-holding, gentry Presbyterianism had waned in the later seventeenth and early eighteenth centuries. Though the social stratum from which justices were drawn certainly included Catholics and Dissenters, the vast majority of those who fell within it should not have been excluded by these tests. Even active Dissenters were not excluded—so long as they were willing to practise 'occasional con-formity', or to run the risk of challenge for non-compliance. Thus, Thomas Butterworth Bayley, who dominated the Salford division of the Lancashire bench (the division which served Manchester and its region) from the 1760s through to his death in 1802, was a trustee of the Cross St Presbyterian Chapel.

In Ireland, where Church of Ireland members formed a distinct minority of the population, similar restrictions applied until 1792. There too, their restrictive effect should not be exaggerated. Since landowning was concentrated in the hands of the Church of Ireland minority, the bulk of the landed class was eligible for office (it has been estimated that, in the early eighteenth century, numerically dominant Catholics owned only about 14 per cent of land, by the century's end—after a series of pragmatic conversions—a mere 5 per cent). A number of historians have in fact argued recently that we misconceive Ireland at this period if we conceive of it as a *distinctively* minority-ruled society. On the contrary, they suggest, it is best con-sidered a fairly run-of-the-mill *ancien régime* society, presided over by a landed elite who were no more distant from the culture of the mass of the population than were landed elites in many other parts of Europe. Be that as it may, Irish religious restrictions certainly excluded some potential office-holders. When in 1792, remedial legis-lation opened up all but the very highest offices to Catholics, some Catholic appointments followed almost immediately—though admittedly, numbers were small. In Tipperary, a county relatively quick to integrate, one Catholic was added to the commission in 1793, four appointed to the grand jury at the summer assizes.

By the end of the eighteenth century, Ireland, with some 3,000 men on the commission of the peace, would seem to have been not too badly served by English standards. But neither these numbers, nor the opening up of the bench to non-Anglicans, sufficed to resolve a larger crisis of authority. Faced with recurrent waves of 'peasant unrest', beginning with the Whiteboy agitation of the 1760s, those with over-all responsibility for government in Ireland repeatedly concluded that the 'civil power' needed strengthening, with new legal powers, and new fiscal and manpower resources. British ministers were sometimes sceptical. They had faced what they took to be analogous situations in England, when local justices despaired of regaining control and wanted the army to do the work for them, and had to be persuaded to

GOVERNING DIVERSE SOCIETIES | 107

take courage and find ways of making civil power work. Since Ireland's domestic institutions mirrored England's, it was tempting to diagnose a failure of will. Within Ireland too, such proposals had their critics, who claimed that authorities sought tyrannical powers, and that special new constabulary forces would represent primarily so much additional patronage for government. Yet in the 1760s, 1780s, and 1790s the Irish parliament did pass new legislation to strengthen justices' hands, and put new police personnel at their disposal, and in the 1810s, Peel, as Irish secretary—having concluded that, as a ruling class, the Irish gentry were indeed fatally wanting—drew up a scheme for the creation of a rural stipendiary magistracy, which was to bear fruit in the post-war years.

In Scotland, the first attempt to establish commissions of the peace, after the union of crowns, had had uneven and slight results. After the union of parliaments in 1707, commissions were issued afresh, and a new statute declared that Scottish justices were to have the powers of their English counterparts. In practice, however, jurisdiction over all serious criminal cases remained concentrated, as of old, in the Edinburgh-based Court of Justiciary, and justices were left with little but administrative tasks. Furthermore, even at local level, they had to work along with other significant county officials: sheriffs depute, procurators fiscal (who managed prosecutions), and commissioners of supply—the latter originally appointed, like English land tax commissioners, to collect taxes for national purposes, but subsequently also acquiring powers to raise taxes for such local enterprises as road building (powers which elsewhere in the British Isles inhered in varying combinations of justices and grand juries).

In England, Wales, and Ireland, whatever their shortcomings, centrally appointed justices did have formal control over the realm as a whole, barring only corporate towns, where mayors and aldermen commonly functioned also as justices. In Scotland before the Forty-Five Jacobite rising, this was not the case. Significant chunks of land in the Highlands, and to a lesser extent in the Lowlands, fell within 'heritable jurisdictions': regalities or baronies in which hereditary title-holders exercised a greater or lesser range of judicial and regulatory powers. In principle this was not very different from the general practice of allocating a range of powers to corporate towns, over the composition of whose ruling bodies central authorities had similarly little control, and indeed some Scottish heritable jurisdictions lay in the hands of corporate bodies, such as that of the city of Edinburgh, and were very much like other urban districts in practice. In the Highlands, however, the system of heritable jurisdictions was intertwined with a distinctive set of social arrangements. To a greater or lesser extent in different Highland regions, the boundaries of heritable jurisdictions coincided with hierarchies of land tenure, based on the exchange of goods and services as well as or instead of on cash payments, and on networks of 'clan' loyalty: *dutchas*.

Clan society was repeatedly stigmatized by Lowland and English critics as inherently disorderly. It has been argued recently that, on the contrary, disorder was most likely to arise when the ideals of clan society were *not* attained: when formal legal power, economic power, and clan loyalties did not coincide, making it difficult for chiefs to bring the disorderly to heel by the negotiative, non-penal means through which Highland peacekeeping had traditionally operated, or when Lowland landlords with Highland property turned a blind eye to their followers' predations upon neighbours for whom they had little regard. Those who argue this however also suggest that the clan system was being hollowed out by a variety of forces during the seventeenth and eighteenth centuries. Clan elites developed a taste for a 'polite' lifestyle—entailing, for example, heavy spending on showy mansions or at the gaming table—and strove to commercialize the management of their estates. The growth of the cattle trade spurred the monetization of the Highland economy. Religious and political division encouraged strife, and sometimes cut across other systems of loyalty—the Jacobite movement was in part a protest movement by clansmen who felt betrayed by chiefs who were surrendering as much to the blandishments of the new social as of the new political order. British government and parliament echoed a long tradition of critical rhetoric when, in the aftermath of the Forty-Five, they diagnosed the clan system and all that gave it a semblance of legitimacy as the heart of the Highland problem, and abolished heritable jurisdictions as one part of a more sweeping programme of forced modernization. This intervention certainly contributed to a process of change, yet—it is contended—did not set it in motion.

Demolishing the old order in the Highlands proved much easier than constructing a new one. This was as true in terms of structures of government as in other respects. The growth of profit-oriented sheep farming spurred a first wave of emigration in the 1770s.

Attempts to maintain displaced populations in 'crofting' communities dependent on potato cultivation, collection of seaweed for fertilizer, and fishing enjoyed only precarious success. Hard times in the wake of the Napoleonic Wars would sap landlord confidence, prompt evictions and a second exodus. Meanwhile, no ideal-type gentry class emerged. The proprietors of vast estates were often absentees. The 'tacksmen' who had managed the non-commercial estate system sometimes mutated into gentry, but often were displaced by 'factors', commercial estate managers. In the absence of other candidates, Highland commissions had to be filled up with such men, or with Church of Scotland ministers, a less gentrified set than their English counterparts.

Central government's control over the commission of the peace gave it some opportunity both to influence the political complexion of local government, and to secure its effectiveness—though as we have seen, means to these ends were not always readily available. In most urban settings—as we have also noted—central authorities had still less power. Their formal powers in relation to town personnel were greatest in Ireland, where in 1672 'New Rules' had given the viceroy and privy council power to vet corporate officers in most of the larger towns. These powers were still sometimes exercised in the eighteenth century, notably early in the century when party tempers ran high. In England during the same years the Walpole regime encouraged legal challenges to some urban corporations; meanwhile, local acts settled urban constitutional disputes in London and Norwich in ways acceptable to government. In all these cases, however, central authorities lacked power directly to appoint their own men: they had to operate indirectly. Interference, moreover, was controversial, often sparking protest. From mid-century, governments relied more on the softer arts of influence.

Traditional forms of urban government can be arrayed along a rough spectrum. At one extreme was the manor. Courts leet and baron provided fairly minimal facilities for urban government, but could be made to serve this purpose. A market charter might contribute further rights and powers—Manchester down to the 1790s made do with little more than manorial and market institutions. The manorial borough—in Scotland, the burgh of barony—might be staffed with more urban officials, with a more extensive range of powers. Moving towards the more developed end of the spectrum we pass through the various forms of corporation: headed by bailiffs or mayors and equipped with one or more governing councils, empowered to make by-laws and maintain civil courts. In most corporate towns, senior urban officers had the powers of justices *ex officio*, and could hold their own quarter sessions for the trial at least of petty, sometimes also of more serious offences. Across this spectrum of urban institutions, power inhered either in lords of the manor, or in officials appointed by them, or in local cliques who reproduced themselves by co-option, or, in some instances, finally, in locally elected officials. Even command of local militias was vested in these locally appointed men.

In terms of the variety of forms urban governments actually assumed, a town's formal position within the spectrum just sketched was not always its effective position. Chartered rights might lie unused, on the one hand; conversely, practices might grow up that were sanctioned by custom but had no other basis. To an important extent, nonetheless, the form of town governments was determined by the historical accident of their having been granted one or another set of powers. In England most notably the result was that there was no systematic relationship between a town's size and the character of its government. Past patrons might have obtained sonorous dignities and extensive powers for the rulers of small towns; other towns— such as Manchester, Birmingham, and Sheffield—grew to substantial, even formidable size without ever acquiring corporate status. In Scotland there were substantial small towns (such as Alloa, a coal port which grew rapidly from the late seventeenth century), which remained in the hands of feudal superiors, and others (such as Paisley, a mushrooming textile town), which remained mere burghs of barony despite swelling population. But the mismatch between town sizes and constitutions was less egregious than in England. This was no doubt in part because in Scotland, corporations were relatively more numerous than in England: Scotland had about one-quarter as many corporations, though it was only about one-fifth as populous. Ireland—though the least urbanized of the three—had about half as many corporations as England; some of these however operated more as political clubs than as governing bodies.

The fossilization of traditional urban forms in apparently irrational patterns can be explained in several ways. First, Charles II's and James II's exercises in remodelling corporations for political

ends—much more hotly contested at the time than their simultaneous remodelling of commissions of the peace—served to bring
all such interventions into discredit: the corporation became a sacred
cow. Secondly, in an era when parliaments entrenched their position
at the centre of public life, in the case of that substantial majority of
corporations possessing the power to return MPs, this power as much
as any other could serve as a corporate *raison d'être*: a reason for
sustaining corporations which served few other purposes. Thirdly, as
governing entities, traditional urban forms, especially the corporation, were in any case falling into disfavour: there was relatively little
interest in creating new ones. Finally, it was unnecessary to create new
ones, inasmuch as alternative ways of governing urban regions were
being devised.

The traditional corporation operated in four main capacities. It
was first a property-owning entity, managing certain forms of property as public facilities—market buildings, harbours, prisons—and
others as a source of corporate revenue. It was secondly a regulatory
body: regulating, or overseeing the regulation of, (among other
things) commerce and industrial production, and street lighting,
cleansing and policing. It was thirdly a court-maintaining body: providing convenient civil and criminal tribunals. It was, fourthly, guard-
ian of the town's interests within the realm: expected to identify and
exploit opportunities to enhance the town's economic position, to
represent its interests to central bodies by lobbying or petitioning—
and in general to win friends and influence people on the town's
behalf, not least by securing appropriate MPs to represent it in
parliament, and keeping them properly briefed.

These were all worthwhile functions, and when traditional urban
governing bodies performed them well, they might hope to retain
local favour. Nonetheless, corporate bodies especially increasingly
attracted criticism on a range of grounds, and, if they were not
judged to be doing a good job in other respects, might face a storm of
criticism—extending in many instances to legal or political challenge.
If both the practice of ruling the countryside through local propertied elites, and that of ruling towns through corporations, can be
dubbed *ancien régime* arrangements, it is notable that the former
survived the period in much better shape than the latter.

One common form of criticism focused on corporations'
exclusiveness. Though a few corporations—including some of the

most prominent, such as London and, after 1760, Dublin—were voted in by a relatively popular electorate, most reproduced themselves by co-option. This being so, it was relatively easy for them to fall under the sway of a single faction. All Scottish corporations were substantially co-optive, and the belief that this had ill-effects both on local government and on the system of parliamentary representation contributed to the growth of a 'burgh reform' movement in the 1780s and again at the end of the Napoleonic Wars.

Religious exclusiveness was the burden of a subset of exclusiveness complaints. In theory, Test and Corporation Acts reserved office in English corporations to Anglicans. In practice, occasional conformity, and willingness to gamble on escaping prosecution operated to give Dissenters representation, even strong representation, on some English corporate bodies. However, the workings of co-option sometimes secured what the law could not. Leeds corporation, thus, acquired the character of a staunchly Anglican preserve in the later eighteenth and early nineteenth centuries, and as such, was a provocation to Dissenters. In Ireland, Catholics were commonly excluded from urban 'freedom', and thus a fortiori from corporate office—a more sharply felt grievance than their exclusion from county benches, inasmuch as they were better represented among commercial than landowning classes. Though they were allowed to trade alongside freemen in return for payment of 'quarterage' dues, the onerousness of these became a focus for Catholic campaigning in the 1760s (in effect, this was the opening salvo of the emancipation movement). The 1792 Act removed the legal bar to Catholics holding corporate office, but inasmuch as corporations continued to decline to admit them to the freedom, this was a nugatory achievement. In the 1830s, when Irish municipal reform came on to the parliamentary agenda, the Protestant bent of Irish corporations was still marked—and was held to their discredit.

A second common basis for complaint, intricately bound up with the issue of exclusiveness, was corporation finance. Income from property and market and other tolls and dues represented most corporations' chief sources of revenue. This was not a sufficient basis for much in the way of corporate enterprise, still less for the provision of any extensive range of public services. In practice, many corporations did spend quite heavily on urban 'improvements', relying on borrowing for funds. A common consequence was a mounting burden of indebtedness. Public doubts about corporations' money-management were not alleviated by their secretive habits. By the end of the eighteenth century, numerous corporations had begun to encounter demands that they increase transparency and accountability. Historically, corporations had often claimed a right to impose rates on inhabitants. However, this rarely seemed an option for an unelected body, in a political culture which set great store by the notion that taxation should be levied by consent.

A third and final problem for corporations was that traditional forms of economic regulation, once one of their primary responsibilities, were also losing legitimacy. Corporations' power to exclude non-freemen from trading was subjected to repeated legal challenge from the mid-eighteenth century in towns throughout the British Isles—and in consequence often abandoned. In the following decades, tolls and dues also increasingly attracted complaint, and were sometimes the subject of litigation. The cost of defending corporate claims in court contributed to the rising expenditure trend.

Where corporations did not exist, these were some of the considerations which would have militated against establishing them. In fact, the issue scarcely arose, since their more valuable functions could in practice almost all be discharged by other means. Thus, certain judicial and administrative services could just as well be performed by men who were nominally county justices (if suitable candidates were willing to serve). Local acts of parliament could moreover be obtained to establish special bodies of men to levy and disburse rates to provide specific public services. (Bodies such as these, pioneered in towns, indeed took over responsibility for the provision of certain services in the countryside too, most notably the provision of transport facilities—roads, improved rivers—but also sometimes care of the poor and adjudication of small debt cases.) Other services might be provided by voluntary bodies, by subscription or by commercial companies: hospitals, schools, piped water. Even in corporate towns with vigorous corporations, many governmental or quasi-governmental functions were discharged by such alternative agencies. In urban areas not subject to traditional governing bodies, these alternative agencies often sufficed.

The enormous diversity of forms of urban public body makes the question, who held power in towns? a particularly difficult one to answer. The traditional corporation was designed above all to recruit from the local trading and manufacturing community, via the system of acquiring 'freedom'—civic rights—on completion of an apprenticeship. Inheritance through a father was another common route. However, it was also possible for corporations to *bestow* freedom, and by this means to incorporate into the system those who would not naturally have qualified. In parliamentary boroughs with freeman franchises, the power to bestow the freedom was in effect a power to create electors, a consideration which clearly shaped its use.

In small towns especially, opportunities to co-opt outsiders to corporate bodies might be used to forge ties with local gentry. More particularly, peers whom towns wished to cultivate might be appointed to such posts as Lord Steward; eminent barristers made Recorder. From the point of view of the 'outsider', the acquisition of political influence might be the point of the exercise, but there were other reasons for landowners to take an interest in towns, not least that town fortunes might be expected to affect the value of both rural and urban property. In elective corporations, office sometimes fell to the man with the popular platform: thus, in the 1770s rake-about-town John Wilkes found himself ensconced among sober citizens on the London aldermanic bench, and obliged (as he complained) to participate in their tedious turtle feasts. The mercantile and trading community might thus share power with other interests. Nonetheless, merchants or tradesmen probably dominated most corporate bodies (though their economic and social profile varied from place to place).

Statutory commissions elected by ratepayers—or, in some cases, comprising all of those who met specified property qualifications who cared to act—might by contrast contain a more heterogeneous cross-section of propertied urban residents, including more professional men, rentiers, and urban gentry, people not perhaps much concerned with the ordering of the urban economy, but much interested in urban amenities. (Even property-owning women might have a vote in shaping these regimes.) As in the case of commissions of the peace, it often proved difficult to secure the active engagement of the cream of urban society in the work of these bodies—particularly once an initial flush of enthusiasm had passed. Their workhorses were often more marginal men, with fewer alternative means of fulfilment.

Commissions of the peace, corporations, and other forms of town government represented a top level of local government, dependent for much of their efficacy on an infrastructure of supportive institutions, subordinate jurisdictions, and lesser officers—as well as on the availability of finance, and the willingness of the population at large to cooperate or comply with their endeavours. The strength and power of this infrastructure varied significantly from place to place. It was generally strong in England, though most so in small parishes with relatively few inhabitants, least so in large urban or sprawling rural industrial parishes. It was less strong elsewhere—thus in Wales, Lowland Scotland, Ireland—and weak almost to vanishing point in the Scottish Highlands.

In England, the main petty units of local government were two: the manor and the parish. The manor had not lost all significance as an agency for the management of certain economic resources in this period. Especially in open field areas—as over much of the Midlands, until the enclosure movements of the late eighteenth and early nineteenth centuries—manors might play a vital part in determining and policing systems of husbandry. Traditionally, the manor had supplied the constable, who as both 'peace officer' and local tax collector provided a vital prop for both county and national government. As late as the 1840s, when the traditional constabulary system was reviewed, it emerged that a significant proportion of constables were still serving formally as representatives of manors. In practice, however, the constable had by that date commonly been assimilated to the ranks of 'parish officers', the parish having emerged as the key community-level administrative unit.

From the sixteenth century, the English parish had ceased to be a wholly ecclesiastical entity, acquiring a set of civil officers: surveyors of the highways, overseers of the poor. Parish affairs were commonly run by 'principal inhabitants', perhaps including lesser gentry, but more commonly farmers and tradesmen, who footed most of the local rate bill and took it in turns to fill parish offices. One of the most onerous of parish duties was the administration of poor relief. Sixteenth and early seventeenth-century legislation, notably the consolidating statute of '43 Elizabeth' had equipped England with the most comprehensive and generous poor relief system in Europe, a rate-based system of pensions and occasional grants. (*Relatively* generous for its day, this system was nonetheless commonly administered, according to credible contemporary accounts, in grudging and suspicious fashion and—in small towns and rural industrial areas concerned about rising costs—increasingly often with the dubiously welcome offer of accommodation in the local workhouse as an alternative to cash doles.)

English arrangements worked in English circumstances: given a social structure which supported not merely an urban but also a sizeable rural 'middle class', and a highly monetized economy. They did not work as well in other conditions. This is perhaps best illustrated by Welsh examples. Formally, the same laws applied to England as to Wales, and the same poor relief system should have operated there. In fact, however, the relatively less developed rural economy of parts of Wales did not so easily support the same regime. In the early eighteenth century, it was reported from both Brecknockshire and Caernarvonshire that the children of the poor could not be induced to come to school because they had to spend their days begging food at farmhouse doors. In parts of north Wales, justices stonewalled pressure from above to levy rates as late as the 1780s. In the 1840s, there were still regions where rates were paid in kind.

In Ireland, no attempt was made to institute a poor relief system comparable to the English. New provisions for the relief of the poor from the 1770s, designed to check vagrancy, suggest pessimism about taxable resources: alongside partly charitably funded workhouses, a system of licensed begging was envisaged. In the 1830s, Daniel O'Connell would oppose the extension of the New Poor Law to Ireland on the ground that the country was too poor to bear such costs.

Given Irish social structure, the lower echelons of government could scarcely have been filled outside Ulster and the towns had not Catholics been recruited to fill them. It seems that they were. Legislation requiring office-holders to take restrictive oaths explicitly exempted constables, and it has been suggested that most of them were in fact Catholic. Catholics were also explicitly empowered to sit on petty juries—though they had to meet a tougher property requirement than Protestants.

What was perhaps most wanting in the Irish case was the zealous cooperation of the rural middling sort with government. Clearly there was enough cooperation to allow the system to jog along—but not enough to satisfy higher authorities. Irish criminal trial juries proved much readier than their English counterparts to acquit—driving the courts back on the expedient of sentencing large numbers of the acquitted to transportation for vagrancy. Constables might assist with the ordinary business of government—but proved slender reeds when confronted with secretive, intimidatory peasant leagues. Though the Whig opposition continued to insist through the early nineteenth century that Ireland should be ruled in English fashion, ministers increasingly commonly concluded that Irish social relations were simply not such as to make English-style government feasible.

Scotland presented another set of circumstances again, inasmuch as the Scottish institutional structure was different. The Kirk, where it was firmly implanted, was a powerful local institution, but it was not the same animal as the Anglican Church: more fiercely committed to the chastisement of sin, and not convinced of the merits of the English relief regime. Often the Scots poor were offered little more than the relatively meagre proceeds of Kirk collections. Poor rates—sanctioned by law—were more commonly imposed in border and more developed regions than elsewhere, lending support to the view, advanced by some contemporaries, that if Scottish practice differed from English that was chiefly because much of Scotland was backward. Yet it seems hard to dismiss different cultural values from the equation altogether. Especially from mid-century, large landowners, 'heritors', were given special powers under Scots poor laws; this too may have helped to ensure stringency.

In the Highlands, where the Kirk was weaker than in most of the Lowlands, one would expect social and economic circumstances also to have operated to produce a weaker infrastructure. Certainly when hard times struck there were fewer local resources to draw upon. Dearth in the Highlands in 1783 was a problem the national government felt compelled to address by the release of military stores.

The constable was not a traditional Scottish officer, but an import. The same statutes which set up Scottish JPs empowered them to appoint a constable for each parish. As usual, local men of substance—farmers, traders, craftsmen—were the target group. Recruitment proved difficult, nonetheless: the office entailed many burdens and offered few rewards. Struggling to get the system off the ground, some justices resorted to imprisoning the recalcitrant to encourage the rest. In most counties, rotas of service were not consistently maintained: justices would give up the struggle for a few years, and only resume when circumstances made the appointment of constables especially pressing: when vagrancy threatened to get out of hand, or the burdens of war entailed new demands on local government.

In the last few decades of the eighteenth century, it became common for contemporaries to comment on what they perceived to be differences in patterns of governance and society in the different kingdoms of the British Isles—to the extent that local newspapers would carry such items as fillers. One of the comments most commonly made in this context was that Scotland was a more law-abiding country than England, as evidenced by the prison reformer John Howard having found fewer criminals in its gaols. Differences in patterns of conduct cannot be ruled out, but a modern historian suggests that it is more probable that the difference reflects greater reluctance to bring criminal prosecutions in Scotland: given that in the Scottish system prosecution expenses had to be paid out of public funds.

Local government in national—and international—context

Institutions of local government in the three kingdoms had traditionally been overseen by three forms of central body: privy councils, parliaments, and courts—and, with modifications, this pattern persisted throughout into the nineteenth century. English, Scottish, and Irish privy councils had traditionally seen it as their role to keep a watchful eye on local officers of government: whipping them into action when they saw the need, hauling them over the coals if necessary, directing their response to crises. When Scotland was ravaged by dearth in 1697, thus, it was the Scottish privy council which directed what measures should be taken to relieve the poor. Decisions to change the ordinary course of the grain trade in years of bad harvest were always taken by privy councils. Again, throughout the period, the British privy council coordinated measures against 'cattle plague'. Parliaments—which traditionally had met only irregularly, and commonly for brief periods—determined the basic powers and responsibilities of local government through the medium of statutes, and amplified and refined the criminal provisions of the common law. Central courts—or high court judges and other senior lawyers travelling on circuit—presided over most criminal trials for major offences. Though petty civil suits might be brought to local tribunals, vast numbers of these were also pursued in central courts. Inasmuch as it fell to the courts to determine when local government officers had broken the law, they also played a part in supervising government at the local level.

Changes in these patterns from the 1690s were shaped by interaction between a number of different developments. Certain changes in the form and style of central government followed from the growth of the 'fiscal-military' state. Others followed from Scottish and later Irish parliamentary unions: the abolition of the Scottish parliament and privy council, and recentring of Scottish government on Whitehall and Westminster, and, in 1801, abolition of the separate Irish parliament, and establishment of the 'imperial parliament'— though in this case there remained, around the Lord Lieutenant in Dublin castle, a local centre of power. The period saw parliamentary sessions increasing in frequency and length—a change introduced abruptly after the Glorious Revolution, and relatively little varied thereafter. It saw the development in the courts of a somewhat more systematic, policy-conscious approach. Finally, a development with significant effects on the whole character and style of government, it saw the development of a 'public sphere', constituted by face-to-face discussion, discussion in print, and the growth of the practice of voluntary association with a view to influencing or implementing public projects. Within this developing public sphere, English, Scottish, and Irish men, and increasingly also women, engaged with the task of conceptualizing and promoting the 'public good', and, in so doing, participated, more or less consciously, in one of the most characteristic endeavours of the 'age of Enlightenment'.

In several of the states of continental Europe in this period— France, Spain, Prussia, Austria—attempts to increase the fiscal and military resources of central governments prompted the establishment of new central agencies in the localities (*intendants, Kriegs- und-Domänen-Kämmern*), to take on certain tasks traditionally performed in other ways, and to oversee, and if necessary intervene to correct, the functioning of older agencies. In the British Isles, only the Scottish case furnishes some parallels: there, the abolition of heritable jurisdictions after the Forty-Five was accompanied by the establishment of centrally appointed 'sheriffs depute', increasingly recruited from Edinburgh lawyers. In the main, however, even in Scotland the effect of attempts to strengthen the British fiscal-military state was to *weaken* links between the central executive and traditional local government, as new and distinct bodies were established to provide fiscal and military services—the excise service, the standing army—and older pressures on traditional local agencies in this connection, though never vanishing, diminished.

One consequence of the development of new fiscal and military apparatuses was the departmentalization of government, at least in mainland Britain. Though the British privy council retained a role in government, it ceased to be the key organ. Power passed to the Treasury, the Admiralty, and the office of the secretaries of state, and the cabinet emerged as the place in which their efforts were coordinated. Departmentalization was associated with a weakening of traditional central–local links. The cabinet was notably less concerned to oversee local government than the old privy council had been, nor was this a major preoccupation for any of the new departments—at least not until the emergence of the Home Office in 1782, with responsibilities in the fields of law and order and punishment. (The Irish executive, not being the coordinating centre of a fiscal-military state, but rather an appendage of the British one, remained somewhat more traditional in form, down to the 1801 parliamentary union, and indeed beyond. Irish domestic affairs loomed larger on the agenda of the Irish Lord Lieutenant than did English domestic affairs on the agenda of the cabinet.)

In Scotland, despite the introduction of new local government officers, a story can also be told of the loosening of traditional forms of oversight proceeding from the parliamentary union of 1707, and its aftermath. The abolition of the separate Scottish parliament was speedily followed by the abolition of the Scottish privy council. Unlike Ireland, Scotland was not assigned a viceroy. A new commission of Lords of Police proved a complete dead letter. A special Scottish secretaryship of state survived the union by only a few decades. The powerful Campbell family in practice served as government managers in Scotland around the mid-century, but this was an informal, political arrangement. At the end of the century, Henry Dundas, who initially combined responsibilities as the government's Scottish election manager with the post of Lord Advocate for Scotland (a post in which he was succeeded by relatives and friends), perhaps came closest to providing new *official* linkage between British central government and Scottish domestic institutions.

Though a case can be made for a loosening of oversight by central government over local government in this period, it would nonetheless be wrong to envisage local authorities in any of the three kingdoms as floating free of central control, escaping scrutiny, or being cut off from the mainstream of public life. Some traditional forms of oversight persisted. Circuit judges continued physically to link centre and locality. In England, their importance as the eyes and ears of government in the localities seems to have diminished in this period; less so in Ireland, where, in the late eighteenth century, they were asked to report on emigration to America, and attitudes to government policy. By adjudicating on cases that arose from the operations of local government, the high courts also continued to help determine the framework within which local officers acted. In the later eighteenth century, Lord Mansfield, Scottish-born Lord Chief Justice of the English Court of King's Bench, can even be said to have developed this form of oversight. He worked especially hard to systematize, and give publicity to his systematization of, crucial areas of law, including the law of corporations, and the law of settlement. Meanwhile, a growing body of legal handbooks instructed local officers—and their often legally trained assistants, clerks of the peace, justices' clerks—not only in statute law but also in case law bearing on their work.

The absence of any clearly defined chain of command linking cabinet ministers to local government, moreover, did not mean *no* contact, *no* communication between central government and the localities. Even apart from the forms of linkage provided by political and personal networks, the secretaries of state always had the maintenance of order, and facilitating the exercise of criminal justice, as part of their brief. The Lords of the Treasury dealt with a heterogeneous range of measures bearing on the public welfare ad hoc. Though town governing elites were not centrally appointed, towns did not escape these systems of supervision and control. In the 1720s and 1730s, Glasgow and Edinburgh were heavily fined for their failure to contain the Malt Tax and Porteous Riots, respectively. In the 1790s town magistrates worried about Jacobinism both channelled information to and sought help from ministers. In general in times of crisis, all possible linkages between centre and localities might be activated, and central authorities might then shower local authorities with advice and directions, and—much more parsimoniously—practical help: troops to help restore order; special commissions to clear the gaols; very occasionally, special grants. Central grants were given in this period for, among other things, the establishment of schools in the Scottish Highlands; patrols against highway robbers in London, and to facilitate the emigration of poor blacks to Sierra Leone. (In Ireland, where local resources were recognized to be less, such crown and parliamentary grants were somewhat more commonly forthcoming.)

Arguably, the fact that internal governmental structures were *not* reformed in anything like the ways attempted in most of the leading continental states reflected not just the British fiscal-military state having organized itself on other foundations, but also the relative power and efficiency of existing domestic governmental structures. Where these structures were less adequate—as in post-union Scotland—they were reformed. The French Revolutionary and Napoleonic Wars exacted from Britain and Ireland greater and more intense exertions than any wars since those of the 1690s; in terms of the scale of manpower mobilization, greater than those. More than in any wars in the intervening period, this was achieved by central and local government working *together*: mobilizing revenue; manning the army, navy, militias, armed associations; surveying crop yields; numbering the people—and more divisively, spying on dissidents, repressing popular unrest. It was by working together that they coped with the extraordinary challenges of these years.

A distinctive form of mediation between centre and localities, the national and the local was provided by the parliaments of the British Isles: three until 1707, two until 1801, one 'imperial parliament' thereafter. Whereas before 1689 parliaments had met irregularly and often for short periods, after 1689 English parliaments met annually and for at least four months at a time. Meanwhile, Irish parliaments settled down to a pattern of biennial meetings, until in 1782 they too switched to a yearly cycle. The main function of these more frequently sitting and regular parliaments was to pass fiscal legislation and transact other business bearing on matters of state. In practice, individuals and groups took the opportunity to bring a wide range of other business to them. In consequence, they passed unprecedented quantities of legislation bearing on many aspects of the kingdoms' affairs—an increasing proportion of it purely local in scope. Parliaments also began to develop for themselves an investigative role: both British and Irish parliaments in the eighteenth century more than once investigated the state of the prisons; they collected quantitative information on punishments; from the 1690s on Westminster parliaments repeatedly surveyed national poor relief expenditure. When the imperial parliament enquired into post-war typhus epidemics in both London and Dublin, it built upon an already existing investigative tradition.

Measures initiated by other than central government authorities included much legislation designed to promote or regulate specific trades; much criminal legislation; legislation against 'vice and immorality'; legislation relating to vagrants and the poor; for the relief of insolvent (imprisoned or exiled) debtors; legislation relating to road-building and maintenance; local acts establishing turnpike trusts; to improve river navigation or build canals; to establish urban 'improvement' commissions, or enclose common or waste lands. Both British and Irish parliaments passed dozens—ultimately, the imperial parliament was to pass more than a hundred—such acts every year, and still other proposals were canvassed but did not win approval. The initiative for such measures sometimes came from local government bodies—county benches, corporations; sometimes from men with experience in local government; sometimes from charitable or other voluntary bodies; guilds or other commercial associations, groups of landowners, or individuals with a mission or a problem. Legislating was not cheap, especially when measures were judged 'private' and not 'public': there were often lawyers' costs to be paid as well as parliamentary fees; perhaps also the cost of maintaining a lobbyist or agent in Westminster or Dublin. Expenditure might run into hundreds of pounds. However, the parliaments' relative accessibility did give groups and individuals a chance to tinker with their legal and institutional environment, whether in pursuit of some conception of the public interest, or their own interest—if at the price of being exposed to scrutiny and debate, and having to win the support of enough members of both houses to survive to the end of the process.

To what extent did the abolition of Scotland's separate parliament exclude Scots from these opportunities? A Scottish parliament would surely have provided a forum for the extended discussion of Scottish circumstances, as the Westminster parliament did not. The Convention of Royal Burghs and the General Assembly of the Church of Scotland provided national bodies where concerns could be aired, and certain kinds of action initiated. But neither had the sovereign powers of parliament. Meanwhile, the Westminster parliament was dominated by MPs whose thoughts rarely strayed north of the border. Much of the time they do not even seem to have asked themselves the question, is this legislation intended to extend to Scotland? It was left to the Scots to work out what was and—given the different Scottish legal inheritance—what could be so extended.

This is not to say that Scottish affairs entirely dropped from sight, however. One historian has stated recently that between 1727 and 1745 (that is, between the accession of George II and the Jacobite rising) 'only nine acts of parliament dealt specifically with Scotland, seven of them of little consequence'.[1] True as far as it goes, this leaves much unsaid. Most public general acts passed in this period—some two hundred—dealt with Britain or the British Isles as a whole, including Scotland. Mostly fiscal or military in character, British acts also included the odd domestic measure, such as the 1736 Witchcraft Act, decriminalizing witchcraft as such. Scots lobbied behind the scenes to shape such legislation, as well as speaking up in debate. The total of nine also ignores local acts, though some twenty were passed relating to Scotland in these years: for example, empowering Scottish burghs to raise local rates for improvements, or improving the navigability of Scottish rivers. Scottish acts were still undeniably few compared with English acts: some eighty specifically English general acts and three hundred English local acts passed in these years. In part this probably did reflect squeezing out of the Scots. But it also reflected their preferences in operating the new system. After the union, for instance, Scots usually preferred to leave the development of Scottish civil and criminal law to Scottish courts: better thus, they seem to have calculated, than to expose their principles and practices to tampering by underinformed English MPs.

It took the Forty-Five to make Westminster MPs focus—and then only transiently—on the state of Scotland, more particularly, of the Highlands. By contrast, in the post-1801 imperial parliament, Irish

---

[1] T. M. Devine, *Exploring the Scottish Past: Themes in the History of Scottish Society* (East Linton, 1995), p. 44.

affairs maintained a somewhat higher profile. Ireland, of course, represented a more substantial chunk of territory and population; by the time of the union, Ireland's population was between one-third and one-half that of mainland Britain. Ireland had, moreover, for the previous century had a regularly meeting, vigorously legislating parliament: its representatives brought a well established legislating habit to Westminster. On top of this, the task of governing Ireland was generally perceived as a challenge. Recurrent waves of peasant unrest had been extensively reported in the English press. At the time of the union, the rebellion of 1798 was a very recent event. Ireland seems often to have been perceived as an underdeveloped country: full of promise, though with a problematic cultural heritage. The challenge was to nurture its development without replicating some of the more problematic features of developed England. The question, should the English poor law be extended to Ireland? was confronted within a few years of the union. But prevalent opinion had it that the poor law had been a bad thing for England, encouraging the growth of a dependency culture. The Scots were thought to be better off with their somewhat different arrangements. In this context, it was resolved not to repeat the error in Ireland. Instead, more appropriate forms of relief were sought. In 1805 parliament approved the use of local rate monies (in Ireland alone) to support medical 'dispensaries', to augment existing infirmary provision.

The importance of parliaments in British and Irish governance lay not only in the business they formally transacted but also in the kind of political culture they helped to nurture: one in which public affairs were open to public debate. Broadsheets and pamphlets addressed to parliament, suggesting alternative ways of approaching matters currently under consideration, were already a feature of the publishing scene in the late seventeenth century. As the eighteenth century progressed, they issued in increasing numbers, and became a more substantial genre. Some reflections on questions of governance swelled to the size of treatises, even multi-volume treatises. Both British and Irish parliaments became more relaxed about placing their proceedings in the public domain as the century advanced. They authorized the publication of their journals, formal records of business, and of numerous committee reports; they allowed the press to cover parliamentary debate. (Court proceedings were also increasingly reported in print. Criminal trials at London's Old Bailey, taken down in shorthand, were published from the late seventeenth century. High court civil cases were increasingly reported in newspapers in the later eighteenth century. Reports of civil proceedings provided an alternative perspective on the issues of the day: in this context, business and matrimonial matters were given special prominence.)

The historian Franco Venturi, surveying Europe from an Italian vantage point has remarked that a key feature of Enlightenment culture was the reflective discussion of questions of governance.[2] Common articles of faith were, on the one hand, the significance of legislation in shaping society, and, on the other, the need for the legislator to understand society's own internal 'laws' in order for his own efforts to work to good effect. The British and Irish were well placed to participate in debates as to how governments might, and might not, promote human betterment. Although the nature of British and Irish government did not make easy the promotion of wholesale reforms from above, in the manner of some later eighteenth-century European 'enlightened despots', there was plenty of interest in the wider European debates associated with such efforts: debates about the best way of punishing crime, for example. (Cesare Beccaria's celebrated treatise on crime and punishment was translated into English within three years of its first Italian publication.) In the person of John Howard the prison reformer, whose prison tours extended not only throughout the British Isles but also across continental Europe, Britain indeed itself produced one of the great philanthropic heroes of Enlightenment Europe.

At the level of the written word, the Scots were certainly the most effective contributors to European debate—at least until Jeremy Bentham's writings began to attract wider notice. The more European orientation of Scottish higher education no doubt assisted this. But, paradoxically, the distancing of the Scots from major institutions of government may have assisted too. Much English writing about social issues immersed itself in the particularities of English statute law, and the debates to which that had given rise. The Scots wrote more philosophically. Contrast, thus, Lord Kames's essay on crime and punishment with undersecretary of state William Eden's treatise on the same subject, or Westmorland justice Richard Burn's *History*

---

[2] Franco Venturi, *Utopia and Reform in the Enlightenment* (Cambridge, 1971), see esp. pp. 7, 99.

of the Poor Laws with Edinburgh minister John McFarlan's widely translated *Inquiries concerning the Poor.*

As integral to the development of the public sphere as the growth of print culture was the rise of associational culture. Societies for the reformation of manners, which proliferated in both England and Ireland in the 1690s and early eighteenth century, were an early and particular example of the form. Mainly concerned to promote prosecutions for immorality (in such guises as prostitution and Sunday trading), they were conceived by some of their elite sympathizers as only one part of a broader ameliorative programme, other parts of which included prison visiting and the promotion of charity schools (the latter conceived in Ireland not merely as moralizing but as Protestantizing forces—though in truth the proselytizing Irish Protestant was inclined to confound the two). Subscription charity—'joint stock philanthropy', as it has been termed—emerged as a powerful engine of social action at about the same time.[3] Infirmaries in England, Scotland, and Ireland were commonly funded by a combination of substantial benefactions and regular subscriptions (in Ireland they also received some public funding).

Some elite societies were primarily think-tanks and lobbies, such as the Highland Society, with branches in London and Edinburgh, which in the 1780s lobbied for the restoration of Jacobite estates, and removal of restrictions on wearing the kilt, yet at the same time for the further development of the Highland economy. The London-based Society for Bettering the Condition of the Poor, which flourished from the 1790s through to the early nineteenth century, had something of the same character, though rather more of its energies were devoted to mobilizing philanthropic effort—to promote soup kitchens, various schemes to enhance the viability of the cottage economy, and elementary education. (Like many of the more successful English societies, it spawned an Irish imitator.)

Whereas official structures of government offered few opportunities for women, the new public sphere offered more. Having some philanthropic presence even in the early eighteenth century (a society of ladies promoted the first, Westminster infirmary), women became more visible as philanthropic entrepreneurs as the century

---

[3] The parallel is drawn in D. Owen, *English Philanthropy 1660–1960* (Cambridge, Mass., 1964), p. 12, though he did not himself use the shorthand phrase.

progressed. Some took to print: Sarah Trimmer to dispense advice to other philanthropists (in her *Oeconomy of Charity*), others, most famously Hannah More, to address the objects of philanthropic effort (in her case, to discourage discontent). In the context of the anti-slavery campaign, which took off as a public cause, chiefly in England, from the 1780s, women began to emerge not only as practitioners of practical philanthropy and as writers but also as fund-raisers, canvassers, and campaigners.

Social issues: case studies

In broad terms, the tasks of domestic governance were much the same throughout the British Isles. As we have noted, however, structures of government, public cultures, and traditions of action also differed from place to place, between and also within the three kingdoms. Varying social structures, social relations, and systems of values moreover meant that demands made on government, and 'problems' presented to it, varied from region to region, as well as over time. The final section of this chapter explores some of these differences through two case studies.

The first, focusing on attempts to regulate the production and consumption of alcohol, presents us with differences in patterns of behaviour between regions as well as kingdoms. It also allows us to glimpse policy-making processes in operation. Regulating the production and consumption of alcohol was a revenue issue, inasmuch as taxes on beer, wine, and spirits contributed significantly to government income. It was also at least potentially a moral and social issue, inasmuch as alcohol consumption was suspected to be—and no doubt in some cases was—associated with idleness, vice, and the neglect of family duties.

In England, the concentration of most brewing and distilling in substantial plants helped to make domestic production relatively easy to tax. Preventing illegal production was essentially the responsibility of the excise service—although, outside the metropolis, excise officers had to bring prosecutions before justices of the peace. All retailers were supposed to be licensed. The licensing of alehouses and inns was the responsibility of justices of the peace. Their powers in this regard were clarified and extended by parliament in a sequence of mid-century acts.

At two periods during the eighteenth century, alcohol consumption became the focus of special concern. The first lasted through the 1720s and 1730s, with a small reprise around 1750. In this instance, concern focused above all on excessive gin drinking, especially in the metropolis. At this time, English grain production was outstripping domestic demand; the gin trade provided one outlet for the surplus. Gin sellers moreover were not required to obtain licences from justices; this made the trade both easy to enter, and attractive to those who wished to operate at the poorer end of the market. Critics charged that heavy consumption of cheap gin was destructive of popular health and morals. At mid-century, it was suggested that the stagnation of population in the metropolis over the previous few decades might be traceable to this source. The mid-century resurgence of concern about gin was also associated with more general anxieties about high levels of crime in the metropolis, especially violent crime; it was suggested that among other things a clamp-down on idleness and on 'disorderly' entertainments might alleviate that problem. A key opinion-forming body throughout was the Society for Promoting Christian Knowledge, the SPCK, which, since its foundation in 1698, had emerged as a wide-ranging social reform gingergroup. Some members of this society were highly critical of what they saw as Robert Walpole's morally lax style of government. As they saw it, the evil resulted partly from the government's willingness to condone excessive gin consumption on account of the revenue it produced. As a result of their campaigns, duties were raised in the 1730s and again in the early 1750s, and justices' licensing powers were tightened up, though the growing pressure of population on grain supplies and falling real wages may also have operated to aid the reformers' cause (to the extent that the 'gin craze' was ever a real matter of popular conduct, and not just a 'moral panic').

In the 1780s, concern was nationwide and differently targeted: focusing primarily on the proliferation of alehouses, conceived as a spur to idleness, disorderly habits, and relief-dependence in poor families. Poor alehouses may also have attracted suspicion as harbourers of vagrants: there was much concern about high levels of vagrancy in this decade. The campaign against overnumerous and disorderly alehouses formed a part of a larger 'reformation of manners' campaign, other favoured objects of which were the invigoration of policing, establishment of Sunday schools, and of friendly societies. Initial pressure to clamp down on alehouses may have come from assize judges, reflecting government concern—but it is clear that justices of the peace throughout the country took up the issue and ran with it. In county after county in the early to mid-1780s, they passed special resolutions, one or more of which usually focused on alehouses. Numbers of licences granted were in truth reined back sharply at this time, and remained relatively low for several decades thereafter, despite accelerating population growth—until in 1830 laissez-faire ideology inaugurated the era of the unlicensed 'beer shop'.

These two campaigns, interesting in their own right as campaigns, despite the differences in their concerns, also clearly shared certain preoccupations. The real focus of concern, in both campaigns, was the working-class consumer, the wage-earner upon whose willingness and capacity for labour the health of the economy was in important part seen to depend. These consumers were conceived as potentially rowdy, licentious, and indeed criminal. They or their families were potential claimants of parish relief.

In Ireland, despite similarities of enforcement structure, and some similarities in patterns of concern, patterns both of official action and of consumer behaviour differed. Although laws, on the English model, had passed during the seventeenth century, empowering sub-sets of justices of the peace selectively to license houses for the sale of beer, wine, and spirits, according to one historian of the subject, in contrast to England, Irish practice was generally permissive throughout the eighteenth century: little effective was done to control the drink trade.

Despite continuing lax enforcement, concern rose at the end of the century, in response to a perceived increase in the consumption of whisky. This in turn seems to have been associated with the rise of a large illicit distilling industry in the north and west of Ireland. Excise rules had been changed in the 1770s to encourage concentration of production on the English model. In less developed districts, peasants however could not afford to abandon their now illegal small stills—a vital source of income with which to pay rents. When war in the 1790s racked up levels of duty, the competitive position of the illegal product was strengthened. While the excise service struggled to put down the illicit trade, the Irish parliament produced new legislation, directed especially against poor whisky houses, or 'shebeens'. Through the first few decades of the nineteenth century, concerns about the debilitating effect of whisky drinking was given further edge by the belief that shebeens were the characteristic meeting places of peasant secret societies. Nonetheless, it is suggested, only from the 1830s, with the development of effective police forces, did legal controls begin to bite.

In Scotland—following representations from the General Assembly of the Church of Scotland, keen to tighten up on moral discipline—legislation of 1756, noting that Scottish justices lacked the licensing powers of their English counterparts, bestowed comparable powers. It has however been questioned whether Scots justices' habits of business would have made possible the systematic discharge of these responsibilities. As in Ireland, consumers often favoured whisky over beer. As in Ireland also, the high tax regime of the French Revolutionary and Napoleonic Wars encouraged the rise of an illicit distilling industry in marginal districts—the Highlands—the more so because of other pressures on the Highland peasant economy. (At the end of the wars, the Highland Society was to cooperate with government in finding ways to discourage illicit distilling, as one part of its larger programme of economic modernization.)

It appears thus that while in more extensively proletarianized English society concerns focused primarily upon the debauching of the consumer, in the more variegated, part-peasant, part-proletarian societies of Scotland and Ireland, although concerns about consumers were certainly voiced, a distinct dimension was added by the entrepreneurial activities of 'peasant producers' with both the incentive and the opportunity to evade excise enforcement, who channelled illicit produce on to markets in any case much less tightly regulated than the English one.

Our second 'case study' will focus on major episodes of social unrest: a source of further insight into patterns of social difference and their complex ramifications.

Even in heavily policed modern societies, the police may lose control of streets or neighbourhoods, to tumultuous or violent protest, systematic defiance of the law, or vigilantism. In relatively lightly policed early modern societies, control was not always easily maintained, and could be very difficult to regain once lost. The use of troops to regain control, though it could be effective in breaking the back of protest, might lead to greatly increased death tolls; troops moreover were not effectively equipped to institute peace in deeply troubled or divided societies.

The most serious and prolonged episodes of unrest generally took the form of some section of the populace taking the law into their own hands. This sometimes involved attempts to prevent authorities or others acting to execute the law, as in the case of militia riots, which disrupted the process of conscription, or turnpike riots, when tollgates were destroyed. It sometimes involved unauthorized people acting out their conception of what was lawful or fair, in defiance of the authorities: attempting to stop the export of grain or fix the price of bread, in years of bad harvest, or to fix industrial wage levels, or prevent the use of machinery seen as taking away jobs. (Often of course both elements were present in some degree, different aspects of a complex event.)

It has been argued that behind all popular disturbances there lay some 'legitimising notion',[4] and this seems fair enough, at least in the case of the most serious and prolonged disturbances: they could scarcely have attracted broad-based support and been sustained had that not been so. It is important however to prise this apart from the notion that popular disturbances, though challenging to the authorities, were intrinsically orderly. In the sense that some rationale, some instrumentality generally governed the actions of participants, this was perhaps true. Furthermore, some such exercises did minimize violence, their relative orderliness both a legitimating strategy and an attempt to ward off retribution. In other instances, however, violence was used as a tool: buildings were showered with stones or set on fire; people beaten up or threatened with death. People could get killed in the process. There were cases in which killing was deliberate.

The most common and widespread of the more serious disturbances arose out of food shortages in times of harvest failure, industrial disputes, and disputes over the terms imposed on small landowners or tenants: rents, tithes. Sometimes conflict was tinged with a political colouring: Jacobitism or Jacobinism. Sometimes, especially in Ireland, it had, or was thought to have, sectarian undertones.

[4] E. P. Thompson, *Customs in Common* (Harmondsworth, 1993), p. 188.

Episodes of crowds taking the law into their own hands in connection with harvest failure occurred throughout the period. Adverse weather conditions—in the early 1690s, around 1710, in the late 1720s, around 1740, in 1756–7 and 1766, the early 1770s, early and late 1780s, around 1795 and 1800, 1810–13, and again at the end of the wars—all precipitated confrontations in one or another part of the British Isles. Areas of disorder were not necessarily the hardest hit. 1783, thus, was a terrible year in the Highlands, but little disorder is recorded, apart from an attack on retailers in Inverness. Disturbances arose not so much when people were hungry as when they saw an opportunity to alleviate their hunger. These opportunities presented themselves when grain, destined for towns or populous regions, moved through areas themselves suffering from food shortage. Not infrequently they focused on ports. Alternatively, they might focus on market places, where grain was for sale at inflated prices, or on urban granaries. Frustrated consumers might march out into the country-side, to see what farmers had in store and what they planned to do with it. Those taking part in these disturbances were characteristically townsmen or women—often the shoppers for their families, women might well be on the front line—or industrial workers—weavers, miners; people dependent for food on what their wages would buy them.

Problems of documentation of course complicate any attempt to map the geography of such disturbances. Such work as has been done nonetheless suggests that in mainland Britain, in the first half of the eighteenth century, disturbances were concentrated on the coasts, on major rivers—Severn, Thames, Trent, Ouse—and in the industrial regions of East Anglia, also a major grain-growing region. The second half of the century was marked by the growth of disturbances in the increasingly populous industrial zones of the Midlands and North, and south Wales. Though the largest Scottish towns saw some dis-turbances, here disorders were most common along the east coast, whence grain might be shipped to England. Irish experience has not been comprehensively studied, but there were certainly similar dis-turbances there. In 1729 and again in 1740–1, these were apparently concentrated in port cities: Dublin, Waterford, Clonmel, Cork, Limerick, Galway, Sligo, Belfast, and Drogheda—though famine, associated with the failure not only of grain but also potato crops, hit hard across the land. The famine of 1740–1 is estimated to have caused more deaths in Ireland than its more notorious successor of the 1840s.

Official responses combined assistance, negotiation, and repression. Over time, official willingness to try to redirect the grain trade, or fix prices for consumers' benefit, declined in favour of other forms of assistance: charitable subscriptions to subsidize food for the poor; soup kitchens. Magistrates and constables did what they could to contain and disperse disorderly crowds, but troops were often called in: regular army soldiers, militiamen or volunteer forces. In the context of general rises in prosecutions for crime in these years, it was common also to make a special example of some rioters. In some years of especially widespread disturbance, as in the 1750s and 1760s, special commissions were set up to try rioters expeditiously. In the 1790s, however, when disturbances were even more widespread, the authorities seem to have felt the need to economize on special judicial effort: special commissions were reserved for the most troubling episodes, as when grain rioting was combined with militia mutiny.

Major industrial disturbances in this period characteristically arose out of disputes between domestic workers, often textile workers, and their employers, although other sorts of employment context could give rise to large-scale confrontations too: thus disputes between miners and their employers, or between Tyne keelmen or East India Company sailors and theirs. Workers often hoped that authorities would intervene: to help them obtain better wages, regulate working practices, prevent the introduction of certain forms of machinery, or change trade policies so as to enlarge markets. This being so, their protests sometimes focused on unhelpful authority.

Major cities were sometimes disturbed, even convulsed, by industrial disorders. Spitalfields silkweavers in London, and the woollen weavers who clustered around the area of the Liberties in Dublin, both reacted vigorously and angrily to worsening conditions in their trades in the later eighteenth century. Their proximity to power helped ensure that they made an impact—both for better and for worse from their point of view (Spitalfields weavers obtained an act empowering magistrates to help fix wages, in 1773, but not before some of their number had been the subject of exemplary hangings). In Norwich, a well-established worsted centre, in the 1750s, protesting weavers set up camp on Mousehold Heath outside the town. Manchester experienced industrial protest at the same time, and in the later part of the century the newer industrial towns—such as Stockport and Paisley—came more to the fore.

Many disturbances, however, took place not in major towns, but in rural industrial regions: the environments in which most of the industrial workforce lived and worked. As in the case of grain rioting, the geography of industrial disturbance was structured by a combination of vulnerability and opportunity. Workers were most vulnerable when most dependent on industrial employment, when not cushioned by access to the land and its produce. Protest, however, also presupposed the possibility of improving one's condition by exerting pressure. Small masters who marketed their own work might lack the obvious targets available to those who worked for a large 'putter-out'. The workforce, moreover, needed to be sufficiently concentrated and cohesive to be able to sustain collective action. In the early eighteenth century, outside the towns, these conditions were best met in the industrial west of England: the textile districts of Gloucestershire and Wiltshire, where a form of proto-trade-unionism was already well established by 1700. Only in the second half of the century did the industrial West Midlands, Yorkshire, and Lancashire also see large-scale industrial disputes. Both south-west and northern districts saw machine-breaking (most famous in its northerly manifestation as 'Luddism'), in the late eighteenth and early nineteenth centuries. Scottish weavers, in the textile district centring on Glasgow, first turned out in force in 1812.

By contrast, although efforts to promote the linen industry in the Scottish Highlands in the eighteenth century had met with some success, this was not a zone of industrial disturbance—any more than was rural Ireland, despite the presence of a similarly implanted linen industry there. In the greater part of these regions, industry was probably simply not sufficiently central to the support of the community to provide a focus for collective action. This was not the case in parts of Ulster where, furthermore, a substantial proportion of linen weavers were not independent producers but wage-workers. Here however social conflict in the closing decades of the century chiefly took the form of sectarian conflict between Protestant and Catholic weavers and small farmers.

The official response to industrial, as to harvest-related disturbances had several different facets. Employers as well as workers might be judged at fault; magistrates might therefore interpose themselves as mediators. 'Combination' was however officially frowned upon. In both Britain and Ireland, the eighteenth century saw the passage of several acts against combinations in particular trades. Workers often proceeded in a peaceful, negotiative manner—though sometimes they sought to pressure recalcitrant masters by destroying working equipment. Violence more commonly ensued when protest focused on the introduction of machinery. In these cases, troops might be deployed. From the later eighteenth century, parliament showed itself increasingly unsympathetic to workers' calls for the regulation of industry: no restrictions were placed on the use of new forms of machinery; parliament refused to sanction wage regulation and, in 1813–14, repealed the apprenticeship clauses of the Elizabethan Statute of Artificers. The effect of this was to make industrial conflict in part a war of ideas.

A third source of major and sustained disturbance were disputes over access to land, or the terms of access to land, for example, over rents and tithes. Not surprisingly, the geography of these conflicts was quite different from that either of industrial disputes, or harvest-related disturbances.

England and Wales saw no major popular disturbances associated with these issues in this period. This is certainly not to imply that there were no conflicts over land or land use. Land reorganization associated with fen drainage, questions of access to woodland, and the enclosure of commons and open fields all provoked dispute and sometimes violent conflict. But though they might be sustained for years, even decades, these conflicts were commonly highly localized. Conflicts over fen drainage, which might affect a whole swathe of communities, probably had the greatest drawing power (in 1699, the privy council responded to riots in Lincolnshire by putting justices of the peace on alert in the Isle of Ely, Cambridgeshire, Huntingdonshire, and Northamptonshire).

In Scotland, land-related protest was similarly muted. The Galloway 'Levellers' revolt'—a protest against the enclosure of land for cattle grazing which broke out in Kirkudbrightshire and Wigtownshire, in the south-west, in 1724–5—was concentrated in a relatively small region, about 25 square miles. (It attracted special attention at the time because the self-proclaimed Levellers' identification with the radical Covenanting tradition helped win them support from elements in the Kirk.) Massive changes in land use associated with the growth of sheep farming in the Highlands from the later eighteenth century, prompting forced resettlement, and a first major wave of Highland emigration, provoked strikingly little active resistance—a reflection, it is often suggested, of the overwhelming legal, economic, and cultural power of the great Highland landowners. (The displaced might however look to heaven to exact retribution they felt unable to administer themselves: oral historians have found their descendants cherishing to this day stories of 'clearing' landlords or their factors coming to sticky ends.)

Ireland was the site of the most extensive and persistent land-related disturbances in this period. There is little evidence of these in the early eighteenth century, one episode of attack on cattle hus-bandry in Connaught apart. They enlarged in scale (or at least, began to attract more notice) in the 1760s in Munster (in the counties of Cork, Waterford, Limerick, and Tipperary) in the shape of the 'Whiteboys', and shortly thereafter in Ulster, in the shape of the 'Oakboys' and later the 'Steelboys'. Thereafter this form of peasant self-help, under various names, was to recur up and down the coun-try for decades: in south Leinster in the 1770s, Munster in the 1780s, and again in the 1790s, in the northern parts of Connaught and in Munster again in the first decade of the nineteenth century, in west-ern Leinster and Munster again in the final years of the war (and indeed beyond that).

In form, these disturbances commonly involved secretive, and apparently oath-bound groups of small farmers, farm servants, industrial workers, and the like threatening with violence (and, in the face of non-compliance, perpetrating violence upon) those who determined the terms of access to land, and did not mete out what the protestors were prepared to accept as fair treatment. Their targets were not commonly large landlords, but the headtenants or middle-men from whom smaller landholders sublet, or tithe-proctors who contracted to collect tithe—or people of the same status as them-selves who cooperated with unfair practice, renting land from which previous tenants had been 'unfairly' evicted, for example. For the purposes of taking action, a local group would operate under the leadership of a 'captain'. Action groups were commonly small and local—but such units replicated themselves over large areas, recog-nized a common identity and practised some forms of cooperation. These practices were overlaid upon a popular culture in which sometimes long-running, sporadically violent conflicts between local groups—'faction fights'—were endemic, and in early nineteenth-century Munster the two seemed to fuse in the struggle between Whiteboyish 'Caravats' and their marginally socially superior antagonists, the 'Sharavests'.

Much of the violence took place between co-religionists, in most cases Catholics, even though the social order against which the protest was directed was dominated at its higher levels by Protestants. This did not stop some observers interpreting it as a form of anti-Protestant insurgency. Sometimes movements similar in form did have a more sectarian colouring. In Ulster in the 1780s and 1790s, nervous Protestants clashed with Catholic 'Defenders'. Political or at least quasi-political movements could be built around similar social forms. This was especially marked in the 1790s, when the north of Ireland saw the appearance of a peasant movement influenced by the ideals and practices of the United Irishmen. Habits of peasant protest formed a basis for mobilization in a militant challenge to the state, the Rebellion of 1798.

These Irish peasant movements had certain points in common with movements of popular protest in mainland Britain. The habit of forming anonymous bands and taking direct action under the leadership of a 'captain' was not unique to Ireland. Oath-bound groups were certainly a feature of some industrial protest on the mainland. However, the Irish context was distinctive in certain respects, which help to account for the distinctive features of these disturbances. First, though 'peasant farmers'—people farming a few acres or less of land, at least partly on a subsistence basis—were by no means extinct in England, this form of social and economic organization was more widespread in Ireland, and to much of the population, few alternative styles of life immediately presented themselves. Population growth, and the growth of commercial farming—cattle farming in the 1760s and 1770s; later, grain growing for English markets—placed this peasant economy under pressure, reducing the availability of land and tending to raise rents. (Munster, the most common site of disturbances, was also the region where commercial agriculture most flourished.) Resort to direct action reflected lack of confidence in any other forms of recourse. On the other hand, contrasting the militancy of the Irish peasantry with the passivity of their counterparts in the Scottish Highlands, we might suggest that Irish willingness to resort to direct action also reflected the self-confidence, strength of horizontal solidarities, and weakness of vertical deference among both Catholic and Presbyterian rank and file.

From the point of view of those responsible for maintaining law and order in Ireland, the same cultural gaps which helped to nurture such movements impeded both understanding, and the formulation of an effective response. The world of the native Irish was hard to penetrate, and the footsoldiers of local government, constables and the like, all too prone, or thought to be all too prone, to intimidation, if not co-option. Hence resort to informers, and repeated attempts to strengthen the articulation of the machinery of peacekeeping.

Some faith was also placed in the power of judicial terror: the exemplary hanging. In the context of the first outbreak of Whiteboyism, in the 1760s, a frightened Tipperary ruling class persisted, despite a notable lack of encouragement from higher levels of government, in indicting, convicting, and obtaining a death sentence against a Catholic priest they suspected of complicity in the disturbances—a striking reflection of tensions between different levels and systems of authority in this, the most internally fractured of the kingdoms of the British Isles.

Figure 5 The main hall of the Bank of England as portrayed in Rudolf Ackermann's *The Microcosm of London* in 1810. The Bank was not only a powerful engine of credit but also a standing symbol of London's pre-eminence as a financial centre.

4

The wealth of the nation

Martin Daunton

The Malthusian race

Thomas Robert Malthus, the great and gloomy economist, compared the economic and social history of the British Isles in the eighteenth century to a race between a hare and a tortoise. The hare of population growth could always outstrip the tortoise of food supply, with very serious consequences for the wealth of the nation and the welfare of the British people. Malthus assumed that any gains in the supply of food would be hard won and slow, as a result of ingenuity and back-breaking toil in winning more crops from the land, or by extending cultivation to marginal soils on the uplands. By contrast, it was only too easy to produce more children. Hence Malthus's dread that an increase in the population would both force up food prices and drive down wages as a result of competition for work.

If Malthus was right, the welfare of the people of Britain could not rise above a level set by the balance of people and land. Any period of agricultural surplus and low food prices might simply encourage people to marry earlier and have children, from which two outcomes might follow. One possibility was that couples would continue to produce offspring, heedless of the consequences, until the hare of population growth was halted in its tracks by the 'positive check' of famine and disease. The second option was much to be preferred. As Malthus put it, 'If we can persuade the hare to go to sleep, the tortoise may have some chance of overtaking her.' A 'preventive check' on population growth depended on the 'prudential restraint' of the population in delaying marriage until there was some prospect of supporting a family in reasonable conditions and maintaining a respectable social position. In the words of the Book of Common Prayer, so well known to the Reverend Thomas Malthus, matrimony 'is not to be enterprised, nor taken in hand unadvisedly, lightly or wantonly, to satisfy man's carnal lusts and appetites, like brute beasts that have no understanding; but reverently, discreetly, advisedly, soberly and in the fear of God'. Malthus hoped that men of all social ranks would carefully consider the implications of marriage. A gentleman's son would wish to maintain his status; a farmer's or tradesman's son would consider his chances of obtaining a farm or starting a business; a labourer's son would be anxious that his exertions could save his family from 'rags and squalid poverty, and their consequent degradation in the community'. Malthus hoped that men and women would control their carnal lusts until they could afford to marry and ensure that children would have a decent start in life. Self-restraint and foresight were therefore crucial in preventing the hare of population from outstripping the tortoise of agriculture, and so preserving a precarious prosperity. What Malthus did not foresee was the possibility that a much larger population could achieve a higher standard of welfare.

The first edition of Malthus's *Essay on Population* appeared in 1798, and in hindsight might seem an unduly pessimistic account of the British economy, at a time when cotton factories and iron furnaces, turnpikes and canals, steam engines and coal mines offered new possibilities of production and growth. Should Malthus's gloom be simply dismissed as a failure to realize that society was passing through a fundamental transformation, what later commentators were to term an industrial revolution? In fact, there were good reasons for his pessimism. The *Essay* appeared at a time when food prices were rapidly rising, and threatening the welfare of the people. Malthus was well aware of the problems of rural poverty in southern England, where he feared that prudence and the 'preventive check' were being subverted by the poor law. Agricultural workers in the southern counties were given relief according to the number of their children and the price of bread, so removing (in his opinion) the incentive for them to control their 'carnal lusts'. Kindness to the poor merely made things worse, for they had more children and so forced up food prices for everyone and dragged down wages, with the result that prudence and deferment of the immediate gratification of marriage became less appealing. Although Malthus's logic was faulty—the high costs of poor relief in the south were a *result* of overpopulation and poverty rather than a cause—he did have a point. Rural labourers in the southern counties of England *were* in a miserable state, and the spectre of the 'positive check' of famine still haunted two kingdoms. Scotland was hit by a serious famine in 1697/9, and again in 1739/41 and 1782. Ireland was badly affected in 1740/1, 1755, 1766, 1800/1, 1817/19, and most notoriously in the Potato Famine of 1846/8. Was Malthus right to stress the limits to the wealth of the nation and the welfare of the people rather than the possibilities of growth and prosperity?

The growth of population

At the start of the eighteenth century, there was greater reason for optimism, for the hare of population growth was slumbering and the tortoise of food supply had a sizeable lead. The population of England declined or stagnated in the later seventeenth century, and prudential restraint was in the ascendant. Marriage was clearly not undertaken unadvisedly or wantonly, and celibacy was commonplace. In 1701 an astonishingly high proportion of the English population—about one-quarter—reached their early 40s without marrying, and the average age of women at their first marriage was as high as 26 or 27. Procreation was spurned even by peers of the realm who had less immediate reason for prudence: peers born in the first quarter of the eighteenth century could manage to produce only 0.79 sons each and by no means all survived to adulthood. Many landowners therefore died without a direct male heir. Population growth resumed at a low rate in the first half of the eighteenth century, and then accelerated in the second half of the eighteenth century, with a spurt to a new level from 1786. Malthus had every reason to fear that prudence was being forgotten in the 1780s and 1790s in a rush to procreate. The population of England rose from 5,100,000 in 1701 to 5,800,000 in 1751, a level it had previously reached around 1300 and again around 1650. On these occasions, the population could not be sustained, and it fell as a result of the positive check of food shortages and disease, and the reassertion of prudential restraint. The late eighteenth century was different, for the population of England passed through the previous barrier, surging to an unprecedented level of 8,700,000 in 1801.

Bachelors and spinsters went out of fashion in eighteenth-century England. The proportion of people unmarried in their early 40s slumped to about 7 per cent in 1801, and the average age of first marriage of women fell by about two and a half years to around 23 in the early nineteenth century. The change in the proportion of the population marrying, and the fall in age of marriage, were undoubtedly the major influences on population growth, by increasing the number of years during which a wife could bear legitimate children. However, fertility *within* marriage also rose over the eighteenth century. Despite the lack of reliable methods of birth control, couples were able to 'space' their children in response to economic circumstances, by reducing the frequency of intercourse or relying on more imaginative strategies which were denounced by Malthus. Further, extended breastfeeding delayed ovulation and hence prevented a further conception. In the course of the eighteenth century, the 'space' between births declined by about two months, so that marital fertility rose and reinforced the effect of more people marrying at a younger age. Mothers had a better diet as a result of the availability of more food at lower prices, so that there were fewer still births, and babies were healthier and heavier, and hence more likely to survive infancy. Clearly, the aristocracy regained its desire to procreate, for peers born in the second half of the eighteenth century each managed to produce an average of 1.4 sons, who had a better chance of surviving to inherit the estate.

Malthus's explanation of the changing popularity of marriage assumed that decisions were made by a rational, prudent man who asked himself whether his assets and earnings could support a wife and child. The prospect of higher real wages would therefore allow him to marry earlier, so that low food prices in the early eighteenth century weakened prudential restraint, as well as improving women's diets so that more conceptions resulted in live births. But marriage is much more than the outcome of economic calculation by rational economic men; it was also a cultural and social act, involving courtship rituals, concern for sexual reputation, and negotiation between families. As Innes shows, it attracted the attention of the government. Marriage decisions were affected by the social structure and cultural setting. In the case of small family farms or independent artisans, marriage was not feasible until an opening appeared, and adolescents and young adults spent their adolescence and early adulthood as servants in husbandry or apprentices, working in the households of other families in return for a small wage, board, and lodgings. Such a system allowed surplus labour in one family to be transferred to cover deficits in other families. A decline in the significance of small farms or of artisan production, and a growth of waged labour, weakened these constraints on marriage. Certainly, service in husbandry declined in the later eighteenth century as a result of changes in the structure of farming and in price trends. On large arable farms in southern England, the demand for labour was seasonal, and farmers hired men and women from a pool of workers which was sustained for the rest of the year by the poor law. Men and women in these areas had little cause to delay marriage, and prudence had little appeal when there was no chance of ultimate independence. Poverty and hardship might therefore encourage early marriage. Service survived in the pastoral areas of the west, where the demand for labour was more constant over the year, and small family farms survived. Again, the growth of industrial outwork in small domestic workshops encouraged early marriage, for a domestic worker in, say, the hosiery trade in the villages of the East Midlands, had every reason to marry as soon as possible in order to get more hands to assist in the production of stockings.

Middle-class families needed capital and credit, and marriage had considerable importance in bringing in funds through dowries and marriage settlements, and giving access to credit networks. Marriage was part of the acquisition of reputation and creditworthiness, and women played a major role as the link in a culture of sociability with other families and with the social world of the town. Marriage therefore had its practical value, but it was not simply an economic transaction. Even in the case of landed families, marriage was not simply a dynastic alliance designed to build up ever greater estates or to acquire large dowries from the new riches of commerce and finance. Indeed, such an ambition was often undermined by the rise of a more egalitarian family structure. Aristocratic families had the appearance of blatant patriarchy, for the landed estate invariably passed to the eldest son or, in the absence of surviving sons, to a more distant male relative—a phenomenon which provided Jane Austen with the plot for *Pride and Prejudice* where the unfortunate Mrs Bennet had five daughters and no son. As Mrs Bennet complained, it was cruel for the estate to pass to a Mr Collins 'whom nobody cared about'. In reality, Mr Bennet would require Mr Collins to make annual payments to his daughters and widow, precisely because he cared for them more than for a distant relative. These charges often had scant regard for the ability of the estate to bear the burden, and the heir might, in the words of Lord Winchelsea, become 'the slave of the family' to support his younger brothers, widowed mother, and sisters. The emergence of a more affectionate and egalitarian family, where younger sons and daughters were valued more highly and estates were encumbered with charges to support them, encouraged an active land market to clear debts and obligations. The emotional history of families might therefore affect the economy, as much as economic considerations might affect the incidence of marriage.

Marriage was the most important factor in explaining population growth, assisted by the rise in fertility within marriage. Nevertheless, mortality should not be ignored. As we have seen, fertility and mortality were interconnected, for the reduction in gaps between births was arguably the result of a decline in still births, which was linked with a greater chance of survival in the first months of life. The infant mortality rate in England fell from an exceptionally high level of about 191 deaths in the first year of life for every 1,000 live births at the start of the eighteenth century, to 136 at the start of the nineteenth century, and there were also significant drops in adult rates. The fall in death rates was particularly striking, for the movement of large numbers of people from the countryside to towns meant that ever more people were living in dangerous environments. In the rural parish of Hartland in Devon, 85 infants in every 1,000 births were dead before the age of 1 in the first half of the eighteenth century. Even in a small town—Gainsborough in Lincolnshire—272 babies out of 1,000 died before their first birthday—and deaths were even higher in larger towns and London. In the metropolis, burials exceeded baptisms by 26 per cent in the first decade of the eighteenth century, and 44 per cent in the 1740s. London only grew by mopping up a considerable part of the natural population growth of the countryside. By 1800 baptisms overtook burials in London, a remarkable change which reflects the decline of infectious diseases and the efforts of improvement commissioners in cleaning and paving urban streets.

Although London and the large towns remained centres of disease and poor life expectancy compared to the countryside for another century, their mortality did fall over the eighteenth century, and they were no longer 'devourers' of men, women, and children.

English population growth in the eighteenth century was held down not only by the higher mortality rate in towns, but also by migration. Around one-fifth of the natural growth of population in England between 1695 and 1801 was exported overseas, and above all to North America. Apart from the convicts who were transported to North America and Australia to atone for their crimes, most migrants were not drawn from the poorest members of society. The largest group were young, single men with a skill, largely from southern England, who sought a new life in the colonies as 'indentured servants', agreeing to work for a master for, say, four years to pay for their passage across the Atlantic. They could look forward to setting up as skilled artisans catering for the needs of affluent consumers in the prosperous towns of the eastern seaboard. A smaller stream of migrants were families, mainly from the north of England and Scotland, whose ambition was to establish independent farms, re-creating on the peripheries of the empire the social world which was being destroyed in Britain.

In Scotland, the growth of the population in the later eighteenth century was considerably *slower* than in England. The population of Scotland was somewhere around 860,000 in the first half of the eighteenth century, and reached 1,625,000 in 1801—an increase of 28 per cent compared with 45 per cent in England. The explanation was in part a higher rate of mortality, and more importantly the prudential restraint of the Scots. Bachelors and spinsters continued to be common and the age of marriage remained high. Meanwhile, Irish population growth outstripped the rate in England, growing from something over 2 million after the devastating famine of 1740/1 to 5 million in 1800. Malthus was convinced that the explanation of this remarkable increase was found in the feckless behaviour of the Irish in embarking on early and improvident marriage. Irish women married on average around the age of 22, and population growth was fastest in the poorest areas where prudence had little appeal. As one commentator remarked, 'the wretchedness of living conditions made marriage seem a welcome relief.' The threat of famine was ever-present, but for most of the time Irish cottagers were kept alive, and in good health, on an unremitting diet of potatoes and skimmed milk left from the production of butter. Despite their squalid hovels and ragged clothes, Arthur Young reported that the poor of Ireland were 'as athletic in their form, as robust, and as capable of enduring labour as any upon earth'. The pressure of population on the land meant that there were surges in mortality in periods of crisis, and there were already signs at the end of the eighteenth century of a modest increase in the age of marriage to limit population growth. More significantly, large-scale migration started from about 1800, both to North America and to Britain. Irishmen endured labour as 'navvies' who dug canals, or toiled in building London and the other expanding towns. As Adam Smith remarked, the Irish porters and prostitutes of London were 'the strongest men and the most beautiful women perhaps in the British dominions'. Others were less impressed by the strength and allure of Irish migrants, and despised them as no better than the heathen native peoples encountered in the further reaches of the empire. Daniel O'Connell, the Liberator of the Irish Catholics, pointed out in 1829 that the Irish were treated as 'white-washed negroes', a telling comment which reminds us that the Gaelic-speaking Irish and Highland Scots were often seen as 'savages' to be civilized in the same way as native Americans or Africans. But the situation was full of ambiguity, for the Irish and Highlanders were both subordinate at home, and active participants in the imperial project abroad, as soldiers in British regiments.

Agriculture

The race between the tortoise of agricultural output and the hare of population fell into two clear phases. In the first part of the race, until the middle of the eighteenth century, food supply was ahead of population. In the second half of the century, the hare of population started to pull ahead of the tortoise of food supply. The contrast between the earlier and later eighteenth century is obvious from the movement of grain prices. In 1700 Winchester College paid 32.6 shillings for a quarter of wheat, and in 1750 only 27.6 shillings; by 1800, the price had risen to 148.5 shillings. The difference is also clear from the loss of self-sufficiency in grain. In the early eighteenth century,

Britain exported wheat, rising from 49,000 quarters in 1700 to a massive peak of 950,000 quarters in 1750. By the 1780s and 1790s, Britain relied on *imports* of grain, amounting to as much as 1,243,000 quarters of wheat in 1800. Here was the context for Malthus's gloom: a rapid increase in food prices, a loss of self-sufficiency, and a threat to the standard of living and welfare of many people. Could it be that population growth was simply leading to more misery and poverty, as it had in the fourteenth and seventeenth centuries when disease had ravaged the country? There was no need to look back into history, for anyone in search of immiseration had only to look across the Channel to France, where the failure of Paris's food supply was one element in the collapse of order and the lurch into revolution, or across the Irish Sea. The supply of food, at a reasonable price, was crucial to social and political order in all pre-industrial societies.

Despite Malthus's understandable gloom, his expectations were falsified in Britain. Population growth continued at a rapid rate, reaching an unprecedented level well above the peaks of the early fourteenth and early seventeenth centuries. Although poverty and social unrest remained very real concerns for the next thirty or so years, food prices actually started to fall with the end of the wars with France in 1815, and a serious *collapse* in the welfare of the people was avoided. Agriculture *was* able to feed more people up to 1800, by the application of great effort and at the expense of higher prices and rents, with major changes in the social structure of the countryside which were regretted both by conservatives and radicals. An understanding of the achievement of agriculture in feeding the people is essential to any appreciation of British history in the eighteenth century, to the welfare of the British people and domestic order, and to the ability of the state to extract revenues to fight wars.

The increase in English agricultural output was in part the result of a change in land from low to high intensity uses. The Fens of eastern England were drained from the seventeenth century, and fishing, fowling, and reed cutting gave way to arable crops with high yields—a change provoking riots by those who saw their traditional livelihood disappearing. Forests were cleared, and land was taken into cultivation on the margins of Dartmoor or the Pennines. The reclamation of land continued over the century, especially in the period of rising prices at the end of the century when marginal land was brought into cultivation at great expense. Further, more land was used within the existing area of cultivation, by reducing the amount of fallow land, and replacing permanent pasture and rough grazing with arable rotations. Flocks of sheep or herds of cattle were sustained by growing fodder crops such as turnips; the animals provided manure for the soil, and nitrogen-fixing crops such as clover helped to raise yields of grain. Farmers switched to more productive crops, with a decline in the acreage of rye and a rise in wheat and barley. They grew winter and spring sown cereals, so that output was less likely to be affected by one poor harvest. From the mid-eighteenth century, the potato was adopted, and produced about twice as many calories as the same area under wheat. Farmers gave more care and attention to the selection of seeds, and they spent time and effort in careful preparation of the soil, harrowing and weeding to give crops a better chance. Breeders also improved livestock, so that sheep and cattle gained more weight and reached the market faster. By these means, the output of the land was increased, and by the 1730s and 1740s grain yields were pushed above the best levels achieved in the middle ages. Unlike previous periods of population pressure, when farmers switched to arable cultivation to feed the people and reduced the number of animals, in the eighteenth century new rotations could sustain *more* animals.

These changes meant that agricultural output rose over the eighteenth century, without necessarily increasing the productivity of *labour*. The extension of the area under crops might simply require more workers, and some of the techniques designed to raise yields were very labour-intensive. Turnips were hoed, sheep and cattle fed in stalls during the winter, manure hauled to the fields. The success of English agriculture was not simply that it managed to feed more people by means of unremitting labour in the fields; it was also able to release workers from the fields to work in industry and live in towns. In England in 1700, there were about 182 people for every 100 in agriculture; by 1800, there were 276. By comparison, in France the numbers supported by 100 people in agriculture were 158 in 1700 and still only 170 in 1800—a difference which indicates a massive discrepancy in the productivity of agricultural workers in the two countries. How did English agriculture manage to raise labour productivity to such high levels?

The increase in grain yields contributed to the improved productivity of the workforce, by encouraging a change in the use of hand tools. When grain yields were low and labour cheap, it made sense to use short-handled sickles: a worker cut a small area in a day, with little wastage of precious grain. When yields were higher, it was possible to use long-handled scythes, which increased the productivity of labour at the cost of wasting grain. Such simple and unspectacular changes in hand tools allowed workers to cut a larger area in a day, and they were better fed so that they could keep up the pace of work for a longer time. Agricultural labourers in medieval England cut about the same area of grain in a day as workers in early nineteenth-century Europe; in England, they were able to cut three times as much. Furthermore, English farmers had more animals to help them work the land than their counterparts in Europe, and slow oxen were replaced by faster horses which had the further advantage that they could be used for a wider variety of purposes. Organizational changes were also important, for an increase in the size of farms and better organization of the workforce led to gains in efficiency. On the Leveson-Gower estate, for example, the proportion of land farmed by large tenants with 200 acres rose threefold between the early eighteenth and nineteenth centuries, creating a much more polarized social structure.

All of these changes depended on the emergence of a highly commercialized agrarian economy, a shift in the cultural assumptions of farmers who aimed to increase their cash incomes by specializing and selling crops rather than aspiring to live off the farm. In France, peasant farmers kept family members on the farm, viewing their holding more as a means of sustaining family members, even if the productivity of additional workers was low. By contrast, English farmers were more likely to shed labourers as soon as their marginal productivity started to fall, which was encouraged by the existence of the poor law to provide support for those who left the family farm. The change was not the result of the imposition of a cash nexus on unwilling farmers in response to landlords' demands for higher rents. On the contrary, the process started when rents were static or even falling in the later seventeenth and early eighteenth centuries, and applied to small owner-occupier farmers who did not need to find additional cash to pay rent. Rather, there was a greater responsiveness to a much more commercialized culture and a more active market, captured by a shift in terminology, from 'husbandman' who carefully nurtured the soil, to 'farmer' who tried to make as much profit as possible. As a result, English agriculture could sustain more people off the land than in France, but at what cost? A more polarized agrarian society, and displacement into disease-ridden towns was not everyone's preferred choice.

These gains in the productivity of land and labour were connected with considerable changes in the institutional and social structure of English agriculture. The proportion of land in the hands of great landowners rose, and of small yeomen farmers declined. Although yeomen might own the freehold of their land, many held it from landlords on forms of tenure which gave them a degree of security and a right of inheritance. These tenures took a variety of forms, whether a lease for a long period of years or a number of lives, a copy of the manorial roll, or custom. The annual rent was low, and the tenants paid larger 'fines' at intervals, for example to add a new life or term of years to the lease, or when a new tenant entered the holding. In the early eighteenth century, rents were falling and landowners had little incentive to press for short lets. A legal challenge to customary tenures would be expensive and uncertain, and landlords would be forced to rely on modest annual rents and to forego periodic fines before existing leases expired and short leases, with higher rents, were introduced. In the early eighteenth century, yeomen farmers therefore had security, which gave them an incentive to improve their land and raise yields, in the knowledge that any gains would go to them in profits rather than to the landowner in higher rents. Indeed, landowners might decide that the easiest option was to sell the freehold to the copyhold and customary tenants. These yeomen farmers were highly commercial and market orientated, and rural society started to polarize as a result of their efforts, as successful farmers bought out their neighbours.

By the end of the eighteenth century, the pattern was changing and the initiative was shifting to large landowners. The pressure of growing population, and the consequent increase in prices and rents, meant that landlords had more incentive to challenge existing tenures, and to forego 'fines' as lives fell in and long leases drew to a close. Long leases gave way to short leases, allowing landowners to increase their rents at short notice to the full market or 'rack' rent in order to take advantage of rising prices.

The nature of enclosure also changed in the later eighteenth century. At the beginning of the period, enclosure was often a piecemeal process, undertaken by agreement within the village or by fencing some land from common grazing on adjoining waste. The process did not usually involve tension, for it was often in areas with a good supply of grazing land. Even where villagers did lose their right to keep animals on the common fields after the harvest, they were usually compensated by the provision of a reasonable amount of common land set aside from the enclosure. In the later eighteenth century, enclosure increasingly relied on parliamentary procedures which forced through change against the opposition of significant elements in the community. At this stage, enclosure was more likely to cause tension, for it applied above all to the Midlands, where pasture was in short supply and grazing on the open fields after harvest was crucial. Enclosure meant the destruction of various property rights, which was bitterly resented. Women were no longer able to supplement family incomes by gleaning and foraging or keeping a cow on the common fields. Enclosure meant that more families became dependent on the wage of a male, landless labourer who was seasonally unemployed, and dependent on the poor law for support. Enclosure also meant that existing leases were cancelled, and landlords could introduce short leases with rack rents.

As a result, landlords were the major beneficiaries of the rise in prices in the late eighteenth century, and their share of the output of agriculture rose. They rearranged their estates to create larger tenant farms on rack rents, with a decline in small yeomen farmers with customary tenure or freeholds. The growth of great estates was not the result of marriage alliances, for we have noted that the demographic and emotional behaviour of landowners tended to break up holdings. Rather, it was the result of the piecemeal purchase of small amounts of land from yeomen farmers or from heirs who preferred to sell off their inheritance. Generally, larger owners were able to borrow more readily, and the active market in land and in mortgages meant that they could buy up smaller properties in a gradual process of accumulation. These changes provoked the anger of William Cobbett, who wished to return to a golden age when England was still a land of prosperous yeomen farmers and contented cottagers. In part, he was constructing an image of an idealized past in order to attack the political and social system of the early nineteenth century, which neglected the forces for change within agrarian society. After all, yeomen farmers were themselves responsible for creating a highly commercialized, capitalist economy. Cobbett's idealized vision could appeal to Tory squires resentful of the great landed magnates in their Palladian palaces and with access to the resources of City finance, and to radicals demanding the return of land to the people. But it was not simply a matter of political rhetoric and the construction of a mythical past: there were indeed changes in the late eighteenth century which allowed landlords to raise rents and take a large share of the proceeds of agriculture. The 'improvements' celebrated by so many agricultural societies and commentators were contested. What appeared to Arthur Young or John Sinclair as a beneficial search for efficiency, appeared to John Clare, the poet of the rural poor, or Cobbett, as a grim record of dispossession and greed, trampling on the rights of the poor.

In defence of the great landowners, it could at least be argued that they invested some of their rents back into the land as well as into their art collections, parks, and houses, reorganizing their estates to create larger and efficient farms. As a result, the supply of food was increased and the welfare of the population did not collapse. When food prices started to fall at the end of the Napoleonic Wars, landowners were quick to complain, fearing that they would be forced to meet interest payments on their earlier loans out of reduced rents. The process of post-war adjustment to lower price levels was extremely fraught, placing the government in a difficult position. A drop in prices would have serious consequences for agriculture and its ability to feed a large population, but any measures designed to mitigate the fall in food prices could easily be interpreted as special pleading by great landowners at the expense of consumers. These issues were to dominate British politics up to the 1840s.

Changes in agrarian society took their own distinctive form in Scotland. At the beginning of the period, clans still lingered in the Highlands. The clan system was based on 'a pretence of blood', a belief that members of the clan should act as members of a family owing loyalty to the chief in return for protection and hospitality, a relationship summed up in the concept of *dutchas* or trusteeship of the clan's territories. The chieftains did not 'own' the land of the clan, but granted land to 'tacksmen' who in turn sublet land in return for rent and service. Payments were made, at least in part, in food and cattle which gave the chief a store for hospitality, to maintain retainers and to cover food deficits. As a result, the economy was not highly commercialized. By the early eighteenth century, the clan system was already fragile, for the chieftains were uneasily part of two worlds, of the Gaelic Highlands and the cosmopolitan society of Edinburgh and, after 1707, London. The notion of *dutchas* as trusteeship gave way to *oighreachd*, a concept of legal title to the land which was apparent when the second duke of Argyll, the chieftain of clan Campbell, started to reorganize the clan lands around 1710 in pursuit of money rents rather than his standing within the clan. The position of the tacksmen was eroded, and farms were let for the highest rent. Such changes towards a commercialized society destabilized Scottish society, leading to support for the Stuart pretender across the seas in France. Allegiance to the old royal family of Scotland would allow them to restore their *dutchas* in the kingdom, as trustees of Scotland in the same way as the chiefs were supposed to act as trustees of their clan—an act of restoration of the older order abrogated by the chieftains as well as a reassertion of Scottish political identity which had been submerged in the union. The failure of the rising of 1745, and brutal oppression in its aftermath, meant that the elite of the clans had little option except to complete their assimilation into the new order, with clansmen converted into useful members of the British empire. The change was personified by Simon Fraser, baron Lovat, who was beheaded for high treason for his part in the Forty-Five. His eldest son, also Simon, was pardoned in 1750 and he went on to lead the Fraser Highlanders in North America in 1757–61 and during the War of American Independence. Within the Highlands, clan loyalty was replaced by a search for rents. From the 1760s, the great landowners 'cleared' their Highland estates of people to make way for great sheep runs, dispossessing the tenants and subtenants, and forcing them to emigrate or to resettle on small crofts where they eked out an existence and provided a cheap labour supply. Meanwhile, the duke of Argyll mixed with the nobility of Britain, with his town houses in Edinburgh and London, and his elegant country seat at Inveraray.

The clearances were often harsh and brutal, destroying the traditional agrarian structure, and turning the crofters to the consolations of a harsh, unforgiving religion. Change in the Lowlands of Scotland was less brutal, but no less sweeping. Scottish law did not recognize customary tenures, and it was possible for landowners to change the tenure at a stroke. At the end of the eighteenth century, the pace of change accelerated: larger farms were created, and subtenants or cottars who had been granted small plots in return for seasonal labour were forced to migrate to the industrial towns or overseas. The Scottish countryside was left eerily empty compared with England. Scottish farmers came to rely on a small, regular workforce rather than on seasonal labour supported for the rest of the year by the poor law or by weaving and spinning. When William Cobbett visited Scotland, he was struck that the people had been 'studiously swept from the land'.

Such a comment could not have been made of eighteenth-century Ireland, where 'clearance' awaited the devastation of the famine of 1846/8. Despite Ireland's unenviable reputation as the land of the potato, it was also a major exporter of livestock and dairy products and, increasingly, grain to Britain. In the mid-1790s, Ireland supplied about 17 per cent of British grain imports, rising to 57 per cent at the end of the Napoleonic Wars and an astonishing 80 per cent in the mid-1830s. The explanation was in part economic policy, and in part the distinctive structure of Irish rural society. The import duties on foreign grain imposed by the corn laws did not apply to Ireland, which could therefore benefit from rising demand from Britain. Despite its wet climate, grain yields in Ireland were on a par with England. Clover was a natural crop in the emerald isle, so that nitrogen was returned to the soil. And the potato formed a crucial part of the rotation system, to feed both animals and humans. Farmers had a cheap and abundant workforce, based on *conacre*, a form of bonded labour in return for small plots of potato land. This labour was used in a highly intensive way, preparing the ground for crops with the use of spades, and collecting and carting materials to improve the fertility of the soil. The Dublin Society's reports on Wexford in 1807 expressed astonishment.

Throughout the whole of this country, . . . all is labour; whether employed in digging the marle from the pit, whether in drawing the limestone a vast length of often a miserable road, whether in dredging the wet and oozy mud from the beds of rivers, whether, in the midst of wintry storms at the dead of night, dragging the uprooted sea-weed from the roaring surf, drenching them in its waves and threatening them with destruction! All is a constant round of industry almost unequalled, and strongly impressing on the admiring observer the ardent wish, that their labour may meet with its due reward.

Unlike in England, the emphasis was on improving the productivity of the soil through the application of larger amounts of labour, rather than releasing people from the land. The strategy did mean that Irish agriculture was prosperous at the turn of the eighteenth and nineteenth centuries, and considerable quantities of grain, beef, and butter were exported across the Irish Sea.

In hindsight, all was not well. Most landowners were relative newcomers, often absentee, who held vast acreages acquired or expropriated in the seventeenth century from the native Irish nobility or an earlier generation of English settlers. As Innes shows, only 14 per cent of land in the early eighteenth century was owned by the Catholic majority of the population. The landowners were remarkably inactive in improving their estates. Rather than letting farms direct to tenants, they relied on middlemen who were akin to the tacksmen in Scotland, and often drawn from the remnants of the Irish or old English aristocracy. These middlemen did little to invest in agricultural improvement, and they were squeezed out around the turn of the eighteenth and nineteenth centuries as landowners tried to take a larger share of the increasing rents. Unlike in Scotland, the Irish landowners did not transform rural society. Farms were so small and the rural population so large, that there was little they could do. They were often too heavily in debt to cover the costs of reorganization, and relations between landlords and tenants were all too often informed by suspicion and hostility, with outbreaks of protest by the 'Whiteboys' and their successors into the nineteenth-century land wars. The result was a lack of investment by either party. Landlords were more inclined to seek higher rents than higher productivity, failing to introduce radical change in the countryside, which eventually came about when the horrors of the potato famine brought the entire system of labour-intensive tillage crashing down. In Ireland, the crisis feared by Malthus did strike; the sad irony was that by growing potatoes and creating a surplus of grain, Ireland had helped Britain cope with its own massive increase in population at the end of the eighteenth century.

Specialization and commerce

In 1776 Adam Smith laid down an axiom for the wealth of nations: specialization was limited by the extent of the market. When producers can concentrate on what they do best, and buy other commodities from other specialists, productivity will rise and the wealth of the country increase. Smith was attacking the plethora of import and export duties of the so-called mercantilist system for distorting the market, and preventing the allocation of resources in the most efficient manner. As he remarked, it was entirely possible for Scotland to make claret from grapes grown, at vast expense, in heated glasshouses, if the Scots were protected from imports from Bourdeaux. But resources would be better used (and palates better pleased) if the Scots concentrated on making whisky and bought their claret from France. The law of comparative advantage was to become one of the most firmly held tenets of Victorian liberalism, but the wealth of Britain in the eighteenth century might well have been increased rather than diminished by mercantilism and the power of the state.

By the early eighteenth century, Britain was well on the way to becoming an integrated national market in which regions were able to specialize in what they grew and produced best. In the seventeenth century, regional self-sufficiency still made sense, for there could be no certainty that a crop failure in one district would be covered by other parts of the country, in the absence of adequate transport systems and market information. Every part of the country therefore tried to grow enough grain to feed itself, even if the soil and climate were not really suitable. By 1700 change was underway and was carried further in the course of the eighteenth century. Agrarian regions came to concentrate on what they did best, so that the heavy clay soils of the Midlands were turned over to grass, while the light chalk or sandy soils of the downs and East Anglia were used for grain growing, combined with flocks of sheep to manure the soil. Specialization was only possible as a result of changes in the marketing system, which connected with government policy.

All governments in early modern Europe were naturally concerned that disruptions to the supply of food and rising prices at times of shortage would lead to disorder and food riots, with which they were ill-equipped to deal. As Innes remarks, food riots continued throughout the long eighteenth century. However, government policy underwent a significant change. In Tudor and Stuart England, the government's response was encapsulated in the Book of Orders, which regulated the market in order to prevent producers and merchants from exploiting the consumer. The government forbade 'engrossing' and 'forestalling' (that is, purchasing goods ahead of the harvest and at the farm), and insisted that all grain should be purchased in public, at pitched markets. The price of bread and the wages of labour were regulated by the local justices of the peace in order to protect consumers and workers from exploitation. It was a vision of social order based on deference in return for paternalistic protection of the poor by local squires or urban elites, and the strategy made a lot of sense in the absence of a standing army or police force. But the central government and 'modernizing' members of local elites came to a different conclusion, increasingly insisting that the best way of securing a regular supply of food at a reasonable price was by encouraging an active market. The tussle between the two approaches was long drawn out. Although the laws against engrossing and forestalling were repealed in 1772, regulation of wages and prices still remained on the statute book and consumers could also appeal to the common law. However, legislation increasingly reflected the desire to create an active market and a commercial solution. Far from standing aside and assuming that the market would solve the problem, the government took active steps to encourage the development of a dynamic and *stable* market for food, which caused tensions when local justices faced immediate problems of order. The policy had two strands. The first was the corn law, an import duty on grain, adjusted according to the price on the domestic market. When the price was low and supplies at home abundant, high import duties were charged; when the price rose and grain was in short supply, duties were reduced. The second strand was the payment of export bounties to domestic farmers when the price of grain fell below a certain point. The aim was to ensure that grain prices did not rise to such high levels that consumers would suffer hardship, or fall so low that farmers would be hit. By keeping grain prices within fairly narrow bands, farmers would be encouraged to grow as much grain as they could to supply the domestic market, without the fear that prices would collapse during a glut as a result of a good harvest or an influx of imports. When food riots did occur, they were not simply an expression of outrage by traditionalist consumers against the incursions of commerce and the market. On the contrary, the worst outbreaks were in highly commercialized and industrialized districts which were highly dependent on the grain market.

Although the corn laws were to acquire a reputation in the early nineteenth century of blatant class legislation designed to protect the agricultural interest, for the most part eighteenth-century governments had a shrewd sense of the limits of their power and the need to preserve social order. Malthus was not alone in defending the corn laws as a way of encouraging self-sufficiency in grain in order to avoid the dangers of reliance on unreliable imports, and of exposing the country to serious food shortages. The approach favoured by Malthus was to maintain a balance between industry and agriculture, rather than to become over-dependent on one at the expense of the other. In the nineteenth century, attitudes started to shift, with a realization that Britain would need to rely on a constant and reliable flow of food imports, which could only be achieved by extending the policy previously applied to the domestic market. The answer was to create a steady demand for foreign food, and so encourage specialist producers and merchants to meet the needs of Britain. In the eighteenth century, such a policy was inconceivable, and the general view was that the best security against famine and social disorder was the creation of a highly commercialized agrarian system *within* Britain, supplemented by imports and exports to keep prices within reasonable limits to satisfy consumers *and* producers. British agriculture was far too important to sacrifice, and the availability of imports was restricted until new areas of the world were opened up by settlement and improvements in transport.

In most of continental Europe, nations were not treated as single markets and internal tariff barriers were imposed to produce revenue. By contrast, there were no internal barriers within England by 1700, with the exception of the duty on coal imported into London by sea which provided revenue for major public works in the metropolis. In 1707, the Act of Union between England and Scotland removed tariffs between the two kingdoms, and made the Scots part of the imperial system of protection. The economic effect of the union was contentious, for its critics feared that it was in the interests of England, designed to open up markets for producers south of the border and to make the Scots contribute to the costs of wars. Supporters of union claimed that it gave the Scots access to a larger national and imperial market, offering them an escape from a serious economic crisis caused by harvest failures in the 1690s, the collapse of their own imperial adventure in Central America, and the decline in trade to Europe. Clearly, the union did offer economic benefits to Scotland, with the growth of Glasgow as a major centre for the tobacco industry, and the involvement of many Scots in imperial projects in India and the Americas. After the suppression of the rising of 1745, the Scots were left with little alternative except to throw in their lot with the union, which did recognize the distinctive nature of Scottish society. The Scots allocated spending on welfare in a different way from the English. South of the border, most social spending was on poor relief, both to supplement the wages of able-bodied men and to support the 'impotent poor' of the old, sick, widows, and children. North of the border, the poor law was much less generous and was usually not financed by taxes. Where the Scots *did* spend was on education, from the universities of the Scottish Enlightenment to the parish schools. The Scots had one of the highest levels of literacy in Europe, far exceeding the English. And the Scots also retained their distinctive and flexible banking system, which contributed to the provision of money and credit, and the rapid development of the Scottish economy in the later eighteenth century. The Scottish economy gained access to the markets of the union and the empire, while retaining distinctive features which contributed to the rapid commercialization of Scottish society and a convergence with English levels of income.

The economics of union were also hotly contested in Ireland. The kingdom became ever more dependent on Britain as a trading partner, sending 79 per cent of its exports to and receiving 74 per cent of its imports from Britain in 1780. The parliament in Dublin did not welcome such a high level of integration in the 1780s and 1790s, and attempted to encourage a greater degree of self-sufficiency—a policy which caused considerable concern to the authorities in London, especially after the rising of 1798. When union was proposed in 1800, the initial intention was to remove all duties on trade between Britain and Ireland, but Irish manufacturers and artisans were outraged. Although they were happy to see the end of duties on imported raw materials and on their exports of manufactures, they were anxious to maintain import duties on British manufactures. The Irish contribution to taxes was also a matter for controversy. The Irish had a small national debt at the time of union, for they had not contributed to the costs of warfare in the eighteenth century. Rather than harmonize Irish taxes with Britain, the Irish contribution was fixed in an attempt to hold down the transfer of revenue from Dublin to London. In the event, the Irish debt mounted very rapidly, leaving Ireland close to bankruptcy. When the Irish and British national debts were merged in 1817 in order to solve the problem, Ireland still retained a degree of fiscal separation, for it was politically dangerous and economically unrealistic to impose the same taxes as in Britain. However, the Irish did not simply escape paying taxes at the same level as in Britain, for army regiments were garrisoned in Ireland. Here was a major theme in the history of eighteenth-century Britain: the costs of warfare and the growth of the fiscal-military state.

Britain was at war for a large part of the 'long eighteenth century' from 1688 to 1815, with a seemingly insatiable appetite for men, money, and materials. There was always an incentive to pass some of the costs to the periphery of the empire, but the revolt of the American colonists showed that the political dangers might outweigh the fiscal benefits. Despite the successful transfer of some of the costs of imperial expansion and warfare to India at the end of the eighteenth century, there was no escape from the need to raise large sums at home—a task central to Britain's defeat of the French and acquisition of empire. The ability to raise money to fight expensive wars, and to maintain naval fleets and dockyards, depended on a steady flow of tax revenues and the ability to borrow large sums to cover the sudden surges of expenditure in periods of war. The British government squeezed more revenue from the country than the French, at less political cost.

In the course of the eighteenth century, the government took an increasing share of the country's income, doubling from about 4 per cent before the arrival of William in 1688, to about 8 per cent over much of the eighteenth century, and as high as 20 per cent during the Napoleonic Wars. The land tax ceased to provide sufficient revenue, and did not rise over the eighteenth century despite the considerable increase in agricultural profits and rents. It was supplemented by a range of assessed taxes on conspicuous consumption such as male servants or carriages. Import and export duties offered an alternative source of revenue, which could tap the growth of foreign trade.

However, these duties were highly complex and poorly administered, and reform was difficult because the rates impinged upon a wide range of trades which were alert to their own economic interests. The bulk of the additional revenue came from stamp duties and, above all, excise duties, collected by an efficient bureaucracy, from a relatively narrow range of goods, produced in a relatively few centralized plants, such as beer and glass. These taxes could be collected without major disputes, provided that the government did not go too far in extending the range of duties with the possibility of freeing itself from the need for parliamentary approval. The fiscal system had a reasonable degree of legitimacy, for customs and excise duties were negotiated in parliament with the representatives of trades and regions, and the land and assessed taxes were administered and collected by representatives of the taxpayers in the localities. On the whole, Britain avoided the sale of offices, a reliance on tax farmers, and the granting of exemptions, which led to such tension in other European countries. The additional costs of the long wars with revolutionary and Napoleonic France did force William Pitt to introduce an income tax in 1799 in place of the land and assessed taxes, which expired on the return to peace in 1816. Consequently, taxes at the end of the war were even more dependent on excise and customs duties—a situation resented by industry, trade, and poor consumers who felt that they were being taxed to maintain hangers-on at court.

The government borrowed huge sums in the eighteenth century to finance war, on the security of the tax revenues of the country. In much the same way that landowners mortgaged their estates to secure funds to buy more land or rebuild their houses, the government mortgaged tax revenues to fight the French and extend their empire. Lending to the government rested on trust, on the belief that taxes would be paid, that the government would honour its promise to pay interest, and that it would not default. The loans did not mature at a fixed date when the capital sum was returned, so that lenders who wished to get their money needed an active market where they could sell their loan stock. Here was the basis for the growth of the City of London as a major financial centre. The Bank of England was established in 1694 to administer the loans, and a market for stocks developed at Jonathan's coffee house, which evolved into the Stock Exchange. The government relied on loan contractors, financiers such as Samson Gideon, the Rothschilds, or Barings, who agreed to take large blocks of loans at a discount, so relieving the government of risk; the contractors then hoped to sell the stock to individuals at a profit. The emergence of a monied interest was open to criticism for subverting the social order, introducing sordid interests to corrupt the virtues of a society of disinterested, independent landowners. The demand for government loans has also been criticized by some later commentators for starving industry of funds, and so holding down the rate of economic growth. Such fears were countered by the patriotic success of the fiscal-military state in defeating the menace of the French from Louis XIV to Napoleon. Neither is there much sign that industry was starved of funds, for its greatest need was credit and liquidity which was probably stimulated by the war and by the creation of a dynamic financial market in the City of London. The incidence of taxes did benefit landowners at the expense of domestic producers and working-class consumers, and the scale of government debt in 1815 did result in considerable payments of interest to rentiers—a source of considerable resentment.

The fiscal-military state therefore had major consequences for the development of the British economy. It helped to create a major financial centre in the City of London, and warfare contributed to London's growth as the centre of world commerce at the expense of Amsterdam. The navigation laws insisted that the production of the Caribbean, North America, and India—sugar, tobacco, muslins, spices—should pass through British ports in British ships, and merchants from Europe came to purchase goods. The government encouraged the emergence of London as the great entrepôt of world trade by allowing merchants to hold goods in bonded warehouses, where their liability to duties was reduced on condition they were re-exported. Of course, the navigation laws were also open to challenge from those who felt that duties and regulations distorted the economy, or at least gave special advantages to monopolists. The charter of the East India Company gave it a monopoly of trade with the East, which was bitterly resented by merchants and shipowners who wished to enter the lucrative trade. Taxes also fell more heavily on trade and production than on land, especially after 1816, so fuelling resentment from industrialists and the poor, who felt with some justice that the economy was being distorted. The result was a demand for retrenchment in government expenditure and the introduction of free trade, in the belief that government spending and intervention were preventing the efficient allocation of resources.

What the supporters of free trade in the nineteenth century overlooked was the possibility that state power had encouraged the growth of industries. The cotton industry was in the forefront of the campaign for free trade in the second quarter of the nineteenth century, when it was the world's dominant producer—a position it owed to some extent to protection in the eighteenth century. Indian muslins were imported into Britain by the East India Company, with the danger that the domestic woollen textile industry would suffer. The government was concerned at the prospects of unemployment, social unrest, and the increasing costs of relief—as well as by the need to find bullion to pay for imports from India. The government therefore imposed restrictions on the import, and even wearing, of cotton cloth to protect the woollen textile industry. It also encouraged the growth of a domestic linen industry, both to replace imports from Germany and to stimulate employment in Ireland and Scotland as a means of containing unrest. The result was unexpected: the limitation of imports allowed the emergence of fustians, a mixed cloth using cotton and linen, which formed the basis of the Lancashire cotton industry. The government was therefore motivated by wider concerns than using duties to produce revenues and to benefit monopolists; it wished to maintain social stability and limit the loss of bullion. State power contributed to the growth of the cotton industry, a point overlooked by industrialists in the early nineteenth century.

A highly commercialized, integrated economy required the provision of financial services to make buying and selling feasible. A manufacturer of cotton cloth in Lancashire purchased raw cotton from a merchant or broker in Liverpool, and would usually delay payment until the yarn was spun and woven into cloth. The manufacturer offered the merchant a bill of exchange, promising payment of, say, £100 in six months, so escaping the constraints of the usury laws with their upper limits on interest rates. Similarly, when the manufacturer sold his output, say of cotton cloth, the purchaser might offer a bill for six months, until cloth was sold and the proceeds received. However, the manufacturer might need ready cash in order to pay his workers, so he might discount his bill, accepting an immediate £95. The bill could be held to maturity for a decent return of £5 over six months—always provided that the whole pyramid of credit did not crash, and that all parties to the transaction could be trusted. The credit system was connected through London. Country bankers in agricultural districts such as East Anglia sent surplus funds to London after the harvest, where the bankers in the City purchased bills of exchange from industrial districts such as Lancashire.

The acceptance of bills of exchange and the emergence of paper money issued by the banks is much more than a tedious technical issue of interest only to financial historians. It was as much a cultural and social phenomenon. The system of credit rested on reputation, a judgement on the value of other members of the community, on the confidence that the debtor would make payment in due course, that the bill and note were more than worthless scraps of paper. The development of a culture of civility and politeness, the construction of reputation through membership of clubs and societies, by attendance at church or chapel, were essential to credit-worthiness and to business success.

Much credit remained face-to-face, an emotional bond between individuals, resting on reputation within the community. In the course of the eighteenth century, credit was extended beyond personal, face-to-face relations with a consequent need to develop new cultural practices. The development of paper money issued by a large number of small banks meant that traders needed to have confidence that the notes were backed with gold and silver, and could be trusted. In England, the number of 'country' banks grew from about 100 in 1780 to 300 in 1800, issuing their own paper money; in Scotland, gold and silver were virtually unknown, and notes were issued in smaller denominations. Similarly, there was also doubt whether a bill of exchange, passed through many hands to someone without personal knowledge of the issuer, would be honoured—a word capturing the culture of reputation. The emergence of mortgages allowed landowners to raise money to enter the land market, and industrialists were able to borrow on the security of their fixed assets. Mortgages depended on the willingness of the law courts to recognize these new financial instruments, and on the confidence of those with surplus funds to lend, often on the advice of attorneys who had a shrewd sense of the financial position and reputation of borrowers. The ability to grant credit and venture money was crucial to the growth of trade and industry, for the amount of 'circulating capital' in raw materials and goods exceeded the 'fixed capital' in plant and machinery. Credit for the purchase of materials and the sale of goods was central to the growth of the economy, but also meant that the whole complex system of credit was prone to crisis, hitting the innocent as well as the fraudulent or unwise. 'In a Trading Country', remarked one commentator in 1734, 'those who have become Insolvent by pursuing Projects or by any other Losses incident to Trade, ought to be gently dealt with; so even this of venturing another Man's money upon a *reasonable* Project, or Scheme of Trade, ought not to be looked on as a very gross Fault.' From 1706 'honest' bankrupts could be discharged when four-fifths of their creditors agreed; if they had managed to repay 8s in £, they would be given 5 per cent of their estate to start life anew.

Britain in the eighteenth century developed a culture of credit and commerce, based on trust and reputation. As *The Tradesman's Director* put it in 1756, 'what does this *Credit*, or *Trust*, arise from? Why from that *Credit* or *Reputation*, that the Tradesman has acquired by his Industry, Integrity, and . . . other good qualities'. But it also depended on legal enforcement of contractual relations. Credit became more abstract and less personal as transactions became more extended, leading to the emergence of intermediaries and institutions, and the growth of techniques to handle risk with the development of insurance companies and actuaries. Commerce and the market were sociable as well as competitive, and contracts were necessary to maintain cooperation and guard against potential dishonesty which could bring the whole fragile edifice of obligations and trust crashing down.

The development of a highly commercialized national market was only possible as a result of improvements in transport and a fall in the cost of shifting goods around the country. Until the coming of the railway in the second quarter of the nineteenth century, the cheapest way of moving goods was by water. Adam Smith estimated that six or eight men in a coastal sailing ship could carry the same quantity of goods between London and Edinburgh as 50 wagons with 100 men and 400 horses. Not surprisingly, 'it is upon the sea-coast, and along the banks of navigable rivers, that industry of every kind naturally begins to subdivide and improve itself.' At the start of the eighteenth century, the cost of transport on inland waterways was about 1p (2.5d) a ton-mile, and even less in a coastal ship; by contrast, road transport cost about 5p (1s) per ton-mile. As a result, bulky, low-value materials were largely confined to the coasts and major river systems such as the Severn, the Mersey, and the Tyne, and potentially valuable—and cheaper—resources in the inland coalfields could not be used to their full extent. In the course of the eighteenth century, human ingenuity brought the benefits of water transport to previously inaccessible parts of the country. The process started by 'improving' rivers—building locks, straightening bends, and increasing depth. In 1694, for example, powers were obtained from parliament to make the Mersey navigable as far as Warrington, so allowing the movement of large quantities of bulky coal and salt. The next stage was to extend the river systems by the construction of canals. In 1754 the corporation of Liverpool, with the support of leading merchants, obtained powers to build the Sankey navigation in order to open up cheaper supplies of coal; and in 1759 the duke of Bridgewater started work on his own canal to carry coal from his estate to Manchester and Liverpool. These canals initially extended the reach of existing natural waterways, bringing a larger part of the country into connection with the river systems and the major ports. In 1772 the process of linking river systems started when the Mersey was joined to the Severn by the Staffordshire and Worcestershire canal. As a result of these improvements to rivers and canals, restraints on inland manufacturing districts were lessened, and urban and industrial growth was possible on the inland coalfields where the pithead price of coal was lower. Meanwhile, changes in ship design meant that smaller crews could handle larger cargoes with considerable savings in costs at sea. Harbours were improved by the construction of breakwaters, quays, docks, and warehouses, so contributing to the improved efficiency of shipping by reducing the time spent idle between voyages. A more active market in freights and in marine insurance, based at the Baltic and Lloyd's coffee houses in the City of London, meant that ships were able to find cargoes and take greater risks. The sociability and gossip of the coffee houses and exchanges, the technical skill of engineers, and the organizational efficiency of harbour masters, contributed to a reduction in transport costs which was as important as changes in the system of production.

Astonishing though the engineering feats of Thomas Telford or James Rennie were to their contemporaries, French engineers could point to equally impressive feats on their canals. More innovative, if less visible, were the institutional and organizational developments which permitted the plethora of schemes to improve rivers and construct canals. The improvement of rivers implied a tussle between interests, for millowners could lose their source of power, or bridges might need to be replaced. Unless means could be found to arbitrate between these interests, there would be stand-offs and a failure to overcome problems. Here was the role of parliament, building up and extending the active social and political life of the counties and towns. An associational culture of commerce, sensibility, and reputation, the growth of a 'public sphere' of discussion and compromise, made possible these large-scale developments, permitting the negotiation of agreements and the raising of considerable sums of capital. In the absence of such a culture of trust and civility, such expensive developments with their potential for conflicts of interest, and their need for considerable sums of money, would not have been possible. A variety of institutional forms emerged. In some cases, public bodies took the lead. At Liverpool, the corporation took over responsibility for the docks from trustees in 1762, and borrowed money on the security of the rates. In other cases, river improvements were undertaken by trustees or commissioners, sometimes with rights extended to property owners throughout the county. The emergence of specific bodies for specific purposes—improvement commissioners for a river or harbour, the construction of a new bridge or paving of streets—was a central feature of investment in eighteenth-century Britain. With the exception of the duke of Bridgewater's enterprise, canals were built by joint-stock companies established by private acts of parliament, to give power to acquire land along the route. The canal companies raised capital by selling shares to the public, so that most industrialists did not need to use their own scarce resources. As in the case of enclosures, parliament established a framework of rules and arbitration to settle disputes over the valuation of property and the terms of compensation, and prevented a minority from blocking the scheme.

Water transport made sense where high volumes were produced at a single point, such as a coal mine or iron works, or where a producer needed large quantities of raw materials, such as the Potteries of Staffordshire. However, the production of many commodities was scattered over a wide area, and roads were much more important than Adam Smith allowed. Wheat and barley for London's bread and beer arrived by barge along the Thames or the rivers Lee and Stort, or by coastal vessel from East Anglia, Kent, and the south coast, but farmers needed to get their grain to malthouses and granaries by road. Many industrial commodities, such as small ironware or cloth, were produced by scattered domestic workers, and in any case had a high value which could bear the cost of transport. Where commodities were expensive, the speed and flexibility of road transport might make more sense than slower water transport. And some parts of the country were simply inaccessible by river and canal, despite their attraction as the source of ores or waterpower. Improvement of roads was of great importance—and depended on institutional and financial innovation rather than technical breakthroughs. The maintenance of roads was the responsibility of parishes, which could call on residents to supply labour and carts or to pay a local rate. The system had serious shortcomings, for parishes might resent repairing roads for through traffic between major towns or between an industrial area and the nearest river. One response was to give the Quarter Sessions power to order parishes to make repairs; another was to hand responsibility for the major routes to turnpike trusts which would impose tolls on users. The first turnpike trust was established in 1663 for part of the Great North Road between London and Edinburgh, with a widespread creation of trusts from 1695. The turnpikes initially covered the most heavily used roads around London and the large towns, and the major routes from London. By 1750, members of society could travel the entire route from London to Bath on turnpiked roads. In the 1750s and 1760s, a denser and more integrated system developed. Except for the strategically important routes to Ireland and in the Highlands where the government paid subsidies and the roads were heavily engineered, most turnpikes simply paid more attention to the surface than parish officers. In order to hand over public roads to trusts, parliamentary approval was needed, and care had to be taken that they did not abuse their power to charge tolls. The trustees were forbidden from making a private profit, and parliament laid down a fixed scale of charges, with lower levels for local users. The income from the tolls was then used to provide security for loans from local people who were looking for a safe investment. The improved roads stimulated the development of faster and more regular services for goods and passengers, provided by a proliferation of carriers, stage coaches, and fast, subsidized mail coaches. These concerns were often impressive in their scale, requiring relays of horses along the route, with inns for passengers and the collection of goods, and stables and repair shops—formidable organizations to meet regular timetables.

From an organic to a mineral economy

Malthus's vision of the economy assumed that sources of energy were limited and difficult to increase, for they depended on a *flow* from organic sources. The labour of humans and animals depended on the availability of food to provide them with sufficient calories for sustained work in the fields or in industry. Wood provided fuel for domestic heat and cooking, and for industrial processes such as brewing beer or smelting iron. These organic sources were supplemented by wind and water, which powered mills to grind corn or crush seeds, to power fulling mills in the woollen industry and bellows in iron furnaces. It was difficult to increase the flow of these sources of energy. The supply of grain could only be raised slowly, and care had to be taken not to cut more wood than the annual growth which would threaten future shortages and rising prices. Wind power was spasmodic and unreliable. Water could be stored in mill ponds, but at considerable expense and with the likelihood of conflict with other users; the search for fast-flowing streams forced industrialists to remote locations, with consequent problems of labour recruitment and transport.

These constraints were removed by the use of coal, which allowed great increases in the *stock* of energy. During the eighteenth century, coal was applied to an increasing number of processes, and mine-owners adopted new techniques to win coal from deeper and more difficult seams. Hard-headed, shrewd, practical 'viewers' such as John Buddle in the north-east of England grappled with the engineering problems of sinking shafts, providing ventilation, pumping out water, and hauling coal to the surface. Their success is apparent in a tenfold increase in coal output between 1700 and 1830, and a fourfold increase in consumption per head of population from about half a ton to two tons. By 1800 British coal output was five times as much as in the whole of the rest of Europe. This impressive increase in output was linked with a drop in the real cost of coal, for coal prices fell more than other prices in the first half of the century, and then rose less until the early nineteenth century. The massive injection of a stock of energy at a lower real price was a major reason for Britain's ability to escape the Malthusian crisis.

Coal was initially used to supply domestic heat and fuel; to heat pans of sea-water to produce salt, of fats to make tallow for soap and candles, or of molasses to refine sugar; and in forges to heat iron and other metals. It was more difficult to use coal where higher temperatures were needed to smelt metals, for the fuel came into contact with the ores and introduced impurities. In the late seventeenth century, the 'reverberatory furnace' offered a solution in the copper industry. Coal was burned in the base of a conical furnace, and heat was reflected onto pots containing the raw materials, which were not in contact with the fuel. However, these furnaces could not produce sufficient heat to smelt iron, which continued to rely on charcoal until the development of new techniques in the 1760s and above all the 'puddling' process in the 1780s. Until this point, Britain imported large quantities of bar iron from Russia and Sweden, where abundant supplies of timber gave a cost advantage; the bars were then converted into a huge range of metal goods in the rolling mills and forges where coal could be used to heat the iron. By the end of the eighteenth century, the application of coal to smelting meant that Britain was a major producer and exporter of cheap iron.

The gradual spread of coal had major consequences for the British economy. The Great Northern coalfield in the north-east of England sent vast quantities of fuel down the coast to London, which freed the metropolis from constraints and contributed to its emergence as the largest city in Europe, with all that implied for the growth of a market for food and a culture of cosmopolitan consumption. London was like a phoenix, reborn out of fire: ashes from its hearths were mixed with clay dug out for the foundations of new buildings, in order to produce bricks for elegant squares and functional warehouses. The pits of the north-east used steam engines to pump out water, to pull coal up the shaft, and eventually to replace horses on colliery tramways connecting pits to the river Tyne. Here was the nursery for George Stephenson and the development of steam locomotion. Coal was transported in coastal ships, plying their trade from the Tyne, Wear, and Tees to the pool of London. Meanwhile, on the Tyne cheap coal was used to make salt and glass—a pattern soon to be followed along the Mersey and Clyde. The poverty-stricken, benighted society of south Wales was transformed in the eighteenth century. Copper ore was shipped to Swansea from the deep mines of Cornwall, where sophisticated high-pressure steam engines were at the cutting edge of technology. At Swansea, the ore was smelted using huge quantities of cheap coal, producing a poisoned landscape. Copper was used to sheath the bottom of ships travelling to the tropics, or to make pots and pans for brewers, sugar refiners, and kitchens. It was mixed with tin to produce brass, which could be used for a vast array of luxurious and commonplace commodities—for buckles and candlesticks, for chronometers and scientific instruments—in the craft shops of London and Birmingham. The business success of Matthew Boulton, well-known as the partner of James Watt in the manufacture of steam engines, depended on selling brass fittings for the adornment of the houses of Georgian London. Meanwhile, ironmasters from the Midlands and iron merchants from London moved to the desolate uplands on the northern fringe of the south Wales coalfield, initially in search of iron ore and wood, but soon to exploit the abundant coal reserves. Merthyr Tydfil became a 'labyrinth of flames', the greatest iron-producing town in the world. The consumption of coal helped to remake the geography of Britain, both in the dramatic creation of new industrial centres and in less obvious ways. Woodland was no longer coppiced on the same scale to produce charcoal for fuel or timber for construction, so that land could be released for food. Coal and steam power meant that animal energy was not needed to pump and haul—with the result that there was more food for humans. Although steam power had still to transform manufacturing industry in the early nineteenth century, mineral energy had contributed to preventing the collapse of welfare as population growth accelerated.

Towns, industries, and services

These changes in agriculture and in the provision of energy meant that more people were supported off the farm than ever before in Britain, or anywhere in the world. The growth of population over the eighteenth century was remarkable; it was more rapid than elsewhere in Western Europe, without a disastrous collapse in the standard of living. Equally impressive was the release or, in some cases, expulsion, of labour from the land on an unprecedented scale. Britain experienced an urban revolution in the eighteenth century. In 1700 about 13 per cent of the population of England lived in towns with a population of 10,000 and above, which was the same level as in the rest of North and Western Europe. By 1800, 24 per cent of England's population was living in towns of 10,000 and above, compared with 10 per cent in the rest of North and Western Europe. London overtook the other great cities in the area, replacing Amsterdam as the commercial and financial hub, and pulling far ahead of Paris. By 1800 its population was about a million, with over 6 per cent of the population of the United Kingdom compared with only 2.5 per cent of France's population in Paris. In Europe most urban growth was in the large cities and capitals, and smaller towns declined. By contrast, the urban hierarchy in Britain was remade, with the emergence of large cities such as Manchester and Birmingham, and the growth of a plethora of small towns. Britain became the most urban country in Europe.

What did this massive structural transformation imply for the wealth of the nation? Were the people moving from an efficient agricultural sector, surrendering their common rights for a miserable existence in towns, condemned to work in low productivity industries and services? Of course, many migrants to towns did find themselves in 'sweated' trades, and artisan skills were eroded in some trades as tasks were subdivided and cheap (often female) workers were substituted. Many men and, above all, women worked in domestic service, where there were few opportunities for increased efficiency. Indeed, the employment of a lady's maid or a butler was more a sign of status than a desire to raise the marginal productivity of the household. The towns offered casual occupations, selling flowers or sweeping the streets, with the danger of sliding into petty crime and prostitution. Not surprisingly, the social problems of towns troubled contemporaries and placed huge demands on urban government, charities, and improvement commissions to pave and light the streets, to remove waste, to deal with crime and public order, to build hospitals for the cure of the sick, the reform of fallen women, and the care of abandoned children. As we have noted, life expectation was lower in the towns, and the death rate often exceeded the birth rate until the end of the century. Migrants from the country were therefore trading higher urban wages for a shorter life for themselves and especially their children.

Relatively few people moved into factories with powered machinery, and the major application of steam power to manufacturing was a feature of the mid-nineteenth century. Many more workers were engaged in hand production, either for trades such as textiles and metal goods to supply the national and export market, or in supplying clothes, shoes, or furniture to a local market. This last group was still the largest in 1800, with few opportunities for gains in productivity by the application of power or specialization. But it would be a mistake to assume that labour released from the land was simply condemned to low productivity in services and 'traditional' handicraft trades. Economic efficiency did not necessarily entail the development of large, capital-intensive factories, for towns themselves were highly effective economic units. Towns could be feared as a source of moral danger, where country innocence was corrupted in pleasure gardens and theatres; they could also be arenas for display, sociability, and civility, fostering a consumer culture and providing the social context for credit through participation in clubs, societies, and charities. Information on market trends was swapped in the coffee houses and exchanges, where merchants gathered to read newspapers and catch up on the movement of shipping or the latest fashions. In the coffee houses of the City, specialist markets for marine insurance or buying and selling shares developed. Artisans shared skills and techniques, spreading new materials and processes from one trade to another in the industrial districts of Birmingham and London. The dense social life of towns was part of their economic efficiency, and towns were also centres of consumption and emulation, the stimulants of fashion and taste. Permanent shops were more efficient than itinerant traders, markets, and fairs.

Hand production should not be castigated as inefficient compared with factory production, for it had the virtues of flexibility and responsiveness to changing tastes and fashions. In Birmingham, simple hand tools could be used to punch metal into a wide range of shapes; alloys could be used to imitate expensive gold and silver; papier mâché could be made to resemble fine japanned ware. Despite the lack of any striking technical breakthrough, these trades were able to popularize luxury commodities, extending the culture of consumption and civility to new levels of income. Chinese porcelain was imitated in the Potteries; silverware was copied as Sheffield plate; exquisite Indian muslins were mimicked in Lancashire. By turning cheap materials into desirable consumer goods, apparently traditional methods of manufacture could add a considerable amount of value. In many cases, the handcrafts were using materials produced in industries where the impact of new technology was more striking. The Birmingham trades, for example, were intimately linked with the copper and brass industries of Swansea. Unattainable luxuries were transformed into desirable marks of status or even into affordable necessities.

The movement of labour from agriculture entailed a major change in the regional economies of Britain. East Anglia was an important textile-producing area at the start of the eighteenth century, and 'deindustrialized' in the course of the century, in order to concentrate on growing food for the London market. Meanwhile, other regions embarked on a process of industrial development, specializing in particular commodities for national and international markets, forming craft regions around a regional capital which provided financial, commercial, and industrial services. Birmingham was the hub of the small metal trades of the West Midlands, Manchester for the cotton industry of Lancashire, Nottingham and Leicester for hosiery in the East Midlands, Leeds for woollen textiles in the West Riding. These craft regions had a political identity, lobbying parliament for legislation to meet their needs, whether it be the demands of the West Riding woollen industry for stricter laws against 'embezzlement' of materials by the domestic workers, or pressure from manufacturers in Birmingham for an assay office to guarantee the quality of goods produced in the town.

These craft regions were highly distinctive, not only in their specialization but also in the organization of production and their capacity for change from 'outwork' to factories. In some cases, production was based on independent artisan producers, who owned the materials and tools, and sold the finished article on their own account. Such a pattern applied to the woollen industry around Leeds. In other cases, the materials were owned by a merchant who 'put out' wool and yarn to domestic workers, in return for a payment according to the amount of goods produced. Such a pattern applied to worsted cloth around Leeds. These differences affected the social structure of the districts, and influenced the emergence of factories.

In the case of the woollen industry around Leeds, independent artisans cooperated to establish mills with powered machinery, to assist in particular stages of production. Artisan households were thus freed to spend more time on other tasks, so that powered machinery fitted into the system of production, and did not cause disruption. By contrast, the production of woollen textiles in the Cotswolds was based on putting out, organized by wealthy 'gentleman clothiers' based in small towns such as Painswick or Stroud. They put out materials to a range of specialists, and mechanization of one stage of production simply led to technological redundancy and social tension, and hence to outbreaks of machine breaking. The money accumulated by the 'gentleman clothiers' was shifted into other forms of investment rather than reinvested in industry. Where circumstances were more favourable, the profits and organizational skills of the putting-out merchant manufacturers formed the basis for the growth of factories, as in the worsted industry around Halifax, or the cotton industry in Lancashire. Coordinating and controlling scattered domestic workers caused considerable problems to the putting-out merchant-manufacturers. Time and energy were lost in getting materials to and from the workers, and it was difficult to control the quality of the goods or the extent of 'pilfering' or 'embezzlement' of materials. The workers felt that they had entitlements to remnants of material, which they could sell on their own account; the putting-out merchants interpreted the practice as theft, and it was redefined as a criminal act rather than a breach of contract, to be punished in the last resort by hanging.

The problems of outwork could be eased by bringing workers together in a centralized plant, even before the use of powered machinery. However, the emergence of centralized production was not simply the result of a desire to impose control on recalcitrant workers. There were also technical reasons for the construction of factories with powered machinery. It was easier to devise machines to spin cotton than wool, and the desire to build cotton mills with powered machinery often entailed a move into remote upland districts to obtain water power, which caused problems in recruiting labour. On the other hand, powered machinery allowed expensive men to be replaced by cheaper, and more easily controlled, women and children. Whatever the motivation, large putting-out merchant-manufacturers had the skill and capital to construct factories, which usually *supplemented* domestic production. The emergence of factories might force domestic workers into ever longer hours at lower rates, creating a spiral of self-exploitation which led to poverty and potentially to riot and disorder. The merchant-manufacturers could hire and fire domestic workers at will, without cost to themselves, and so cover fluctuations in demand and ensure that their expensive mills were kept in production.

Factory production was intimately connected with the need for workers to follow set hours so that plant was not brought to a halt by absenteeism. Factory masters therefore imposed a new attitude to work, with bells to mark the start of the day, and fines for late arrival. The imposition of time discipline in schools and the teaching of reliability by Methodists were all part of the process of creating an orderly, disciplined workforce. Outworkers had more freedom to set their own time and pace of work, and many commentators in the early eighteenth century assumed they simply stopped work when they reached a conventional standard of living. Higher wages therefore seemed dangerous, allowing workers to down tools earlier in the week, and enjoy themselves in the ale house or leisure. On this view, low wages were necessary to ensure that workers were diligent. By the late eighteenth century, most commentators argued a different case, that higher wages gave an incentive to work harder in order to consume a wider range of goods. Such a change in attitudes to work and consumption did not depend simply on the desire of factory masters to impose time discipline. Domestic workers had more freedom than factory workers to determine their own time-budget, so that they might deal with a domestic chore or help in the harvest. Such behaviour would disrupt production in a factory, but did not mean that domestic workers had a high leisure preference. In fact, their work intensity increased over the eighteenth century as a result of a desire to purchase more consumer goods.

Such a change helps to resolve a paradox that real wages were static in the later eighteenth century as a result of increasing food prices, yet more goods were being produced and purchased than ever before. The answer is that Britain was experiencing an 'industrious revolution', driven by the commercialization of society and the growth of an active market. This was a cultural phenomenon, involving a series of changes in the behaviour of households as both producers and consumers. Households opted to specialize in the production of goods for the market, as a result of their growing preference for market-supplied goods and services compared with goods and services produced within the home—and especially for the new 'exotic' imports of sugar, tea, and coffee. Hence, women might reallocate their time away from unpaid tasks in the household in order to enter the labour market and a commercialized economy. This was part of the general shift towards specialization, of reliance upon the market rather than own-use production—a change only possible as a result of the emergence of an integrated, national market which made it safe to rely on the supply of goods from other regions of the country. This reallocation of time and energy amounted to an 'industrious revolution' which brought more resources into production, by making seasonal agricultural labour available for industrial outwork; it also redeployed labour from non-traded to market activities. Such a shift depended on the existence of an active market to make a wider range of goods constantly available, to provide an incentive and stimulate emulation. Attitudes to wants and desires changed. Work did not stop when a conventional level of consumption was reached, and more people were caught on a hedonic treadmill of desire. As Sir James Steuart commented in 1767, 'men are forced to labour now because they are slaves to their own wants'. Households wished to buy more marketed goods, and therefore deployed their resources to provide more goods and labour to the market. More people joined the labour market to produce marketed goods, and more women and children were employed in domestic industry even before they were used in the new factories. As a result, household earnings rose faster than wage rates. The rise of an acquisitive society was not the result of imposition of work discipline by factory masters, or even the manipulation of taste by advertisers and retailers. Their endeavours only made sense if households had already started to adjust their behaviour, so providing an incentive for producers and retailers. At the centre of the process were decisions within households, and especially by women who were at the intersection of reproduction, production, and consumption.

Conclusion

By 1815 the race between the tortoise of agricultural production and the hare of population growth was more evenly matched than pessimists might have feared. The hare had not fallen asleep, and population growth far surpassed previous levels. By dint of ingenuity and hard work, agriculture was able to feed the population without a serious collapse of welfare, at least in Britain—the situation in Ireland gave more cause for concern. At the end of the Napoleonic Wars, food prices actually started to fall. Such an outcome was highly significant, for historical precedent would suggest that prices would continue to rise, and impose restraint on population growth. Although a marked improvement in the standard of living of the majority of the people was to wait for another two or three decades, with a period of considerable social and economic tension in the interim, the British economy had broken through previous barriers on output and population, and had undergone a major structural change from a rural to an urban society. The agrarian world had become more polarized with the dominance of great aristocratic landowners, and the power of the monied interest of the City of London caused concern in some quarters. Yet at the same time, Britain had developed a culture of credit, of commercial civility and sociability.

Figure 6 Hogarth's 'Gin Lane' of 1751 was a classic piece of bourgeois improving culture, providing an apocalyptic vision of the degenerative effects of gin drinking on females and families in lower-class London.

5

The culture of improvement

Peter Borsay

There was no one cultural system that embraced the kaleidoscopic character of eighteenth-century Britain. Too many people—living in widely contrasting locations—felt, thought, and acted in different ways for that to be possible. Yet there was a group of core beliefs that permeated the fabric of life throughout the British Isles, and exerted a powerful impact over its cultural identity and development. It is dangerous to prioritize any one of these beliefs and proclaim it the elusive 'spirit of the age', but if there is a single idea that occupied the cultural high ground, that resonated most closely with the timbre of the time, and set the agenda for the future, then improvement—interpreted in the broadest sense—could claim to be it. This is not to say that in some crude quantitative way it represented the 'majority' culture. Many of the population may have felt indifferent or even hostile towards it. But the sheer ubiquity with which the notion, or ones allied to it, surfaced in the discourse of the powerful and prosperous of the period, and the frequency with which they mobilized the idea—to persuade, cajole, and justify—suggests that this was a concept of peculiar force. As the Scottish philosopher David Hume declared in 'Of Refinement in the Arts', 'The spirit of the age affects all the arts; and the minds of men, being once roused from their lethargy and put into fermentation, turn themselves on all sides, and carry improvement into every art and science.'

Improvement, as it came to operate in its purest form in eighteenth-century Britain, contained several basic elements. A commitment to change was fundamental. Not limited change, which stopped when a specified goal was reached, but an endless process of alteration and transformation. Nobody could rest on their heels. There was no end game, other than perhaps salvation, only a series of targets that once attained were replaced by others. Meliorism was also critical; a faith in the human capacity to better the self and the world, and a responsibility to pursue change that achieved this end. Finally, there was morality. Improvement was an ethical as well as a material category. The notion of improvement had long been in use in the narrow economic sense of enhancing profitability, but its emergence as a wider cultural concept dates from the later seventeenth century. It was at this point, in the return to 'normality' after the trauma of the Civil Wars and Interregnum, that a series of phenomena—commercial expansion, urbanization, the Scientific Revolution, Protestant theology, and an expanding middling order—fused together to create a dynamic new idea. Earlier in the eighteenth century the seeds of this idea were still in the process of growing and maturing, but by the end of the century the plant had blossomed to touch seemingly every area of life, so that it now formed the core element in the British Enlightenment. This movement is usually portrayed as a European and especially French affair. Yet there was a good deal in common between the European and British experiences, and England was often seen on the continent as a model of enlightened culture, with the great French *philosophes* openly acknowledging their debt to figures such as Francis Bacon, Isaac Newton, John Locke, Joseph Addison, and Richard Steele. However, Britain diverged from the Gallic notion of Enlightenment in that secularism was not part of the agenda, and the British Enlightenment did not end abruptly in 1789 or 1793, but rolled into the nineteenth century as the continuously evolving idea of improvement became the cultural dynamo of the Victorian age.

The emergence of improvement as a dominant ideology derived from three of its characteristics. First, its plasticity. Betterment was a defining feature, but what form this should take was not predetermined. Improvement was able, therefore, to provide a matrix for a range of related but more specific cultural ideals—such as taste, politeness, civility, sociability, sentiment, and sensibility—whose currency waxed and waned during the course of the century. In this sense improvement was a super-concept, capable of embracing multiple and even contradictory ideals, and able to maintain its internal essence while altering its external shape to accommodate changing cultural fashions. This sense of universality and sustainability itself imparted authority to the notion. One closely allied concept, which reached its apogee of influence among English and Scottish thinkers (such as Richard Price, Joseph Priestley, Lord Kames, David Hume, and Adam Smith) between the 1730s and 1780s, and which could be easily implanted into the improvement package, was the idea of progress. Its ascendancy reflected the victory of the Modern over the Ancient camp in the intellectual debate that raged in Augustan Britain, and in its English formulation established the doctrine of indefinite progress that gave improvement its inexhaustible driving power. As Priestley argued, 'mankind, some centuries hence, will be as much superior to us in knowledge and improvements in the arts of life, as we are now to the Hottentots, though we cannot have any conception [of] what that knowledge or what those improvements will be.'[1] The second key to improvement's dominant position was its plurality of appeal. Though it was the culture of the powerful and wealthy, these are relative terms; within even the lower orders there were those, in comparison to their peers, who were prosperous and influential. A culture of improvement could therefore attract all those who perceived themselves as successful, or aspired to be so. Third, and perhaps most important of all, an improving culture bridged the material and spiritual spheres. On the one hand, it was a powerful tool to enhance or sustain personal and corporate power, wealth, and status. On the other hand, its underlying moral and religious dimension helped to cleanse gain of its material stigma, and sustain improvers with an inner spiritual dynamic. It was this fusion of materialism and altruism, Mammon and God, which allowed improvement to become the leitmotiv of Georgian Britain. The following aspects of this culture will be explored here: its material and mental forms; the mechanisms deployed to inculcate and impose these forms; its varying impact in the contexts of space, gender, status, and class; and the presence of alternative or counter modes of belief.

---

[1] Joseph Priestley, *Experiments and Observations on Different Kinds of Air* (1774–86), preface, in J. T. Rutt (ed.), *The Theological and Miscellaneous Works of Joseph Priestley* (25 vols.; London, 1817–32), vol. xxv, p. 378.

Forms of improvement

One of the reasons that it is possible to talk of a *culture* of improvement, and not just a series of specific improvements, is the way in which the notion infects such a multitude of areas of experience. Among the earliest and most persistent of usages was in connection with agriculture and land. Andrew Yarranton's *The Great Improvement of Land by Clover* (1663), and John Houghton's periodical, *A Collection of Letters for the Improvement of Husbandry and Trade* (1681–3, 1691–1703), formed part of a tradition of improving literature that reached something of a climax in the late eighteenth century in the prolific output of the agricultural publicist, Arthur Young. A commitment to the idea of innovation and experimentation in husbandry lay behind the formation of a gamut of societies and boards. One of the first was the socially exclusive The Honourable Society for Improvement in the Knowledge of Agriculture, founded in Scotland in 1723. This was the country which also spawned Sir John Sinclair, whose passion for improvement contributed to the formation of the Board of Agriculture (1793, of which he was the first president), the British Wool Society (1791), and the British Fisheries Society, and led him to oversee the compilation of the twenty-one volume *Statistical Account of Scotland* (1791–9). It was a measure of the extent to which the itch for innovation was not just economically driven that one of the most fertile areas of estate development was horticulture. From the 1750s onwards the fashion-conscious gentry, employing the services of modish gardening practices like that run by Lancelot 'Capability' Brown, began to jettison the geometric garden for the landscape park, under the self-conscious banner of improvement. When in Oliver Goldsmith's play *She Stoops to Conquer* (1773), Miss Neville casually curtails a scene with the remark 'But my aunt's bell rings for our afternoon's walk round the improvements' (Act I), the audience would have intuitively understood not only the form of the recreational facility but also its emblematic qualities.

The eighteenth century was characterized by a remarkable surge in inventiveness and innovation in what may be broadly termed economic practice, technology, and infrastructure; turnpikes and canals, steam engines and textile machinery all spring to mind. It is traditional to account for and interpret these developments in terms of purely commercial logic. Yet so often in the period the symbolic meaning equalled, and frequently exceeded immediate practical value, and ideas ran ahead of implementation. In his *Tour through the Whole Island of Great Britain* (1724–6), Daniel Defoe delivered an extended and effusive paean to the wonders of turnpiking. Upon Watling Street, he enthused, 'there are wonderful improvements made and making ... no public edifice, almshouse, hospital, or nobleman's palace, can be of equal value to the country with this, nor more an honour and ornament to it.'[2] Significantly, this account preceded by some decades the great bulk of turnpike legislation, the 1750s and 1760s representing the peak in this respect. The great intellectual breakthroughs that laid the theoretical foundations for modern science, with the new emphasis on empiricism and mechanism, were essentially a seventeenth-century phenomenon. The eighteenth century's contribution was to popularize these ideas, and begin their implementation in a new scientific methodology of experimentation, that in the field of chemistry, for example, led to Joseph Priestley's discovery of oxygen, Joseph Black's theory of latent heat, and Henry Cavendish's discovery that water was a compound and not an element. But even here the practical lagged behind the cultural, with science being an intellectual, and for most people simply a fashionable pastime, with few workaday implications. Much the same could be said of medicine, where aspirations for improved treatment generally exceeded hard outcomes, though mass inoculation for smallpox undoubtedly saved many lives. The growing interpretation of insanity as a flaw in upbringing—in Locke's view due to a faulty association of ideas—rather than a consequence of demonic possession, led in the late eighteenth century to the introduction of a treatment regime of moral management. This, whatever its practical results, demonstrated a belief in the human capacity and responsibility to improve an imperfect world.

In Georgian Britain the form of medicine most in vogue among the well off was water treatment at one of the proliferating specialist spa or seaside towns. This reflected a much wider process by which the town emerged from the later seventeenth century as a centre of

---

[2] Daniel Defoe, *A Tour through the Whole Island of Great Britain*, ed. G. D. H. Cole and D. C. Browning (2 vols.; London, 1962), vol. ii, p. 124.

improving culture. The physical manifestation of this was everywhere to be seen. In Scotland and Ireland hundreds of small new, or heavily remodelled, settlements were established, especially between the mid-eighteenth and early nineteenth centuries, displaying features of classical town planning. Inveraray, for example, was laid in about 1740 as an elegant replacement for an older squalid-looking settlement, and Westport (Co. Mayo) from about 1780 to a design based on a central octagonal space with radiating streets lined by simple symmetrical buildings. In England there was less need for new towns as such, but planned extensions were being added to many, as they were to the older centres in Scotland and Ireland. In the metropolitan capitals the results were hugely impressive, the rash of squares in the West End of London, the New Town in Edinburgh, and the spacious developments to the east of the old city in Dublin providing a prototype for smaller-scale additions to provincial towns. In Dublin a major influence in remodelling the city was the Wide Street Commission, introduced in 1757, but it was simply part of a broader movement to establish urban improvement commissions. The first were set up in Westminster in 1725 and Salisbury in 1737, and by the end of the century 160 such bodies had been founded in England to implement schemes of street paving, widening, cleansing, and lighting. However, such formal mechanisms represented only the tip of the iceberg in a process of physical refinement that brought enhanced amenity and a touch of the Italian Renaissance to even small towns. The arcaded and pedimented brick town hall (1745, further improved 1828) and modest classical houses of the tiny Welsh county town of Montgomery show how deep change was penetrating the urban fabric of Britain.

The built environment was only one aspect of an improving urban culture. The town became the focus for the creation of an integrated package of polite leisure, which included theatre, music, assemblies, lectures, clubs, coffee houses, walks, pleasure gardens, and modish sports like horse racing. These activities were made available in a public commercial format which widened access to them and transformed their social function. Towns were also, in their role as centres of production and sale, the location of what has been called a consumer revolution, based on luxury goods such as books, newspapers, prints, paintings, domestic artefacts and furnishings, clothes, and personal accoutrements. Many of these products, even if made and purchased in the town, were consumed outside it, spreading their influence across the country as a whole. That this influence was an improving one cannot be assumed; indeed, contemporary Jeremiahs were only too quick to seize on the corrupting consequences of consumerism. But underpinning this efflorescence of leisure and luxury was the notion that consumption of the appropriate activities and objects in the appropriate way was a life-enhancing experience. This was because material forms of culture were perceived not simply as phenomena in themselves, to be enjoyed for their own sake, but as vehicles for deeper psycho-moral systems.

These can be detected in a series of keywords and concepts whose regular presence in the refined discourse of the eighteenth century is freighted with meaning; politeness, taste, sentiment, sensibility, sociability, and civility. All contained elevated goals, the pursuit of which led to human betterment; in this sense all represented mental forms of improvement. In 1712 Addison conceived of taste as a superior faculty, which though it 'must in some measure be born with us, there are several methods for cultivating and improving it, and without which it will be very uncertain, and of little use to the person that possesses it'.[3] The emphasis was upon persistent cultivation of the innate faculty through exposure to suitably elevated models, such as provided by Addison and Steele in the papers of *The Spectator*. This externalization of standards was also evident in politeness, where the arts could be deployed as a means for refining the collective persona. As Jonathan Richardson argued in 1715, if understanding 'paintings and drawings were made part of the education of a gentleman . . . the whole nation would, by these means be removed some degrees higher into the rational state, and make a more considerable figure among the polite nations of the world'.[4] Though the aim of the exercise was to cultivate character as a whole, politeness focused on external behaviour—manners, conduct, and accomplishments—as the means of achieving this. This remodelling of the exterior self reflected the pressure for a cultural system that stressed universal human characteristics, that possessed signs and symbols which could be readily understood and shared, and that reduced friction in social intercourse. The adoption of such a system was in part a response to the

[3] Joseph Addison in *The Spectator*, No. 409, 19 June 1712.
[4] *The Works of Jonathan Richardson* (London, 1773), pp. 271–2.

bitter ideological divisions which had divided the British elite in the seventeenth century, and the need to create a public sphere of cultural activity in which the wounds which had opened up could be healed. Thus, ideas which also flourished were those of civility, seen as embodying the shift from man as savage individual living in a state of conflict and chaos (the parallel with the Civil War years would not have been lost) to a corporate being living in ordered harmony with his neighbours; and the concept of sociability, materialized in institutions like the assembly and the club, and multi-dwelling architectural units like the uniform terrace and square.

Ideas of this type held sway throughout the period, but from the mid-eighteenth century they were joined and challenged by new notions. The emphasis on reason and external behaviour always ran the risk of neglecting the interior self and its emotional energies. With the need to civilize the public conduct of the ruling orders now less pressing, after several decades of polite reprogramming, attention could be devoted to cultivating this inner, private area of the human psyche. Presaged in the novels of Samuel Richardson, the medical theories of the physician George Cheyne, and in the visual output of William Hogarth, but brought to fruition in the writings of Laurence Sterne and Jean Jacques Rousseau, there developed the cults of sentiment and sensibility. These asserted the importance of feeling and the human heart as sources of pleasure and judgement, and paved the way for the rise of romanticism. The emphasis on inner self, emotion, and an implied anti-intellectualism, gelled closely with a rising tide of piety and religiosity, which emerged as early as the 1730s with the evangelical revival and the appearance of Methodism. Self-improvement was a central feature of the latter, and a moral/religious dimension underpinned improving culture as a whole. Scientific research was justified throughout the period as a means of reasserting and celebrating the existence of God through an enhanced understanding of the natural world. It must be remembered that Newton devoted by far the majority of his writings to theology, and saw his scientific work as a means of affirming rather than questioning a divine presence in the universe. Fashionable culture fed on underlying forces of piety. Handel spectacularly revived his flagging fortunes in the 1730s by switching from Italian opera to oratorios, thereby tapping into the rising tide of bourgeois evangelicalism. One project with which the composer was closely associated was Thomas

Coram's Foundling Hospital, established in London in 1739. Handel, who became a governor of the hospital, gave regular benefit concerts in the institution's chapel, where performances of the *Messiah* developed into an annual ritual. Leading artists of the day—including William Hogarth, John Michael Rysbrack, Thomas Hudson, Allan Ramsay, and Thomas Gainsborough—also produced works gratis for the new hospital, several on religious subjects. In Dublin the Rotunda Hospital, designed by Richard Castle and opened in 1757, was home to a maternity charity founded by Bartholomew Mosse. It was adjoined by commercial pleasure gardens, receipts from which were used to fund the project, and from the 1780s by the New Assembly Rooms. This close association of fashionable leisure with piety and philanthropy, a state of affairs repeated frequently, reflected the moral and religious function of culture, and greatly reinforced its improving role.

Inculcation and imposition

That the notion of improvement came to permeate the cultural fabric of Britain was not something that happened by a vague process of osmosis. A wide range of formal and informal mechanisms operated by which people were encouraged and persuaded, and where necessary forced, into accepting the improving agenda. Legislation was always a possibility, though one that needed to be deployed carefully. Widespread use was made of acts of parliament to facilitate physical improvement schemes where property rights were involved, such as street widening, urban reconstruction, land enclosure, turnpikes, and canals. Legislation in the fields of leisure, manners, and conduct was less frequent. Moral panics could lead to short bursts of activity, aimed at extirpating a perceived threat to the well-being of the social body. Thus, in the late 1730s there were acts regulating the theatre, gambling, and horse racing, and in the early 1750s to control gin drinking, marriage-making practices, and bawdy houses. Where serious issues of social policy were felt to be at stake, then parliamentary intervention was considered appropriate. But by and large cultural reform was pursued much more effectively outside the formal mechanisms of the state. The key vehicle, from an organizational point of view, for disseminating improvement was the club and society. The eighteenth century saw a remarkable proliferation of such bodies. By no means all could be said in principle, and even less in practice, to be elevating. Often the consumption of social drugs—alcohol, nicotine, and caffeine—and the relaxed conviviality these induced, appears to have been the main objective. Yet the inherent commitment of these gatherings to sociability meant that they were seen as powerful vehicles for improvement, and most espoused objectives that sought to better or enrich the human condition. The trend spread throughout Britain. The Dublin Society was founded in 1731 to promote Irish agriculture and manufactures, and during the 1740s absorbed a local academy to provide a training for arts and crafts. Critical to the renaissance of Welsh culture in the eighteenth century were three London clubs—the Society of Ancient Britons (1715), the Honourable Society of Cymmrodorion (1751), and Gwyneddigion (1770)—though from the 1770s and 1780s a range of locally based secular societies were becoming common. The breeding grounds of the Scottish Enlightenment, the universities apart, were the intellectual societies established in Aberdeen, Glasgow, and in particular Edinburgh. In England the range and geographical spread of societies and clubs was quite stupendous. At the top of the pile were grand organizations like the Royal Society (1660) and the Royal Academy (1768). The latter was part of a self-conscious strategy, led by the institution's first president Sir Joshua Reynolds, and articulated in his *Discourses* to the Academy, to raise the status of British art and elevate national taste. Beneath these august assemblies a galaxy of other groups emerged; book clubs, music clubs, antiquarian and scientific societies, literature and philosophical societies, floral societies, political clubs, debating societies, corresponding societies, freemasons, county improvement societies, box clubs, bellringing societies, social reform societies, and so on. The networking potential of these organizations, given their duplicate membership, their formal interaction with each other, and their sheer number was formidable. It was in the close human contact that they fostered—supported by complex bonding rituals and the gregarious ambience of the coffee house, inn, and alehouse—and in the regular debates and discussions that they engaged upon, that notions of sociability and improvement leapt the divide between theory and reality.

Some of the journals of the period organized pieces of their material around the club motif. The *Spectator*, for example, purported to record the discussions of a 'society of gentlemen'. This was a literary conceit, but serial publications, some of which contained space for readers' correspondence, constituted a sort of informal society of their own. Certainly, it is difficult to imagine most formal clubs operating without some textual input. Print was in fact fundamental to the formulation, evolution, and dissemination of an improving culture. It provided the means by which novel and sophisticated ideas could be transported rapidly and effectively across large geographical and social spaces. For example, the spread of correct classical architecture, with its radical and refined approach to design, to the far corners of Britain, and to relatively modest levels of the housing market, is hard to imagine without the rise of the pattern-book. This was possible because of a revolution in the provision of print. The lapsing of the Licensing Act in 1695, allied to rising levels of literacy and wealth, led not only to an increase in the volume of printed material, but also its range and accessibility. Religious works continued to be of major significance. Sermons were the single most important category of output. But to these were added a widening conspectus of secular factual and imaginative literature, that led to the emergence of relatively new forms of publication such as the newspaper, the journal, and the novel. The first provincial paper was probably the *Norwich Post* of 1701, and by 1760 around 150 papers had been started, though not necessarily continued, in over fifty English towns. The proliferation of bookshops and book outlets on the urban high street, and the development of the coffee house (which stocked newspapers and other literature for their patrons' use), book clubs and libraries, greatly enhanced the availability and circulation of print.

Some novels were composed in an epistolary format, such as Samuel Richardson's *Pamela* (1740–1), and *Clarissa Harlowe* (1747–8), and Tobias Smollett's *Humphry Clinker* (1771). In fact it was not that uncommon for real correspondence, like the famous letters of Lord Chesterfield to his son (composed 1739–65, published 1774), and diaries to appear in print. Such a genre had a particular appeal to the reading public, since it reflected forms of personalized literary composition in which all educated people could, and increasingly did, engage. The process of self-reflection and self-representation involved was often motivated by a desire to improve the self. The travel diary, of which hundreds were compiled by young gentlemen and women on their educational tours around Britain and the continent, was a case in point, since it constituted a record of the extent to which the writer had absorbed the cultural benefits of the tourist experience, and done so in an appropriate way. Though private in character, the resulting journals were often modelled on printed guides, which provided a public template of how educated travellers should respond to the world around them.

The ability to peruse newspapers and novels, and to compose letters and diaries, depended on literacy. Education was, therefore, a fundamental tool of improvement. The acquisition of reading and writing skills was a socially selective process. By the beginning of the eighteenth century, it is likely that the upper and most of the middling orders already possessed at least a basic proficiency in this area. Literacy was so fundamental to their economic and social identity that it was difficult to function without it. For the social elite, and those who aspired to join its ranks, academic education focused on advanced forms of learning—in particular the study of and initiation into that most exclusive of languages and cultures, Latin and the classics—which had traditionally been provided at the secondary level by grammar and public schools, and the higher level by the Inns of Court and the universities. In the later Stuart and early Georgian periods these institutions acquired a reputation for intellectual lassitude, and in some cases depravity and barbarity, that led to a shift among the elite towards more personalized forms of learning, especially the employment of private tutors. However, over the longer term the institutions themselves became agents of improvement, as they slowly modernized their curricula, and adopted more polite norms of behaviour. Some enterprising grammar schools, such as Rugby, combined a changing ethos with a more commercialized approach to attracting pupils (by taking on fee-paying boarders), providing a prototype for the modern public school. In their new role the institutions (the Inns of Court excepted) regained their market position, because they married modern attitudes to education with their traditional, and still crucial role of high status collective bonding. The English universities were slow to be drawn into the process of modernization, but the same could not be said for their Scottish counterparts, which were early to adopt Newtonianism, and became leading centres of European Enlightenment thinking and training in the sciences, medicine, and philosophy, establishing a gamut of new lectureships and chairs in these fields, and attracting the likes of William Cullen, Joseph Black, and Adam Smith.

Between the late seventeenth and late eighteenth centuries many among the lower orders—particularly those who were better off, town dwellers, and male—joined the ranks of the literate. What precisely this meant in terms of attainment, and how it was achieved, is unclear. Developments in the Scottish Lowlands rested in part on an established and widespread system of parish schools. Throughout Britain the early eighteenth century saw a move to establish charity schools, but the deliberately limited level of attainment they aimed for, their obvious emphasis on social management rather than education, and declining financial support, restricted their impact. In Wales major advances were achieved from the 1730s by Griffith Jones's 'circulating' or itinerant schools. When in 1761 Jones died, 3,325 schools had been established in 1,600 different places, though during the later part of the eighteenth century the movement began to wane. In Britain as a whole the key to popular and lower middle class literacy was probably a mixture of the commercial sector—comprising of thousands of small schools, such as the adventure and hedge schools in Scotland and Ireland, and the plethora of petty 'academies' advertised in the English urban press—and a strategy of self-help nurtured in chapels, clubs, and pubs. Given that the abilities to read and write are not absolutes, but represent widely varying levels of sophistication, then too much should not be attributed to crude measures of literacy. However, one cannot ignore the implications of a situation in which access to print culture was becoming available to a majority rather than a minority of at least the male population.

One of the features of early modern manuscript and even printed language was its variable and unstable nature. However, rising levels of literacy, allied to the explosive growth of published material, tended to standardize written and—by a knock-on effect—oral usage. Authors, publishers, and readers had a mutual interest in developing a single linguistic currency so as to facilitate communication, and the fixed character of printed matter meant that it could invade linguistic regions and remain unaffected by vernacular influences. The practical advantages of such developments would themselves have been considered improving. But just as important were the moral effects. A universal language eased and encouraged sociability. Moreover, given that the standard adopted emanated from the most advanced and polite centre of culture in the kingdom, London, then standardization was also seen as a mechanism for spreading civilization. In these circumstances, it is not surprising that the important role of language in human progress was widely discussed in the eighteenth century, nor that several attempts were made to compile dictionaries, most famously Samuel Johnson's *Dictionary of the English Language* (1755). In his *Plan* (1747) for this, he proposed 'a dictionary by which the pronunciation of our language may be fixed, and its attainment facilitated', and drew on the analogy of Caesar's invasion of Britain, 'I hope, that though I should not complete the conquest, I shall at least discover the coast, civilize part of the inhabitants, and make it easier for some other adventurer to proceed farther, to reduce them wholly to subjection, and settle them under laws.'[5] The imperial metaphor reminds us not only of the perceived civilizing function of language, but also its coercive potential. This was particularly so in a Britain that was a multilingual society. In 1700 perhaps one-quarter of Scotland was Gaelic-speaking; in Ireland the position was stronger though declining, with around two-thirds of the people using Irish as their ordinary language in the 1730s, and one-half by 1800; Welsh was the strongest placed of the Celtic languages, with up to nine in every ten of the country deploying it as their everyday medium of communication. Measures to promote English and retard the use of native languages, on the assumption that they were primitive modes of expression, were instituted in all three countries. The Scottish SPCK, for example, forbade the use of Gaelic until 1766. Welsh was the one Celtic language which appears, despite many of the gentry's withdrawal from the vernacular, to have successfully managed the crucial transition from an exclusively oral to a print medium. This was due to the energies of a circle of patriotic intellectuals, the circulating schools' commitment to its use, and the establishment in the Teifi Valley, Carmarthen, and Shrewsbury of dedicated Welsh language presses producing popular literature (ballads, interludes, and almanacs) and religious works. Thus, the tools of an improving progressive culture were deployed, ironically, to preserve what some would have seen as a barbaric language.

[5] *The Plan of a Dictionary of the English Language* (1747), in M. Wilson (ed.), *Johnson: Poetry and Prose* (London, 1970), p. 138.

Improvement in context

The notion of improvement commanded widespread appeal, supported as it was by an array of powerful mechanisms to inculcate and
spread the message. However, as the position of language makes clear,
the meaning and impact of improving culture was often complex and
contradictory, varying across a range of contexts. Three of these will
be explored here; space, gender, and status and class. It is possible to
conceive of improvement as a fundamentally urban phenomenon,
and as a tool by which the town exerted power over the countryside.
Towns were self-evidently centres of cultural innovation and gate-
ways for new ideas. Moreover, their very openness to migrants and
visitors, and their concentration of population, encouraged high
degrees of sociability. This made it appear that they were inherently
more advanced and civilized societies, and the rich array of polite
leisure and consumer facilities that sprang up in eighteenth-century
towns simply seemed to confirm this. Hand in hand with this went a
vein of anti-ruralism, such as Addison and Steele's satirical treatment
of the country gentry in the pages of *The Spectator* and *The Tatler*,
Henry Fielding's sending up of the bucolic and alcoholic Squire Wes-
ton in *Tom Jones* (1749), and Richard 'Beau' Nash's determination to
ban country dress and behaviour from the assembly rooms of Bath.
Yet this idea of an urban civilizing agenda has its limits. Improvement, as we have seen, was closely linked with agriculture and gardening, the country houses of the landowning elite contained some of
the most advanced examples of contemporary artistic taste, and by
the latter part of the century changing attitudes to nature were
beginning to reconceive 'wild' and picturesque areas like the English
Lake District, the Scottish Highlands, Killarney, and the Wye Valley,
not to mention the coast and sea as a whole, as improving spectacles.
Moreover, towns imported 'nature' into their midst in the forms of
public and private walks and gardens, and these were seen as exerting
a cleansing impact on what some commentators portrayed as the
corrupting influence of the city.

If the urban/rural dichotomy is unduly simplistic, then a more
meaningful way of interpreting the spatial impact of improvement is
to see it in terms of the centre, metropolitan and middle England,

drawing under its influence the periphery—the English provinces of the North and West, the Celtic 'fringe' nations, and the growing overseas empire. London was the vortex at the heart of this system. In 1800, with a population of around a million souls, it contained over 6 per cent of the entire peoples of the British Isles, was over four times the size of its nearest native rival Dublin, and was one of the three largest cities in the world. Through its bulk and dominant economic, social, and political position, it exerted a huge centrifugal force. Culturally this meant that the metropolis had an irresistible appeal, not least for financial reasons, to the most able and aspiring provincial artists, performers, writers, and thinkers. From Ireland, for example, came Jonathan Swift, Richard Steele, George Farquhar, George Berkeley, Oliver Goldsmith, Edmund Burke, and Richard Brinsley Sheridan. Some migrants might return home, but they, together with the landed elite who attended the London season *en masse*, carried with them the improved taste discovered in the city. This contributed to the broader process by which metropolitan fashions were disseminated throughout Britain, prompting Richard Warner in 1801 to declare the capital 'the central point where arts originate, and from whence they ramify'.[6]

However, persuasive as the notion of cultural centralization appears, it should not be taken too far. The Celtic nations of Britain all possessed and developed a sense of their own cultural identities, which, paradoxically, the centrifugal forces emanating from the capital may have accentuated. The eighteenth-century Welsh cultural renaissance was in part driven by an Oxford-based academic, Edward Lhuyd, and a group of patriot intellectual clubs in London. The members of these societies, temporarily or permanently living at the heart of the great machine, were no doubt acutely conscious of their own separateness, and of the threat metropolitan domination posed to the traditions and identity of their homeland. Their response was to initiate a scholarly programme to rediscover the historic culture of Wales, though it has to be said that this became shot through with a strong element of myth and invention. The gifted if wayward Iolo Morganwg fabricated a number of medieval poems (the earliest first appeared in print as an appendix of the Gwyneddigion society's edition of Dafydd ap Gwilym's poetry in 1789) and prose items, seeking

---

[6] Richard Warner, *The History of Bath* (Bath, 1801), p. 224.

to add that extra boost to Welsh antiquity that James Macpherson had provided for the Gaelic past with his Ossianic counterfeits, published in the early 1760s. Macpherson's poems may also have stimulated a new interest in the Irish Gaelic heritage, which acquired institutional form with the establishment of the Irish Academy in Dublin in 1785. Even more important to Scottish cultural identity, at least in the Lowlands, than the Gaelic revival was the country's distinctive and impressive contribution to the European Enlightenment. Such developments helped build a strong sense of patriotism, that held in check metropolitan Ascendancy, and for those involved inverted notions of centre and periphery. However, for patriotism should not necessarily be read nationalism, since many of those who lived on the Celtic 'periphery' displayed multiple identities or 'concentric loyalties', which embraced *both* a sense of Scottishness/Welshness/Irishness, and of Britishness. Much the same could be said of the natives of the English provinces, 'countries' which possessed their own, often dynamically expanding urban capitals, such as Manchester, Birmingham, and Leeds. Such towns were the focal points of regional identities, and would have been considered by those who used and lived in them as much founts of an improving culture as London. Indeed, it should not be assumed that all ideas were generated in, or even flowed through the metropolis. Britain was saturated by European taste, not least because of the compelling appeal of the Grand Tour. Dublin's eighteenth-century architecture and interior decoration reflected Italian and German influences, imported directly into the city by architects like Edward Lovett Pearce and Richard Castle, and stuccodores like the Francini brothers, Paul and Philip, who were probably born in the vicinity of Lake Lugano. The passion for foreign fashions was so great as to stimulate among the English bourgeoisie an anxiety about its own identity. This expressed itself in bursts of xenophobia, more than traces of which can be detected in the anti-European sentiment to be found in Hogarth's work, such as the skinny Frenchman manhandled by the hearty corpulent English cooper in *Beer Street* (1751). *Beer Street*'s principal role was to act as a counterfoil to the far more powerful *Gin Lane*, an apocalyptic vision of the degenerative effects of gin drinking, and part of a long-running campaign to curb what was perceived as a major social evil. The illustration contained graphic images of female alcoholics and their neglected children; one showed a woman forcing gin down the throat of her offspring, another a drunken adult allowing a child to fall from her arms to its death, and a third a woman being lowered into a coffin beside which sat a tearful baby. The message was clear and stark; the consumption of spirits by women undermined their fundamental role as mothers, and therefore threatened the whole social fabric. *Gin Lane* was a classic piece of bourgeois improving culture. Produced cheaply, it would have hung in many middle and lower middle class homes, a reminder of a woman's primary duty, and an indication of the long-term trend in the period to enhanced female domesticity. The strong emotional images portrayed, tugging at the heart strings of the observer, were also a harbinger of the sentimental revolution of the later eighteenth century, that became particularly associated with women and further accentuated sexual differentiation. Not that men were unaffected by an improving culture. On the one hand, politeness and civility sought to create a new image of male gentility based on intellectual and behavioural refinement, that stood in contradiction to the archetypal representation of the country squire as a man of limited intelligence, and boorish violent habits. On the other hand, there was an increased emphasis in the male persona on utility and productiveness. This was exemplified in Hogarth's moral cycle, *Industry and Idleness* (1747), which traces the careers of two London apprentices, the industrious one becoming Lord Mayor, his idle counterpart ending his life on the gallows. It may also have been reflected in changing sexual mores which increasingly demonized 'wasteful' masturbation and valorized 'productive' penetrative sex.

The domestication, and associated de-sexualization of women—and the novelty and extent of these trends should not be exaggerated—that might be argued to be a consequence of the culture of improvement, has to be set against the opportunities that this culture offered for a more public, active, and independent feminine lifestyle. Opportunities for female middling order education expanded, not only through domestic tutoring, but also by attending the growing number of small, commercially run academies that, on a day or boarding basis, took girls out of the house. Though these schools clustered around London, the resorts, and fashionable county towns, they were also to be found in small towns and even villages, and though the training offered was geared towards genteel accomplishments and marriage, the curriculum also included reading, writing, mathematics, and increasingly other academic subjects.

The development of a world of polite urban leisure and philanthropy drew women into the public sphere. John Macky, writing in the early 1700s of the new rage for assemblies, observed that 'formerly the country ladies were stewed up in their fathers' old mansion houses, and seldom saw company, but at an assize, horse-race, or fair'.[7] Commercial music and theatre not only enticed women away from the home, but also provided new areas of paid professional employment as performers, though in the case of drama this might carry a moral stigma. One of the products of the print revolution was a small but growing body of women writers, able to explore a specifically feminine agenda, and to service an increasingly literate female market. The widening opportunities for consumerism and shopping enhanced the scope for women to make decisions and spend money. The high concentration of fashionable retail and recreational facilities in spas and seaside towns made resorts particularly conducive and empowering to women. Many would visit without their husbands, and many who were economically independent, like well off spinsters, chose to reside permanently in such locations, contributing to their comparatively high female sex ratios.

However, the capacity to enjoy the benefits of an improving culture was conditional upon the possession of wealth. Most women's contact with fashionable society was as a producer, often in desperately poorly paid jobs, rather than a consumer. This all reflected the obvious but crucial point that improvement, for all its emphasis on sociability, was a major tool in the pursuit of status. During their respective seasons, the national capitals, county towns, and resorts were hothouses of competition, as the company, dressed to the nines, jockeyed with each other for the last ounce of prestige. Orgies of consumption, facilitated by a never-ending round of shopping sprees, were engaged in to obtain the required intellectual and material possessions (clothes, jewellery, books, etc.) to vie in the public arenas (assembly rooms, walks, theatres, etc.) for social prestige. Often such spaces were used as marriage markets, for marital alliances were the key to long-term success or failure in the social hierarchy. Marry a wealthy heiress and a gentleman could repair financial losses, shore up a failing estate, and invest further in status objects. Marry his

---

[7] John Macky, *A Journey through England and Scotland* (3 vols.; London, 1722–3), vol. ii, p. 41.

daughter to a titled big-wig and a successful merchant could transform his wealth into social kudos. No wonder that there existed a rule
in the Bath assembly rooms 'That the elder ladies and children be
contented with a second bench . . . being past, or not come to perfection.'[8] It could be argued that all the emphasis on polite behaviour
and sociability on such occasions was necessary simply to keep the
forces of competition in check. For those with high aspirations, land
was the most important form of prestige-bearing consumption. But
it was not simply a matter of amassing multiple acres. What was
critical was that the property possessed or acquired was modelled to
express the superior character of its owner. It was here that improvement played a vital part, with investment in new agricultural practices, house architecture, landscape gardening, and estate planning to
allow the landowner to display his advanced taste and compete with
his neighbours. Urban elites pursued a similar strategy, engaging in
improvement schemes and competitive public building to score one
over their rivals. After Bristol had built a splendid new merchant's
exchange in 1741–3, its great northern rival, Liverpool, also employed
the same architect John Wood to design an exchange (1749–54).

When the town fathers erected impressive new public buildings,
the modish classical style adopted bore comparison with that of
modern country house design, and was a way of the urban rulers
asserting that they and the surrounding rural gentry were part of a
common status system. Increasingly a biological definition of gentility was being challenged and surpassed by a cultural one, which
allowed an expanding middling order access, through an appropriate
use of their wealth, to social kudos. Improving culture was providen-
tially tailored to facilitate this process. It was not by any means an
exclusively middling phenomenon. Many of the landed gentry, as we
have seen, adopted its philosophy and forms with enthusiasm. But
much of its centre of gravity appears urban and bourgeois: the critique of the traditional pastimes and manners of the rural squirearchy; the urban nature of much of the new world of fashionable
leisure; the challenge to aristocratic ideals and fashions embodied in
the notion of sensibility; and the emphasis on moral and religious
reform, industriousness, and sobriety as exemplified in the urban

[8] John Wood, *A Description of Bath*, 2nd edn. 1749 (reprinted 1765 and Bath, 1969), p.
249.

reformation of manners societies and charitable organizations, or the output of Hogarth. Moreover, the Scottish Enlightenment and the Welsh cultural renaissance were primarily a product of middling and professional social groups. Perhaps the very commitment to a notion of continuous progress reflected the restless middle-class psyche, conscious always of its indeterminate position in the social hierarchy, and driven equally by the glittering opportunities for upward, and awful dangers of downward mobility.

One group for whom the culture of improvement would, on the face of it, have limited meaning, was the lower orders. Improvement was a pricey commodity, and was intended to be a tool of social exclusivity. When country squires re-landscaped the parks around their estates in the second half of the eighteenth century, some removing villages and realigning roads, one of the intentions was to put space between themselves and the peasants. When elegant urban squares were constructed, the purpose was not simply to encourage sociability among the fashionable residents, but also, in the words of the architect of Queen Square' Bath (1728–36), to create a 'spot . . . separated from the ground common to men and beasts, and even to mankind in general'.[9] The common people might be embraced within the improving agenda, but it was very much as the passive recipient of some moral or philanthropic initiative, one function of which would be to reinforce notions of social subservience. Such was the theory. In practice, the pleasures and benefits of an improving culture could not be confined to society's upper echelons. The commercialization of polite pastimes pushed down their price and increased accessibility. Alexander Pope's excoriating critique of the literary hacks of Grub Street in *The Dunciad* (1728) can be read as a conservative response to the threat posed by popularization to the exclusivity of elite taste and culture. Similar concerns also lay behind the legislation introduced in 1737 and 1740 to try to curtail the availability of theatre and horse racing. Servants necessarily had close contact with the lifestyles of their employees, and, for example, may have—with approval or otherwise—borrowed their reading matter. There was a healthy market in second-hand fashionable clothing. Popular evangelical religion, such as Methodism, whatever its avowed conservative message, embodied powerful notions of

[9] Ibid., p. 345.

self-improvement. Most importantly, there existed in the upper strata of the working class comparatively well off artisan elements who vigorously embraced an ideology of self-help, in which industry and thrift, consumption, education, morality, and religion all played an important part, but differed from its bourgeois counterpart in its emphasis upon cooperation as the means to achieve personal progress.

Alternative cultures

Improvement may have been the dominant cultural icon of the eighteenth century, but was it the way in which most people actually lived their lives? The very emphasis on ideals and aspirations, and on a never-ending pursuit of betterment, made it a difficult, perhaps impossible ideology, to adhere to. Thomas Turner, a shopkeeper in the Sussex village of East Hoathly, appears an archetypal self-improver; parish officer, upwardly mobile, he was an avid reader of serious literature, and kept a daily diary (1754–65) in which to survey his personal development. Yet what the journal also reveals is his human fallibility, as day after day he is forced to acknowledge his craving for drink: 'I came home again in liquor . . . I do think I am prodigiously silly and apish when I am in liquor, having always, for a great while after, a sting of conscience for the same.'[10] Turner's weakness for heavy drinking may have generated anxiety and guilt, but it was a pattern of living that he continued to choose, and one that was replicated across the length and breadth of Georgian (male) society. For a good many commentators the seeds of such 'problems' lay in improving culture itself. Fashionable leisure and consumerism—for all its emphasis on taste, politeness, sociability, and civility—had its less edifying side, providing a ready vehicle for overindulgence, promiscuity, prostitution, pornography, and excessive materialism. Bitter attacks were launched against the proliferation of luxury, and the corrupting influence of town and city. In the *Rake's Progress* (1735), Hogarth delivered a ruthless exposure of the London West End social round, and Bath attracted a torrent of criticism, castigated variously as 'a sink of iniquity' and 'Satan's stronghold'. However, such assaults

---

[10] *The Diary of Thomas Turner 1754–1765*, ed. D. Vaisey (Oxford, 1984), p. 24.

did not seek to undermine the ethos of improvement per se; rather they represented tensions between pleasurable and purgatorial versions of the same improving culture, both of which—one suspects— it was the norm for an individual to embrace.

Libertinism might seem to offer a clearer cut alternative to improvement. Since at least the Restoration there had existed a rakish strand in elite culture, that celebrated overtly hedonistic values. One form this may have taken were the so-called Hell-Fire clubs, such as the Irish Blasters and the Dublin Hell-Fire Club, notorious for their wining, debauchery, and blasphemy. One such club was rumoured to have been organized by Sir Francis Dashwood at Medmenham Abbey close to his West Wycombe estate, though whether there was any truth in this, or it was simply a political smear, is difficult to judge. Dashwood was a founding member of the aristocratic Society of Dilettanti (1734), Grand Tourists and wealthy collectors, several of whom—such as Richard Payne Knight, important theorist on the picturesque, but also author of explicit studies of phallic worship— also enjoyed a dubious moral reputation. Whether all this amounted to a full-blown alternative culture is dubious. Men like Dashwood and Knight had a serious commitment to the arts and the role of these in developing taste. For such people connoisseurship, and any associated libertinism, could well be a reaction and challenge to the increasingly puritan, professional, and middle-class vein in British culture, rather than a rejection of improvement as such. Nor can the homosexual subculture which emerged in eighteenth-century London, based on molly houses and places of open-air assignation, be interpreted as inherently anti-improvement. A more systematic alternative might be found in romanticism, the first seeds of which were appearing in the eighteenth century. Changing attitudes to nature were a central feature of this, and were presaged in the cult of the picturesque, for which Knight was such an influential propagandist, with its emphasis on rough-hewn natural landscape. Yet as Knight showed at Downton Castle in Herefordshire, and his cousin Thomas Johnes in the even more remote wilderness of Hafod in Ceredigion, natural did not mean unimproved, as they invested huge sums in re-landscaping their estates. Johnes, who planted almost five million trees in the thirty years before 1816, was also a committed agricultural improver, and put money into developing road access and local tourist facilities. This enabled the delights of wild Wales to be enjoyed by a growing stream of cultural tourists, many in search of an antidote to an increasingly urbanized and commercialized way of living. Such wild areas, like the Lake District and the Scottish Highlands, far from being examples of nature in the raw, were the products of a high level of human intervention and invention.

A belief in progress, and the possibilities for human betterment opened up by change, was a feature of English romanticism. Hence the initial warm response to the French Revolution, William Words-worth declaring 'Bliss was it in that dawn to be alive' (*Prelude*, 1805),[11] and William Blake, who was no lover of authorized versions of improvement, exhorting his fellow citizens to 'Drive your cart and your plow over the bones of the dead' (*Marriage of Heaven and Hell*, 1790–3).[12] But romanticism also had its deeply conservative elements, and this reflected a continuous strand in eighteenth-century British culture of nostalgia and historicism. The study of antiquities was popular in gentlemanly circles, though it tended to eschew the empiricism of the late seventeenth century for a more proto-romantic approach which was to make much of ancient Celts, druids, bards, and such like. Interest in the gothic, which never completely died out, enjoyed a concerted revival from the mid-eighteenth century, pioneered architecturally by figures like William Kent, Batty Langley, Sanderson Miller, and most famously Horace Walpole—who also authored the first gothic novel, *The Castle of Otranto* (1764)—in his house at Strawberry Hill, Twickenham (1748 onwards). How far such intellectual and aesthetic movements amounted to a culture of anti-progressivism, and even more anti-improvement, is question-able. In returning to the past it was not necessary to vacate the future. Classicism was, after all, based on a historic culture, and late eighteenth-century radicals were to find sustenance in the myths of Saxon freedom and the Norman yoke. However, there was a pool of conservative gentry, to whom the notion of progress, never mind indefinite progress, would have made little sense. Some were Jacobites, particularly in Scotland and Ireland, where the Stuart cause became fused with nationalism. Some were out and out tradition-alists. Wedded to a unitary paternalist vision of society, and impervious

---

[11] William Wordsworth, *The Prelude*, 1805 text, ed. E. de Selincourt, 2nd edn. ed. S. Gill (Oxford, 1970), Book X, p. 196.

[12] William Blake, *The Marriage of Heaven and Hell*, Proverbs of Hell, in *The Poems of William Blake*, ed. W. H. Stevenson and D. V. Erdman (London, 1971), p. 108.

to the blandishments of polite culture, they remained committed to country sports and customs, and were deeply suspicious of city life.

Many traditionalist gentry, as part of an overall vision of 'country' resistance, also displayed sympathy for so-called folk culture. The Glamorgan gentry patronized the boisterous village wakes, and even established new ones in communities which lacked them. However, such customs were becoming essentially popular in character. As the Newcastle upon Tyne curate Henry Bourne argued of the 'ceremonies' and 'opinions' he recorded in his *Antiquitates Vulgares* (1725), one of the earliest studies dedicated to 'folk' culture, 'though some of them have been of national, and others perhaps of universal appearance, yet at present they would have little or no being, if not observed among the vulgar'.[13] This reflects part of a long-term process, which accelerates rapidly in the eighteenth century, by which the upper and middling orders became detached from, and increasingly antagonistic to, aspects of 'traditional' culture. Underpinning this was the Enlightenment intellectual and moral agenda, which sought to refine and civilize mankind, rejecting folk practices as primitive, and its social agenda, which though it promoted sociability among the elite, was also a tool to differentiate the ruling orders from the common people. In this sense an improving culture and a folk culture were diametrically at odds. The two clashed at many points. Magic and witchcraft, from which the ruling orders were retreating with almost unseemly haste by the late 1600s, continued to inform much of popular custom. Physicality, violence, and apparent cruelty were part and parcel of popular recreations, exemplified in activities like cudgelling, cock throwing, and bull baiting. Speech, song, and visual spectacle, allied to symbolic forms of ritual behaviour, remained the principal means of articulating and communicating the folk idiom. This was primarily a culture of the spoken word and gesture, not of print. It was also focused, in obvious contradiction to the Enlightenment with its internationalist perspective, on the locality and the community. Vernacular architecture, to contemporary educated observers a sign of impoverishment, was a material expression of local character, and village ceremonies were a means by which a community could celebrate its specific identity and the ties which bound it together. Above

---

[13] Henry Bourne, *Antiquitates Vulgares; or, the Antiquities of the Common People* (Newcastle upon Tyne, 1725), p. ix.

all, custom legitimated activity. A community asserted its norms and nature by referring to, and replaying, its past. It also defined itself in terms of the annual seasonal cycle, which constituted the principal chronological structure around which festivities and pastimes were organized. Here were notions of historic and cyclical time which fitted ill with the progressive linear sense of time that was central to the notion of improvement.

Folk or popular culture, and neither term is really satisfactory, thus constituted a real and vibrant alternative to an improving culture, and in the context of the civilizing mission of the Enlightenment was one of the principal phenomena that needed to be improved. Yet it would be dangerous to read the eighteenth century as a titanic struggle between two notions of culture. In practice the situation was much more fluid, complex, and variegated. Not the least of the problems is the extent to which the two cultures shared characteristics, and indeed fertilized one another. A fascination with spectacle, effect, and mystery that borders on the magical infected much of eighteenth-century science, particularly in the way it was presented to the public by itinerant lecturers; nor is it possible in the medical field to divorce the period's obsession with water treatment, at spa and seaside, from the traditional magical healing qualities springs and wells were said to possess. Newspapers, at the cutting edge of the print revolution, traded in the fabulous and exotic as well as the mundane and 'rational'. The *Northampton Mercury* in 1721 included an illustration of an eight-foot sea-monster with 'a head like a spaniel . . . broad flat teeth, fiery eyes . . . lank hair, a large flat nose, hands, arms, shoulders, and all motions like those of a man: a brown skin, full breasts like those of a nurse'.[14] John Wesley managed to combine elements of Enlightenment thinking and a commitment to self-improvement, with a belief in ghosts, exorcism, miraculous healing, and traditional medical remedies that allowed Methodism to bridge improving and popular culture. It is customary to associate the march of reason with a rejection of ritual and ceremony. However, fashionable leisure was intensely ritualized. Resorts—the focal points of polite culture—were saturated with repetitive and coded patterns of behaviour, and replete with symbolic architecture and space. Moreover, improved recreations were closely tied to a cycle of winter

---

[14] *Northampton Mercury*, 17 Apr. 1721.

and summer seasons that reflected the solar calendar. Popular culture, despite its roots in custom and locality, was anything but static and insulated, and was constantly responding to altering external influences. In this sense it embraced rather than rejected change. Fifth of November bonfires, for example, were an invention of the early seventeenth century and an act of parliament to celebrate deliverance from the plot to blow up James I. They had no obvious predecessors in Tudor or medieval England, nor were they related to the Hallowe'en fires found in early modern Wales, and central Scotland. The Fifth of November became a central feature of the Protestant calendar, and was widely celebrated, changing its props to suit altering political circumstances. In the eighteenth century effigies of the Pope were often replaced by hated politicians or local people. As the elite withdrew their patronage of the event, so it became more popular in character, this in turn emphasizing its boisterous nature, and initiating a long drawn out battle, which lasted well into the nineteenth century, to suppress it. The print revolution undoubtedly had an important impact on folk culture, through, for example, the mass printing of chapbooks, ballads, almanacs, and cheap abbreviated novels, not to mention religious literature. English medium publication of 'popular' literature had already become firmly established in the seventeenth century, and a Welsh language strand emerged strongly from the early 1700s. On the one hand, this type of literature sustained fundamental elements of folk culture, such as story-telling and magic. On the other hand, it was a source of standardization and innovation. Eighteenth-century almanacs, for example, reflected polite taste by toning down the astrological element, and increasing instructional features. Indeed, the culture of the common people, a rapidly increasing proportion of whom were located in towns and cities, was constantly being reforged and reinvented in the crucible of commercialization and urbanization.

By the late eighteenth century improvement had emerged as the dominant cultural motif in Britain. This reflected the evolution throughout the century of a broadly defined, flexibly constituted culture of improvement, which commanded widespread support within the ruling orders, in particular among an increasingly influential middling sort. In the evolution of this culture the foundations were laid for what was to become the ideological dynamo of Victorian Britain and its empire. However, improvement was not a monolithic

ideology. Its plasticity was central to its character, and its manifestations and impact varied considerably according to space, gender,
status and class. Moreover, there existed alternative cultural forms,
especially a popular or folk type, that stood for, and sustained, a
world-view that seemed to contradict that of progressivism. Some
contemporaries would have seen the confrontation of the two cultures as an out and out battle, in the case of the improvers a struggle
between the forces of civilization and enlightenment, and those of
barbarity and heathenism. It cannot be denied that some of this spirit
was to infuse the class conflict that gained increasing strength in the
early years of the nineteenth century and the spread of empire later in
the century. But *in practice* high and low culture, the small and great
traditions, interfused and interbred with each other, creating a plural-
istic, multifaceted cultural amalgam that was all the stronger socially
for its mongrel nature.

United Irishmen upon Duty.

Figure 7 Gillray's 'United Irishmen upon Duty' portrays a scene from the Irish uprising of 1798 when the empire was seemingly being torn apart by discord in Britain, rebellion in Ireland, and a worldwide war with the French Republic. The artist's fiercely loyalist propaganda depicted Irish nationalists as murderous plunderers of Protestant families.

6

Contested empires, 1756–1815

Michael Duffy

The restorative political stability created by Sir Robert Walpole was founded upon a policy of peace, but the fall of the master in 1742 accompanied the start of the most extensive period of warfare in British history. In fifty-two of the seventy-seven years between 1739 and 1815 the British state was officially and unofficially at war with rival imperial powers or with rebels within its empire (Table 6.1).

War on this scale changed the nature of British politics and society and transformed its international position. In what became a great Armageddon of *ancien régime* Europe, Britain survived to become leading great power and, in 1814–15, the first modern international superpower.

Such a triumphant result was unexpected, and certainly the rest of Europe did not wish it, making it difficult to find supportive allies. Britain frequently faced defeat. Invaded in 1745, it braced itself for further invasion in 1756–7, 1759, 1779, 1796–8 (the last time invading forces actually landed in the British Isles), 1801, and 1804–5. In its greatest national humiliation of the eighteenth century, in 1782–3, it was forced to concede both independence to its thirteen rebel American colonies and semi-autonomy to Ireland. It was confronted with rebellion in its Caribbean colonies in 1795 and in Ireland in 1798 and 1803. In the 1790s there were those who even feared revolution in Britain itself. Governments faced anti-recruitment riots and anti-tax

Table 6.1 *The Georgian age of warfare 1739–1815*

1739–48	1739–48 War of Jenkins's Ear with Spain
	1742–8 War of the Austrian Succession
	1744–8 War with France
1754–63	1754–5 unofficial war with France in America
	1756–63 Seven Years War with France
	1762–3 War with Spain
1775–83	1775–83 War of American Independence
	1778–83 War with France
	1779–83 War with Spain, 1780–3 with Holland
1793–1815	**'The Great War with France'**
	1793–1802 War with Revolutionary France, 1795–1802 with Revolutionary Holland, 1796–1802 with Spain
	1803–14 Napoleonic War with France and Holland, 1804–8 with Spain
	1812–14 'War of 1812' with the USA
	1815 The 'Hundred Days War' with Napoleonic France

riots in their efforts to fight and pay for the wars; food riots and employment riots when war added to bad weather to produce inflation and dislocate traditional trading patterns; political and religious riots when unsuccessful war discredited the authority of government; and constitutional crises when even the authority of the crown was in danger of being discredited. Over all loomed the escalating costs of war that threatened to drive the nation into bankruptcy. Ian Christie, Linda Colley, and Jonathan Clark have well set out the strength of the underlying ties of stability, continuity, and loyalty of this period, but those who lived through it experienced no assured, smooth path to achieving the status of first international superpower.

The objects of imperial warfare

How did Britain become involved in this traumatic, ultimately decisive struggle? At issue were believed to be national prosperity and even survival. Under threat were the interconnected issues of commerce and naval power, both of which were considered crucial to the success of Britain's political system, its economy, and its power projection. The navy, sustained by maritime commerce, protected Britain, its overseas possessions, and its trade from attack. It preserved the Protestant succession from Catholic, arbitrary, and Jacobite enemies. It rendered unnecessary a large, expensive and politically dangerous standing army. And it was Britain's most potent weapon of war against the trade and imperial possessions of other powers. Thomas Lediard in his *Naval History of England* (1735) voiced an often repeated belief: 'That our trade is the Mother and Nurse of our Seamen; our Seamen the Life of our Fleet; And our Fleet the Security and Protection of our Trade: and that both together are the WEALTH, STRENGTH, and GLORY of GREAT BRITAIN.'

In mid-century such convictions became closely tied to issues of empire. Throughout the century overseas trade grew far faster than that with Europe. In 1700–1 Europe accounted for 66 per cent of the imports of England and Wales and 85 per cent of domestic exports, but by 1772–3, 55 per cent of imports and 51 per cent of domestic exports were in the overseas trades. As the colonial population grew apace, with the North American colonies in particular growing from just over 250,000 colonists in 1700 to approaching 2.5 million in 1775, both colonial produce and colonial markets increased. In this period re-exports of overseas produce increased from 28 per cent to 36 per cent of total exports in official values, while sales outside of Europe, primarily to the Americas, accounted for nearly four-fifths of the growth in English domestic exports since the start of the century. At least half of English foreign-going shipping was engaged in this burgeoning Atlantic trade. With an ever-increasing proportion of government tax revenue coming from trade; with naval power underpinned by this growing merchant shipping; and with the colonial population providing military manpower of which Britain was in need, there was an increasing belief that national wealth and power now depended upon overseas commerce and empire.

The value of these imperial assets were shown in the mid-century wars, when the damage to French credit and trade from the threat to Canada through the surprise colonial capture of Louisburg, coupled with British naval victories in 1747, induced France to abandon its winning position in Europe and make peace by a mutual return of conquests. In the ensuing Seven Years War the American colonies contributed 20,000 men towards the conquest of Canada and

Havana, while British trade, which boomed in the war (exports and re-exports from £11 million in 1755 to £15.7 million in 1763), enabled it again to outlast France financially and win spectacular imperial gains. Kathleen Wilson has demonstrated how empire was taken into the national culture as the embodiment of English national virtues—courage, mercantile enterprise creating and diffusing wealth throughout the nation, liberty, an invigorating 'Country' public-spiritedness to counter enervating 'Court' corruption. These became unifying British virtues as in the 1760s and 1770s Scottish and Scotch-Irish emigrants poured into the American colonies; as all contributed men and taxes to the imperial war effort; as England's sister king-doms took a rising share of the colonial trade and the whole popula-tion became tied into the network of imperial trade and investment. The mid-eighteenth century successes accustomed press and public to take a world-view of an extending empire of expanding British wealth and liberty, in which colonies were seen as bulwarks of trade, prosperity, naval strength, and political virtue for the parent state, and empire became a touchstone of the health, vigour, and power of the nation.

However Britain's main imperial and maritime rivals, France and Spain, also learned the lesson of these events. Each sought to build up their own overseas wealth and to prevent further British advance through strengthening their colonial fortifications, occupying key imperial pathways, and rebuilding their fleets. The ending of the War of the Austrian Succession in 1748 initiated a naval arms race that reached its zenith in the early 1790s and constituted a threat that Britain could not afford to ignore (see Table 6.2).

Table 6.2 *The great naval arms race among the imperial powers*
(Total tonnage of sailing warships above 500 tons in 000 displacement tons)

	1745	1755	1765	1775	1785	1795	1805	1815
Britain	235	277	377	337	447	512	546	609
France	98	162	175	199	268	284	182	228
Spain	55	113	124	198	211	264	139	60
Holland	65	58	66	68	124	76	44	71
Portugal	28	28	32	41	34	50	54	44

Source: J. Glete, *Navies and Nations: Warships, Navies and State Building in Europe and America, 1500–1860* (2 vols. Stockholm, 1993), vol.ii app.2 pp. 553–695.

This naval rivalry was sustained by corresponding efforts to increase overseas trade, in which France achieved some spectacular successes. In mid-century French Saint Domingue overtook British Jamaica as the most productive colony in the Caribbean, and by the late 1780s exceeded the trade of the breakaway United States of America. Whereas in constant prices English foreign trade increased 2.4 times between 1716–20 and 1784–8, French trade more than tripled, within which its transatlantic trade increased tenfold. While French domestic exports to Europe tripled, their colonial re-exports increased eightfold. Between the 1720s and 1780s they rose from 55 per cent of the English total to 90 per cent, and France's total seaborne trade from about 50 per cent of the value of that of England and Wales to over 80 per cent. In proportion to its much larger population, France still had a long way to go to catch up its British rival, but its progress alarmed observers across the Channel.

This imperial commercial rivalry was played out both in war and in the peacetime competition to investigate the unknown possibilities of the Pacific. In the 1760s–1770s the exploratory voyages of Byron, Wallis, and Cook countered those of Bougainville from France; in the 1780s–1790s Bligh and Vancouver were rivalled by La Pérouse and d'Entrecasteaux for France and Malaspina for Spain. Concern to secure access to the trade of the Pacific produced diplomatic crises against Spain in 1770 over the Falkland Islands and in 1790 over Nootka Sound on America's north-west coast. Another naval mobilization against France in 1787 enabled Britain to recover a predominant influence over the Dutch, which not only deprived the French of use of the Dutch fleet but also of the use of Dutch naval bases in the Far East from which they could prey on Britain's eastern empire.

This new age of global warfare forced Britain to create a more coherent war administration with a new office of Secretary of State for War in 1794. Its first incumbent, Henry Dundas, held that 'all modern wars are a contention of purse'.[1] The size of the British purse depended on the extent of its trade, and the capacity of the navy to protect and increase it at the expense of its rivals. This had a decisive influence on British war strategy. In 1801 Dundas told the Commons that:

[1] To William Pitt, 9 July 1794, in A. Aspinall and E. A. Smith, *English Historical Documents*, xi (Oxford, 1959), pp. 123–4.

from our insular situation, from our limited population not admitting of extensive continental operations, and from our importance depending in so material a degree upon the extent of our commerce and navigation, it is obvious, that . . . the primary object of attention ought to be, by what means we can most effectually increase those resources on which depend our naval superiority. . . . Navigation and commerce are inseparably connected, and that nation must be the most powerful maritime state which possesses the most extensive commerce.[2]

It was obvious, he added, 'that upon the possession of distant and colonial commerce the extent of our trade must in a great degree depend.' To preserve and increase that trade by breaking the French attempt to strangle further inland expansion of British North America, Britain embarked upon the military operations on the Ohio in 1754–5 that eventually precipitated the Seven Years War. To defend the integrity of its expanding empire Britain sought to subdue its rebellious American colonists in 1775–6, opening the opportunity for a Franco-Spanish war of revenge. To protect its trade and empire by keeping the Dutch fleet and empire out of French control, Britain went to war with Revolutionary France in 1793. To counter Napoleon's creeping expansion on the continent, which threatened to continue and extend overseas to the Middle East and threaten British commercial control of India, Britain refused to restore captured Malta and renewed war with France in 1803.

The extent of the national war effort

The long series of wars from 1739 to 1815 were therefore a contest of empires, fought with a mounting intensity from 1756. They were responsible, in Linda Colley's words, for 'forging the nation' from the disparate kingdoms and colonies of the British crown by focusing attention on what Britons had in common that they wished to defend against their enemies. Shared values of Protestantism, property, liberty, and empire, combined with active leadership from the ruling elite and a growing appreciation of the virtues of their monarchy

[2] W. Cobbett, *The Parliamentary History of England from the Earliest Period to the Year 1803*, xxxv (London, 1819), col. 1072.

drew the vast majority of the British people together in a sustained collective national war effort.

For a nation traditionally hostile to taxation and to standing armies, the extent of this national war effort is staggering. Popular prejudices against the military were set aside in an unprecedented mobilization of the nation's manpower into the armed forces. Stephen Conway has calculated the national mobilization of males of military age as 1 in 16 in the War of the Austrian Succession, 1 in 10 in the Seven Years War, and between 1 in 7 and 1 in 8 in the American War, while a government calculation during the Napoleonic Wars in 1805 put the nearly 804,000 under arms as more than 1 in 5, and Clive Emsley has estimated 1 in 6 in 1809. While the regular army more than doubled over this period, and the navy more than trebled, the key to successful mobilization was the development of an enormous home army of part-time civilian soldiers. The militia was reintroduced to England in 1757 and trebled in 1796; it was introduced in Ireland in 1793 and in Scotland in 1797. John Cookson has described the measures of 1796–7, which also imposed recruitment quotas for the army and navy on the localities, as 'easily the largest requisition of military manpower the British state had ever made'.[3] Increasingly, moreover, these proscriptive methods were supplemented by volunteers. Volunteer units were formed against invasion in 1779 and there was a mounting response to government calls against successive invasion threats in 1794, 1798, and 1803. Of the 804,000 under arms in 1805, 383,000 were in the Volunteers.

Patriotism, fear of French rule, whether Bourbon Catholic absolutist, or Jacobin republican atheist, or arbitrary Napoleonic imperial, played their part in this great mobilization, as did local social and political considerations. The massive call for manpower against Napoleon's threatened invasion saw Dissenters and urban middling classes seizing the opportunity to play a prominent role commensurate with their rising social position but hitherto denied them by the Anglican and landed rulers of the localities. This large infusion of domestic armed force provided an extra cushion of defence against foreign invasion and released regulars for offensive operations overseas. It provided a force against internal revolution, as when militia regiments helped suppress the 1798 Irish revolt. And it provided a

---

[3] J. E. Cookson, *The British Armed Nation 1793–1815* (Oxford, 1997), p. 36.

nursery for training and recruiting sufficient manpower to fill the losses of the regular army and sustain it at around 200,000 men throughout the long and exhausting Napoleonic Wars. This civilian and local way was found to be a politically acceptable method of expanding the armed forces in a country traditionally hostile to large professional standing armies.

It cannot be said that this extension of popular participation was painless. Each new extension of the militia was accompanied by rioting against compulsory selection by balloting—the nearest that the government of a 'freeborn' people dared get to conscription. There were riots in London in 1794 and 1795 against army recruitment methods, while seafaring communities throughout the empire resisted naval press gangs. Resentment at impressment contributed to c.40,000 desertions from the navy in each war in the second half of the century. Yet this did not stop British naval manpower expanding from nearly 45,000 men in 1748 to nearly 85,000 in 1762, to 107,000 in 1783, and to a peak of 142,000 in 1810. Nor did it significantly diminish the fighting spirit that produced a succession of great naval victories in each of these wars. However the vast influx of merchant seamen eventually infused civilian labour dispute practices. The strikes against shipowners in 1766–9 and 1792 had repercussions in the great fleet mutinies over pay and conditions in 1797 and fleet mutinies over delayed demobilization as wars ended in 1782–3 and 1801–2. Nevertheless, these wars saw the armed forces raised to previously unheard of levels for Britain which, when combined with traditional methods of hiring foreign mercenaries and recruiting from colonial and imperial populations, gave the country far greater direct military muscle than ever before.

Such an unprecedented military mobilization of its people required a far greater mobilization of Britain's wealth for state purposes than ever before. Spending on its eighteenth-century wars jumped from £93.6 million (1702–13) and £95.6 million (1739–48) to £160.6 million (1756–63) and £236.5 million in 1776–83, while the long and finally decisive wars from 1793–1815 cost a massive £1,657.9 million. This required both a remarkable transformation of attitudes, and sacrifices on a scale unknown elsewhere in Europe. Taxes soared from £6.9 million in 1755 to £79.1 million in 1816, and even in deflated 'real' terms (in constant values based on 1700 prices) from £6.83 million in 1755 to £24.64 million in 1803–12. Although part of this can be attributed to economic and population expansion, taxation levels undoubtedly increased faster than physical output from about 1775 and stand in stark contrast to the French performance. Relative to the size of their respective populations and economies, the two wars 1756–63 and 1775–83 took the British tax burden from just above that of the French to nearly double, and then in the great wars from 1793–1815 to triple that of France which grew little from former levels.

The general level of national acceptance of this enormous increase, however reluctant, is extraordinary. Only the thirteen oldest North American colonies refused to comply. Britain made itself the most highly taxed nation in Europe. There were even times, when invasion threatened, that voluntary subscriptions were donated beyond tax requirements—in 1778–9, and most notably in 1798 when £2.2 million were raised by this means. The vast increase was helped by the increasing proportion of revenue raised by indirect taxes, from 65 per cent at the start of the century to 82 per cent before the Younger Pitt increased direct taxes dramatically in 1798–9, so that the impact was spread across a broad range of consumption rather than loaded on incomes. Sensitive political management often replaced the most unpopular new taxes and conceded local control of the assessment and collection of direct taxes (similar to its local methods for increasing the armed forces). Equally significant was the scrutiny of the national finances conceded to parliament and, through the press, to public opinion.

Expanded tax revenues, backed by national consent through parliament, increased the government's ability to borrow. This also eased the burden of new taxes, which did not have to pay all war costs immediately but only the interest on the loans. Whereas £29.7 million were borrowed to meet the costs of the 1739–48 war, £60 million were raised for that of 1756–63, £94.6 million for 1776–83, and £440.3 million for 1793–1815. The funded National Debt increased 80 per cent as a result of the Seven Years War, a further 82 per cent in the American War, and a massive 217 per cent in the Revolutionary and Napoleonic Wars. In 1755 it stood at £71.8 million, and in 1816 it was £733.6 million. This level of state indebtedness horrified contemporaries and at times shook confidence in the credit system. A run on gold in 1797 forced the government to suspend cash payments, but a rallying around by the business community and decisive measures to increase tax levels and so reduce the borrowing requirement enabled the economy to survive and even grow in the new paper-money system. The escalating size of the National Debt again indicates the extent of national investment in these wars. While foreigners also contributed, the vast majority of the sums loaned came from the British public. It did so by buying stock from the banking houses which contracted with the government, though in 1796 Pitt went direct to the public to raise an £18 million 'Loyalty Loan'. By 1815 there was a vast rentier class committed to the regime by having a stake in its success through possession of government securities in the National Debt.

Impulses to the national commitment

This degree of national commitment made Britain a formidable opponent in the second half of the eighteenth century. In 1782, despite all the British reverses of the American War, the French foreign minister still urged his Spanish ally to make a compromise peace, pointing to the exhaustion and lassitude of the French navy 'which contrasts in a disadvantageous manner with the energy which not only the sailors but the entire English nation eagerly manifests'.[4] This was a level of individual patriotic involvement unmatched in Europe until the French Revolution. A visiting German Pastor, Carl Moritz, noted in 1782, that:

when one sees here how the lowliest carter shows an interest in public affairs; how the smallest children enter into the spirit of the nation; how everyone feels himself a man and an Englishman—as good as his King and his King's minister—it brings to mind thoughts very different from those we know when we watch the soldiers drilling in Berlin.[5]

Another German Pastor, Gebhardt Wenderborn, asserted in 1791 that 'even an English beggar, at the sight of a well-dressed Frenchman or any other stranger, still thinks himself superior, and says within himself, I am glad I am not a foreigner.'[6] The superior values that roused the nation were evoked by the Younger Pitt in April 1798 when

[4] See note 14 below.
[5] C. P. Moritz, *Journey of a German in England in 1782*, trans. and ed. R. Nettal (London, 1965), p. 56.
[6] G. F. A. Wenderborn, *A View of England towards the Close of the Eighteenth Century* (2 vols.; London, 1791), vol. i, p. 375.

rallying the country against the threat of invasion: they were 'contending for liberty, for order, for property, for honour, for law, for religion, and even for existence'.[7]

Liberty loomed large in all attempts to stimulate British war efforts. 'No Power can stand the deadly Stroke / That's given from hands & hearts of Oak, / with Liberty to back em!' proclaimed a Hogarth print when invasion threatened in 1756.[8] At the end of the century, a seaman Charles Reece Pemberton, described how:

> as often as he had seen days in the year, the English sailor had been told that he was 'a true born Briton' . . . he was told that peer or peasant, his rights were the same: he was told that glorious independence and freedom from the scathe of tyranny were his inalienable heritage . . . and . . . that an unflinching spirit in resisting oppression, and driving back encroachment, and in insisting on and maintaining all these privileges and blessings, were the characteristics which distinguished a manly Englishman—a bold Briton, from all other men in the universe.[9]

It was emotive language, and historians have not been slow to contrast it with the reality for many unenfranchised working men and women regulated by authoritarian labour legislation and the poor laws. Nevertheless, in a decentralized state lacking a large professional bureaucracy, standing army, or police force, government depended on local consent, accommodation, and participation. Local rulers too had to earn their authority. The public was not just reliant on elections to make its feelings known, but acted by petition, demonstration, and targeted riot. Tension was integral to relationships and part of a bargaining process that was fundamental to British political culture. Both national and local rulers recognized that there were limits to their authority and that they too were subject to the law. At the state trial of radical leaders in 1794 the prime minister himself answered to a defence subpoena to give evidence in court on his former activities as a parliamentary reformer. When juries acquitted the first three accused, the rest were released.

The defence of liberty was a potent rallying call against foreign enemies, but it also made freeborn Britons sensitive to the actions of

---

[7] W. S. Hathaway (ed.), *The Speeches of the Rt Hon. William Pitt* (4 vols.; London, 1806), vol. iii, p. 275.

[8] W. Hogarth, 'The Invasion' (1756), plate 2.

[9] C. R. Pemberton, *The Autobiography of Pel. Verjuice* (London, 1929), p. 147.

their own government. This was spectacularly demonstrated in the 1760s by John Wilkes when he represented the government's heavy-handed attacks on an irritating opponent as a threat to 'The liberty of all peers and gentlemen—and (what touches me more sensibly) that of all the middling and inferior set of people, who stand most in need of protection.'[10] In a series of challenges to government the cry of 'Wilkes and Liberty' triumphed over its use of general warrants as a means of disciplining the press (1763–5), its overturning of the rights of the Middlesex electors in declaring his defeated opponent elected in his stead in 1768–9 (expunged from the parliamentary record in 1782), and parliament's efforts to prevent press publication of its debates in 1771. A London simmering with social and economic unrest in 1768–9 adopted Wilkes as the symbol of irreverent defiance of authority around which a parliamentary reform movement was developed independent of the oligarchic parliamentary elite. Wilkes's imprisonment for seditious libel in 1768 turned him into a martyr for liberty, in which Londoners shared when troops fired on rioting supporters in St George's Fields outside his prison.

Liberty was thus a double-edged weapon. Nevertheless on the two occasions when the public had to decide between alternate causes claiming to champion liberty—when Britain challenged the American Revolution and the French Revolution—patriotism prevailed. While Wilkes and a substantial minority opposed the use of force in America, the majority rallied to the government and this increased when the absolutist Bourbon powers intervened. Francophobia and revolutionary violence made the overwhelming majority profoundly mistrustful of French liberty.

Anti-Catholicism also roused the nation against external enemies and was almost as double-edged. One of Hogarth's 1756 prints depicted the invading French army prominently accompanied by a priest with an axe and a sled full of instruments of torture, idolatrous statues, and a plan for a monastery at Blackfriars. Another threatened invasion in 1779 produced a print depicting the devil, wearing a papal tiara, in league with the Bourbon rulers of France and Spain in *The Family Compact*. Such prejudices, however, caused problems with the Catholic populations of the British Isles, considerable in the Scottish

[10] J. Almon, *The Correspondence of the Late John Wilkes with his Friends*, i (London, 1806), p. 117, n. 1.

Highlands and the great majority in Ireland. Moreover Britain's successful imperial wars brought increasing numbers of colonial French and Spanish Catholics under its control. Government needed to conciliate old and new Catholic subjects to prevent them becoming a security risk, and, after the mid-century wars removed the Jacobite menace, to recruit from all of its available manpower resources.

In the most populous newly conquered colonies, Grenada in the Caribbean and Canada, the Test Acts were relaxed to allow Catholics a share in government. Relief Acts were granted to Catholics in England in 1778 and 1791, and in Ireland in 1792 and in 1793 when they were admitted to the franchise and their embodiment into a new Irish militia followed. Government needs clashed with popular anti-Catholic prejudices. The Quebec Act of 1774 antagonized Protestant British North America, admitting Catholics into a crown-appointed legislative council and allowing Catholic clergy to retain their right to tithes. Demonstrations and petitions scotched Scottish Relief proposals in 1779 and encouraged a similar campaign in England by Lord George Gordon's Protestant Association. This escalated into the Gordon Riots, the most damaging of the century, which raged in London for a week in June 1780 until suppressed by 10,000 troops, with 281 rioters killed and 25 hanged. Rising sectarian violence made Ireland a defensive liability after 1793. The Younger Pitt forced through an Act of Union in 1800, intending a repeal of the Test Acts to follow to reconcile Catholics, and hoping that Irish Protestants would feel protected by junction with the British Protestant majority. However, like his predecessors in the 1770s, he found that his government's pro-Catholic policies ran far ahead of national prejudices. When the king declared his opposition to emancipation, the most powerful and successful prime minister since Walpole conceded defeat and resigned in 1801. Six years later the Ministry of 'All-the-Talents', again seeking to strengthen the war effort, likewise fell in the face of the king's popular rejection of its attempts to enable Catholics to become field officers.

Protestantism nevertheless was a declining force in rousing national unity. The end of the danger of a Catholic Jacobite restoration split the Protestant alliance. Irish Protestants felt able to pursue a more independent line from their British co-religionists, and similarly Dissenters became more restless at their political subordination to Anglicanism. In the 1770s they began their own campaign for relief, culminating in three unsuccessful attempts to repeal the Test and

Corporation Acts in 1787, 1789, and 1790. Many turned to advocating parliamentary reform when they got so little from parliament. Many sympathized with their American co-religionists and opposed the use of force against them in the 1770s. Numbers also sympathized with the religious freedom attained by the French Revolution and opposed war with that regime in the 1790s. The most active religious supporters of the government and the national war effort at all times, were the established church of England and its Scottish counterpart.

Political reactions to the wars

The wars accelerated the growing politicization of the nation. This was reflected by the growth of the press. Stamped newspaper sales increased from 7.3 million in 1750 to 16 million in 1800. The outbreak of the Seven Years War alone raised sales by one-quarter as the press responded to the growing demand for news and opinion in these momentous times and helped disseminate them further through the clubs, societies, and coffee houses of an urbanizing society.

War policy affected everyone. Rising taxation limited private expenditure and hit both investment and trade. Government borrowing competed with the needs of private credit, and the escalating National Debt threatened to destroy confidence in the credit system that lubricated the British economy. Government efforts to solve problems occasioned by the wars aroused major merchant/ manufacturer petitioning movements which helped force the withdrawal of the Stamp Act in 1766, Pitt's Irish Commercial Propositions in 1785, and the Orders in Council in 1812. While the expanding middling classes took pride at their part in the imperial mercantile achievement and the increase of national wealth and the financial strength of state, their sense of new-found status and importance to the nation made them more ready to voice and organize dissatisfaction resulting from the policies and actions of their aristocratic rulers.

Inevitably the fluctuating fortunes of wars, their cost, economic dislocation, and instances of mismanagement aroused discontents among a patriotic people. These were largely channelled into attempts to bring pressure on parliament for economical reform, parliamentary reform, and efforts at a reformation of morals. Protest movements largely looked to purify and reinvigorate the existing system rather than create an entirely new one.

The strongest pressure was for economical reform that would stem the rocketing growth and expense of government occasioned by the wars. Traditional Country suspicions that court/government extravagance and corruption were artificially inflating costs and producing administrative inefficiency combined with concerns that the requirements of war strengthened the power and size of the executive, that this threatened the balance of the 1688 Constitution, and that, in the words of Dunning's Resolution, passed by the Commons in 1780, 'the influence of the Crown has increased, is increasing, and ought to be diminished.' Through a series of public scrutinies—commissions on the public accounts (1780–6) and on public fees (1785–9), select committees on finance (1797–8) and on public expenditure (1807–12)—governments sought to show the public that their money was not being misused. Redundant offices were abolished, salaries replaced payment by fees, but these efforts were overtaken by the needs of the Great War after 1793 (state officials increased from 16,000 to 25,000 between 1797 and 1815) until peace after 1815 enabled horrified public opinion to sweep away both the residue of surviving *ancien régime* sinecure posts and also much of the extended 'military-fiscal' state designed for war, leaving in their place the small-government laissez-faire state of the nineteenth century.

Whereas economical reform was the majority desire of the country, parliamentary reform was the wish of a small, albeit growing, minority which stirred only intermittently, usually when confidence in the effectiveness of economical reform was least and more radical means were felt necessary to advance it. Demand revived in the late 1760s in a London proud of its contribution to victory in the Seven Years War, chafing at the domination of the aristocratic landed elite, dissatisfied with fiscal policies that seemed to exacerbate rather than settle the economic turbulence following the war, and seeking a decisive resolution of the issues raised by John Wilkes. What was new was the degree of organization created by Wilkes's metropolitan supporters. The Society of the Supporters of the Bill of Rights was formed in 1769 to pay Wilkes's debts, but developed a programme of parliamentary reform independently from the control of the political opposition in parliament. However Wilkes's disinterest and splits within the Society limited its impact outside London, and it lost out when attention switched to the mounting American crisis in which the reformers took the unpopular line of siding with the colonists.

The cost and mismanagement of the American War revitalized the movement in the early 1780s, adding Christopher Wyvill's County Association movement to the successors of the Wilkesite Bill of Rights Society—the Westminster Committee and the Society for Constitutional Information. Economic reform, peace, and renewed prosperity then dwindled support until in the early 1790s it revived again, stimulated by the centenary of the 1688 Revolution, by Dissenter disgruntlement at their failed campaign against the Test Acts, and by the example of the new American Constitution of 1787–8 and of the French Revolution. Alongside the reactivated Society for Constitutional Information sprang up new bodies such as the London Corresponding Society and clubs in provincial manufacturing towns that drew in new adherents from the lesser middling classes and artisans, inspired by Tom Paine's *Rights of Man* (1791–2) which castigated their rulers, declared government simple enough for all to participate and advocated a constitutional convention to make an entirely fresh start on the American and French model. Except when economic distress swelled the ranks of their open-air public meetings, they nevertheless remained small in numbers against the groundswell of patriotic support for the war with Revolutionary France and for punitive government action against their potentially revolutionary efforts to gain popular support. Finally it revived again in a less organized but much wider movement in the late 1800s as the result of high taxation and corruption scandals which forced the resignation (and impeachment) of the First Lord of the Admiralty in 1805 and of the Commander in Chief in 1809. Only at this time of economic hardship, sky-high taxation, and with the desired defeat of Napoleon as remote as ever, did a broader popular support start to rally, about 1809–12, behind William Cobbett's message that only parliamentary reform could kill 'Old Corruption' and secure relief from high taxes.

Yet theirs was never the generally accepted solution. They never developed the momentum of the economical reform movement. There were wide divergences of object among parliamentary reformers, usually related to their social position—for annual or triennial elections; more county or more urban seats; major, moderate, or no extension of the franchise; restoration or innovation. The extremism of some impaired the credibility of moderates who might have stood more chance of success. The ideological sympathy of many reformers with the American cause in the 1770s and the French in the 1790s alienated the patriotic majority. The movement depended on economic crisis, when remedies were sought from parliament, for much of its popular support, but this melted away in better times and when government seemed to be conscientiously pursuing economical reform.

The wars also accentuated fears that moral decay might sap the national character, which might become too enervated to overcome their enemies. Those lauding the achievement of a new age of virtue and commerce were challenged by others fearing that it was producing the opposite—luxury, extravagance, venality, political and moral dissolution—leading to national decline and imminent ruin. The dangers were most conspicuously apparent in the vast sums being made from India. If Robert Clive's £400,000 was unique, others made over £100,000 and wealth brought home by these British 'nabobs' was invested in seats in parliament (19 in the 1768 election) to protect their corrupt gains. Horace Walpole lamented in 1773 that England had become 'A sink of Indian wealth, filled by nabobs and emptied by Macaronis [fashionable fops]! A senate sold and despised! . . . A gaming, robbing, wrangling, railing nation, without principles, genius, character, or allies; the overgrown shadow of what it was!'[11] There was indeed pride in having won what Sir George Macartney in the same year was the first to describe as 'this vast empire on which the sun never sets',[12] but a classically educated propertied class knew from Tacitus how the Roman empire had been destroyed by enervating luxury and corruption. It was not simply through chance that Edward Gibbon began to research his *Decline and Fall of the Roman Empire* a year after the Peace of Paris, and the danger was there for all to see when his masterpiece was published in 1776 as the American colonies revolted.

One of the declared objects of Wyvill's County Association move-

---

[11] To Sir Horace Mann, 13 July 1773, in W. S. Lewis (ed.), *The Yale Edition of Horace Walpole's Correspondence*, xxiii (New Haven and London, 1967), p. 499.

[12] Sir G. Macartney, *An Account of Ireland in 1773* . . . (London, 1773), p. 55, quoted in P. J. Marshall (ed.), *Oxford History of the British Empire: The Eighteenth Century* (Oxford, 1998), p. 262.

ment, campaigning in 1779–84 for economical and parliamentary reform, was 'the restoration of the national morals'. A growing number thought such potential cancers needed to be eradicated, and pressed for improved moral standards in government which was to lead to the impeachment of Warren Hastings, former Governor-General of India, in 1786–7, and of Lord Melville, former Treasurer of the Navy in 1805–6. It was also a powerful impulse, together with the religious revival, towards the campaign to abolish the national sin of the slave trade, which was held to make its participants degenerate and contemptuous of individual liberty. William Wilberforce declared, in his *Practical View of the Prevailing System of Professed Christians* in 1798, that 'We bear upon us but too plainly the marks of a declining empire', and felt that divine retribution was falling on the nation for its religious and moral decline. The nation was roused to massive petitions—over 100 in 1789, 519 with 400,000 signatures in 1792, and, after abolition of the British slave trade was finally secured in 1807, an enormous 750,000 signatories sought to ban its international revival in the peace negotiations of 1814.

Problems of empire

One of the greatest impacts of the wars was on the empire for which they were fought. Empire indeed created as many problems as it solved. The great imperial victories of the Seven Years War loaded Britain with debt and new administrative and defensive burdens throughout the world.

As defence against any Bourbon war of revenge and as protection after a 1763–4 Indian uprising, 10,000 troops were left in garrisons across the American colonies after the war. Against colonial wishes, attempts were made to avoid antagonizing the Indian by restricting western settlement. Colonists protested against the imposition of a feared standing army on them, and were incensed when, to help pay for it, the premier George Grenville imposed a more stringent sugar duty in 1764 and an internal stamp tax in 1765, levied by authority of parliament rather than their own assemblies. The response of the older North American colonies accorded with British traditions. The New York Assembly, petitioning against the Sugar Act, declared that exemption from ungranted, involuntary taxation must be the grand principle of every free state without which 'there can be no liberty, no happiness, no security'. An anti Stamp Act Congress of nine colonies in 1765 condemned its 'manifest tendency to subvert the rights and liberties of the colonists'. Riots and a boycott of British goods led to repeal of the acts in 1766, but when a subsequent Chancellor of the Exchequer, Charles Townshend, imposed a series of import duties in 1767 to help pay for colonial administration, resistance was renewed until all but that on tea were repealed in 1770.

The extent of victory in India also caused problems, particularly when in 1765 the East India Company took over collection of taxes in Bengal which, with 20 million population, was bigger than the British Isles. Government claimed a share of these revenues to meet its own financial burdens, and secured £400,000 a year as the price of re-charter in 1767. However famine in Bengal, local wars, and trade depression in the late 1760s–early 1770s, brought the Company to the verge of bankruptcy and jeopardized the British position in India. A government takeover however would have so vastly increased its patronage as to threaten the balance of the Constitution. For another decade governments were shy of such political dynamite. Instead the Company was propped up by Lord North's 1773 Regulating Act with a £1.4m loan and the right to market its tea direct to America. In return a Governor-General was imposed, appointed by the crown but subject to majority decisions of his council.

These decisions were made in an ad hoc way, addressing problems as they arose. It cannot be said that there was any coherent, structured, overall imperial plan or policy. Rather there was a general wish, symbolized by the creation of a new Secretary of State for the Colonies in 1768, to strengthen control over what was a conglomerate assortment of farming settlements, plantation colonies, trading factories, fishing bases, naval bases, a wholly native Indian province in Bengal, and a subordinate sister kingdom in Ireland, all with differing administrative systems, economies, and societies.

It was a situation that could produce discordant policy decisions at the same time, and in 1773–4 this happened in a way which precipitated revolution in America. The decision to give the East India Company a monopoly of the sale of tea in the colonies would raise revenue from the last surviving Townshend duty. Boston rioters therefore dumped the tea into the harbour, for which government punished Massachusetts by the 'Intolerable Acts', altering its charter to give more control to the Governor. At the same time the Quebec Act passed parliament, making concessions to Catholics and instead of a traditional elected Assembly installing one nominated by the Governor. No connection was intended between these measures in London, but connections were made in America. As the South Carolinian 'patriot', David Ramsay, later remembered: 'It was inculcated on the people, that if the ministerial schemes were suffered to take effect in Massachusetts, the other colonies must expect the loss of their charters, and that a new government would be imposed upon them, like that projected for Quebec.'[13]

This was more than the thirteen oldest North American mainland colonies were prepared to stand. Their self-confidence had rocketed along with their population and with the triumph of the Seven Years War, a result in which they believed their military contribution and their booming trade had made the crucial difference, an opinion reinforced by the subsequent success of their commercial boycotts in defeating parliament's attempts to tax them. Moreover with the French expelled from Canada, they had less need to be subservient to British policies that clashed with their interests. Their resistance brought the issue of parliamentary control over the colonial assemblies to the point where the British government determined to resort to armed force to reassert authority. Fighting broke out in 1775 and in 1776 the American colonies declared their independence.

The American War was Ireland's opportunity. There was much in which Ireland could sympathize with the colonists, who deliberately excluded Irish trade from their boycotts of the 1760s. Chancellor of the Exchequer Townshend's elder brother was Lord Lieutenant of Ireland from 1767 to 1772 where he sought to win back political management from local undertakers and to make government less dependent on the financial controls of the Irish parliament. Irish and Americans exchanged protesting manifestos. The Irish Protestant Ascendancy however were not prepared to go down the American path of independence for fear of losing control of the majority Catholic population. They found ways of getting their ends by other means. Volunteers formed to defend Ireland against French invasion

---

[13] L. H. Cohen (ed.), *The History of the American Revolution in Two Volumes by David Ramsay* (Indianapolis, 1990), vol. i, p. 106.

in 1779 were used to bring pressure on the British government, which, afraid of seeing Ireland go the way of America, first removed most of the remaining restrictions on Irish trade in 1779–80, and then in 1782–3 repealed the legislation by which Ireland's parliament had been declared subordinate to the British parliament and Irish legislation subjected to the approval of the British privy council. Taking advantage of America's successful resistance, the Irish parliament thus gained a large measure of autonomy from British control.

Many feared that the empire was disintegrating, but ultimately its *ancien régime* character, so disliked by bureaucratic centralizers in London, proved its major strength. The different circumstances and traditions of the various colonies and dependencies meant that they were developing at different paces and had little in common. Attempts by the rebel colonists to draw support from Canada, the West Indies, and Ireland failed. Only thirteen of Britain's twenty-eight American colonies rebelled and forced their independence in 1776–83. Ireland found alternative ways to what it wanted within the empire. The uncoordinated nature of imperial policy came to the rescue still more strikingly in the 1790s, when it was possible for British ministers to remove liberties from Catholics in Grenada at the same time as they granted further Catholic Relief in Ireland. Revolt consequently broke out among the discontented French Catholic population of Grenada at the earliest opportunity in 1795, and was crushed by a massive concentration of the British army in the following year, while the irruption of discontent in Ireland was delayed until after this crisis was over.

Tensions remained within Ireland where the new access to the empire fostered the growth of Irish prosperity and population and precipitated competition for land between Protestant and Catholic tenants. A land war developed, fought out by secret societies—Ulster Peep o'day Boys and the Orange Order (1795) facing Catholic 'Defenders'. In 1791 the Society of United Irishmen also emerged from radical members of the merchant and professional classes, campaigning for political and religious equality to break the oligarchic hold of the Ascendancy ruling elite. After the recall of a Lord Lieutenant sympathetic to immediate Catholic emancipation in 1795, they appealed to France for aid. When only the weather prevented a French expedition from landing in Bantry Bay in 1796, the Ascendancy embarked on a brutal disarming of the Catholic population that precipitated an unsuccessful, uncoordinated and partial rebellion of Defenders and United Irishmen, belatedly and inadequately assisted by the French, in 1798. A final isolated United Irish rising in Dublin was quickly crushed in 1803.

The quest for a national leader

The fluctuating course of these long and exhausting wars imposed severe tests on national morale. When the Reverend John Brown published his best-selling *Estimate of the Manners and Principles of the Times* in 1757–8, calling for national moral regeneration under the guiding hand of a virtuous great minister, he was reflecting a widely felt need for leadership in these times of crises.

This yearning for a unifying heroic leader recurred repeatedly. The role was formulated in the Seven Years War around the image and achievement of William Pitt the Elder, subsequently earl of Chatham. Pitt was portrayed as 'the Great Commoner', uncontaminated by the corruption of court honours, places, and pensions, and as a self-styled 'independent Whig' unbound by divisive party prejudices but inspired by honest and independent 'Patriot' spirit. Pitt's leadership style was vital to Britain's spectacular success. He exuded self-confidence, communicating energy and courage to others. Intolerant of restraints, he brought to the war a restless, aggressive energy to strike at the enemy as often and as widely as possible. The range of simultaneous British offensive enterprise throughout the world was unprecedented. He made many mistakes, but momentum on so many fronts masked these by producing victories elsewhere.

The Seven Years War was the first that Britain fought predominantly outside Europe, and Pitt secured general national agreement behind this 'blue water' policy. A government of national unity was formed in the alliance of Pitt's 'Patriot' supporters with Newcastle's 'Old Corps' of Walpolean Whigs. The last prospect of a Jacobite restoration faded away, killed by the navy's defeat of the 1759 French invasion threat at Quiberon Bay, while even Tories rallied to Pitt's victorious war leadership and the 'blue water' strategy they had so long advocated. This unifying mood was taken further with the death in 1760 of the German George II and the accession of the

English-born King George III. The new king was himself imbued with 'Patriot' idealism. He 'gloried in the name of Briton', and wanted the best people rather than the best party or faction to govern, removing in the process the tacit ban on Tory gentry holding local office. Old Whig/Tory party distinctions melted away as Whigs and Tories merged into a single ruling class.

National unity forged in the heat of war crisis, however, came apart in the cooling winds of peace from 1763. The Pitt legend became bigger than the big man himself and set impossibly high standards both for him and all who followed. Neither Pitt nor the young and inexperienced king was able to live up to the high expectations aroused by the euphoria of victory. Pitt's arrogant and demanding individualism alienated monarch and politicians, while to the public he appeared flawed when he resigned in a pique with his colleagues in 1761, taking a pension for himself and a peerage for his wife which he subsequently adopted himself as earl of Chatham on returning briefly as the sick and remote leader of a hopelessly fragmented ministry in 1766. The king incurred the distrust of politicians by appearing too much guided by his disliked Scottish former tutor, the earl of Bute, fear of whose influence remained long after it had been discarded. George III's determination to free himself from the party power of the 'Old Corps' of Whigs only produced competing factions and a decade of government instability with six ministries between his accession in 1760 and the appointment of Lord North in 1770.

Both the crown and the politicians suffered from the consequent national disillusionment, circumstances in which a popular counter-hero such as Wilkes could flourish. Yet Wilkes too ultimately failed to live up to the ideological aspirations of his supporters, settling for a lucrative office in the government of the City of London. Within the political elite, part of the 'Old Corps' of Whigs which briefly formed the 1765–6 ministry of the earl of Rockingham blamed national ills and their own exclusion from office on corrupt crown influence. Their propagandist, Edmund Burke in his *Thoughts on the Causes of the Present Discontents* (1770) claimed that the official ministry was a sham and the king was governing through a secret cabinet, backed by a party of 'king's friends'. He identified a role for a party of the aristocratic owners of the country as the natural defenders of liberty against threats from a corrupt executive. Despite the slim basis of truth in his allegations, Burke's pamphlet became the foundation document for a new self-styled Whig party claiming to inherit the pure principles of the Glorious Revolution of 1688. Small in numbers initially and fragmented again in the 1790s, a rump under Charles James Fox and Charles Grey continued and became the basis for the development of the nineteenth-century Whig party. Others, however, were not prepared to accept the claims to such a virtuous role from the owners of the 'rotten boroughs' who returned so many unrepresentative MPs to parliament.

For a while stability and confidence were restored by the financial and parliamentary skills of Lord North, premier from 1770 to 1782. North's conscientious and at times innovative attempts to tackle the problems left over from the Seven Years War deserved better than his subsequent public damning reputation as the man who lost America. Indeed he lacked the drive and decisiveness of the Elder Pitt as a war leader, but, faced with a far more difficult war against the majority population of North America and the combined maritime powers of Europe, it is hard to see that Pitt could have done better, and no one else emerged to do so. In consequence 1780–4 saw a real crisis of confidence in the political leadership of the nation. The established politicians squabbled for power, and former heated rivals North and Fox joined in a coalition to oust the king's choice, Shelburne, and produced a solution to India that gave control over its patronage to parliament which they dominated. A disillusioned public decided that the Coalition was unprincipled, their India Bill beyond consti-tutional proprieties, and their conduct immoral and symptomatic of the evils which had caused failure in the American War. With fears of excessive crown influence reduced by the king's recent political defeats and the start of economic reform, opinion rallied towards George III, particularly when he turned to William Pitt the Younger, 24-year-old son of the Elder Pitt, to defeat the Coalition and their India Bill.

In a period of national gloom, when the *Newcastle Chronicle* lam-ented (19 August 1786) that 'Everything human . . . has its period: Nations, like mortal men, advance only to decline; dismembered empire and diminished glory mark a Crisis in the constitution; and, if the volume of our fame be not closed, we have read the most brilliant pages of our history', it was the Younger Pitt who turned things round and restored national self-confidence.

Pitt was an entirely fresh start: an independent Whig like his father;

too young to have been involved in the political quarrels and disasters of the previous decade; and dedicated to the rule of virtue and reform to purify and reinvigorate the failing system. He carried through measures of economic and financial reform. In the 1780s he urged parliamentary reform (and in 1785 was the first prime minister to do so) to restore confidence between the Commons and ministers, and between the people and the Commons. He took the moral approach by approving the impeachment of Warren Hastings and campaigning for the abolition of the slave trade. In fact his policies diminished the need for parliamentary reform so that his motions were defeated, but he restored national unity and self-confidence instead by his financial policies. He fostered the great outburst of entrepreneurial activity that produced rapid economic recovery after the American War by helping to re-establish business confidence through lowering tariffs, and above all by his 1786 Sinking Fund which promised to reduce and eventually eliminate the National Debt. He brought stability to the empire by increased central control through his 1784 India Act, 1791 Canada Act, and the 1800 Act of Union with Ireland. He revived Britain's international position by joining with Prussia in 1787 to win back from France the predominant influence over the Dutch.

What Pitt did was to appropriate Patriotism from its traditional role as a weapon used to attack negligent and corrupt governments, and deploy it as the characteristic of the king's ministry. In this way he enabled George III to emerge from his earlier unpopularity into a symbol of British values, a transformation enhanced by comparison of his thrift, dedication, and family virtues with the licentiousness of his heir when the latter appeared likely to become Regent during the king's illness in 1788–9. It gave Pitt's government a national support beyond his predecessors that he was not afraid to summon to his aid against all dangers.

Addresses from the localities to the throne were encouraged in 1784, 1788–9, 1792, and 1795. He spoke on behalf of petitioning movements on parliamentary reform in 1783 and 1785, and to abolish the slave trade in 1788 and 1792—the latter three as prime minister and the first to do so. He encouraged the formation of loyalist associations in 1792 and military volunteer movements in 1794, 1798, and 1803–4. He successfully invited national participation in his 1796 Loyalty Loan and the patriotic subscription in 1798. The Younger Pitt, perhaps more than any other politician of the century, stimulated the politicization of the nation and, at least in his own lifetime, ensured that it rallied to crown and constitution against internal radical extremists and external French Revolutionary enemies.

It was largely due to Pitt that Britain was able to respond to the extremity of the dangers in the Great Wars with France between 1793 and 1815 by so vastly increasing national efforts beyond all that had gone before. He was able to persuade the majority of the need to restrict liberty in order to preserve liberty when he introduced punitive measures (moderate by twentieth-century standards) against radical agitation and the small number of revolutionary conspirators during the war emergency. He produced the great patriotic rallying which brought over half the opposition into a government of national unity in 1794 and reached peaks of patriotic enthusiasm in the face of threats of invasion in 1798 and 1803–5. Perhaps most important of all it was confidence in his financial abilities which allowed levels of government expenditure to reach undreamed heights; which sustained financial confidence when Britain was forced to abandon the gold standard to continue the war in 1797; which persuaded the public to accept increased direct taxation for the first time in a century by the incomes tax of 1798–9 that dramatically increased tax revenues; and which contained fears that an escalating National Debt would cause national bankruptcy, thus enabling government to borrow beyond all that had gone before.

Yet even confidence in Pitt eventually wavered when he failed to bring a successful end to the wars, and his second ministry of 1804–6 was on the verge of defeat when he died, exhausted by the effort. Already a crisis of confidence in the national leadership was re-emerging which his successors could not dispel. Corruption scandals, a duel between the two ministers directing the war, Castlereagh and Canning, in 1809, humiliating reverses (at Buenos Aires in 1807 and at Walcheren in 1809), even humiliating victories (when the defeated French army in Portugal was transported home with its loot by the Convention of Cintra in 1808) revived demands for economic, parliamentary, and moral reform. Even the assassination of a prime minister, the competent Spencer Perceval, by a madman failed to move a frustrated and disillusioned public in 1812, a year of economic unrest and Luddite machine breaking in the Midlands. It was the old King George III, who finally lost his mind in 1810 and was replaced by a Regency, who remained as the symbol of national resistance to Napoleonic tyranny.

Ultimately national morale was sustained by a new-found belief in the strength of Britain's resources to continue the struggle against Napoleonic military domination. Intensive investigations into the national capacity to meet the heightened demands of the Great War, which included the first national census in 1801, showed a 500 per cent increase in national income and a 70 per cent increase in population since estimates made a century before. They gave confidence in the sustainability of manpower resources and in the internal dynamic of the economy fostered by the strength of the home market and the growth of manufacturing production and exports (largely to areas from which rivals were excluded by the navy). Although there were petitioning movements to end the war in 1806–7 and 1812–13 in order to facilitate the growth of this economic power as a counter to Napoleon, the majority continued to regard economic prosperity and national independence as so much in danger from the ever-grasping ambition of Napoleon that the war should continue. Rather than the hoped-for virtuous British war leader, it was the sinister 'Corsican ogre' who sustained continued British resistance and enabled Britain's total victory.

Causes of the final victory

Britain owed its *survival* in this long struggle to its national determination to keep fighting, to its financial strength and to its sea power. It owed its ultimate *triumph* to its allies and to Napoleon.

The wars vindicated the national belief in the importance of commerce and naval power. Britain's biggest advantage over its rivals in the naval arms race was the greater size of its merchant marine and resultant pool of trained seamen. A French calculation of 1785 put British merchant tonnage as double that of France, four times that of Holland, and ten times that of Spain. The size of this shipbuilding sector enabled Britain to outbuild its rivals, British private yards increasing their production of ships of the line from 29 per cent in 1688–1755 to 52 per cent in 1756–1815, while others remained reliant on their state dockyards. It saved Britain in the American War when, in persuading the Spanish to negotiate for peace, the French Foreign Minister Vergennes admitted that 'The English have to some degree regenerated their Navy, while ours has been used up. Constructions have not been at all equivalent to consumptions.' Britain's vast reserves of merchant seamen also enabled Britain to sustain its fleets and even expand them through manning the new ships built, whereas Vergennes further confessed that 'the body of good sailors is exhausted and the officers show a lassitude in war'.[14]

However the leverage of naval power was to a considerable extent dependent on the extent of the reliance of Britain's opponents on their overseas trade and the value they set upon their overseas empires. The dramatic expansion of France's overseas trade in the century, and its consequent contribution to state finances and credit, made France particularly vulnerable until, under the French Revolution and Napoleon, France found alternative means of wealth production by plundering its continental neighbours. It took another ten years after Nelson's crushing victory over the combined Franco-Spanish fleet at Trafalgar in 1805 before Napoleon was finally beaten. Even in the best of circumstances the pressure exerted by the navy was largely economic and consequently took time to have effect. When that economic pressure was ignored, the best that the navy could achieve was to safeguard Britain from invasion and to secure and increase its trade and empire so that it had the financial means to continue fighting for as long as necessary.

In 'The Great War with France' (1793–1815) Britain's navy destroyed the fleets of its imperial rivals (see Table 6.2) and cut them off from sustaining their empires. France's wealthy Caribbean empire collapsed to slave revolt; Spain's vast South American empire disintegrated to Creole revolution, leaving Britain the dominant European power in both the Atlantic and the Pacific. Britain seized Cape Town, Ceylon, and Guiana from France's Dutch ally and acquired a virtual protectorate over its remaining East Indian possessions as well as over the empire of Britain's dependent ally Portugal. Nelson's victory at the Nile in 1798 wrecked Napoleon's attempt to carve out a new French empire in Egypt and with the conquest of Malta (1800) made Britain the dominant sea power in the Mediterranean. Napoleon's

---

[14] To Montmorin, 1 Nov. 1781, in J. R. Dull, *The French Navy and American Independence* (Princeton, 1975), p. 316.

eastern threat was used to justify the extension of British dominance over India by defeating its most dangerous native rivals, Mysore (1790–2, 1799) and the Marathas (1803–4) and building up an immense Indian army of 227,000 men (86 per cent native sepoys) by 1815 which gave it complete dominance of the shores of the Indian Ocean. Only the large ex-colonial European populations of La Plata in 1807 and the United States, provoked into war by the arbitrary British exercise of command of the seas in 1812–14, could muster sufficient strength to resist Britain's overseas power.

While the wars remained a contest for empire, Britain was less dependent on allies. The Prussian alliance in the Seven Years War was useful for protecting George II's Hanover, but by the accession of George III (less devoted to the electorate than his predecessor) the nation had become weary of the men and subsidies expended to sustain it. Although allies were eagerly sought in the American War, it was probably a blessing in disguise that none were found, since the costs of two major continental wars (in Europe and America) and a maritime war would have impaired the ability to outlast its European rivals financially that eventually saved Britain from total defeat. As long as Austrian-controlled Belgium remained neutral and free of French influence, as it was from 1757 to 1792, there was little need for Britain to involve itself in European conflict. However Revolutionary France overran Belgium in 1792 and again in 1794, when it followed with gaining control of Holland, its navy and access to its overseas naval bases. In 1796 France continued its expansion into Italy, threatening to achieve dominance in the Mediterranean. Subsequently Napoleon pressed on into Germany and Central Europe where he sought to block out British trade. From the moment it entered the European war in 1793, therefore, Britain was in urgent need of continental allies to help drive France back into its old frontiers. Increasingly Britain financed the European war effort against France: £15.75 million in subsidies and loans in 1793–1802, and a massive £49 million between 1803 and 1815. From 1808 it kept an army under Wellington in the Iberian Peninsula in support of Portuguese and Spanish attempts to assert their independence from French control. The allies it found, however, were reluctant to do all it wanted. Despite the obvious growth of French power, the obvious growth of British imperial power made potential European allies unwilling to reduce France beyond a point at which it could counterbalance

Britain. Even the Russian commander Kutusov preferred to offer Napoleon a golden bridge out of Russia because 'his succession would not fall to Russia or any other continental power, but to that which already commands the sea, and whose dominion would then be insufferable.'[15] The European powers, weakened and exhausted by their struggle with Napoleon, would have preferred to have left the beaten French emperor in 1813–14 with the Rhine frontier and his new fleet at Antwerp to match a British power that at this point was financing fully half of the allied war effort. It was only Napoleon's gambler's instinct to refuse peace and instead seek to turn defeat into total victory that forced them to destroy him, with the result, after his final crushing defeat at the hands of Wellington and Blucher's Prussians at Waterloo in 1815, that they all feared. Napoleon proved to be Britain's most potent ally in destroying all rivals to its position in 1815 as the first modern superpower. As the Prussian general Gneisenau complained: 'Great Britain has no greater obligation to any mortal on earth than to this ruffian. For through the events which he has brought about, England's greatness, prosperity, and wealth have risen high. She is now mistress of the sea and neither in this dominion nor in world trade has she now a single rival to fear'.[16]

[15] Sir Robert Wilson, *Narrative of Events during the Invasion of Russia*, ed. H. Randolph (London, 1869), pp. 233–4.
[16] Quoted in G. J. Marcus, *A Naval History of England*, ii (London, 1971), p. 501.

Figure 8 W. H. Timms's engraving of 'A View of Newcastle and Gateshead', early nineteenth century, presents a flourishing industrial port, equipped with steam as well as sail, as a place of picturesque edification and beauty.

Epilogue

Paul Langford

Waterloo brought to an end a gruelling period of warfare abroad and all kinds of social and political strains at home. The years that followed did not, however, noticeably lessen the latter. Indeed without the distraction of war, the effects of economic and political crisis seemed to many to darken the prospect still further. Yet in retrospect the United Kingdom is generally seen as having entered upon a new era. As the editor of the subsequent volume in this series observes, the nineteenth century was to be Britain's century.

It does not follow, however, that what took place was a radical break with the recent past. On the contrary much of what is taken to be so distinctive about the Victorians can be traced back to eighteenth-century developments that have featured in this volume. For example, their faith in reform, their belief in self-improvement and social improvement, and their leading role in world politics, all had an eighteenth-century prehistory.

Reform, so often pictured as the heroic achievement of the 1830s, overturning decades of reaction and corruption, is more plausibly seen as part of a campaign that went back at least to the 1760s. Electoral reform had commenced with Grenville's Act transferring disputed election hearings from the House of Commons to a committee of MPs chosen by secret ballot and with the first of a series of disenfranchisements of corrupt boroughs, that of New Shoreham in 1771. The economical reform measures of 1782 represented a significant brake on the growth of executive power in parliament. Subsequent measures under Shelburne, Pitt, and their successors, steadily eroded the influence of government on MPs and their electors. Curwen's Act of 1809 making it illegal to sell seats in parliament was passed at a time of so-called Tory dislike of anything savouring of reform.

In short, the reaction over which reformers triumphed in the 1830s was a reaction of the post-1815 years rather than a long-standing rejection of any structural change. That more sweeping reforms were not passed in the late eighteenth century simply reflected the pragmatic arguments of the day and the belief that gradual reform was sufficient to adjust an evolving system of parliamentary accountability to new demands. It would be as plausible to argue that Victorian politics was unreforming because the demands of the Chartists were denied as to view the polity of the late eighteenth century as a kind of English *ancien régime* because the root and branch parliamentary reformers of 1780 were not immediately successful.

The same might be said of other key accomplishments of the so-called age of reform. Catholic Emancipation and the repeal of the Test and Corporation Acts were not herculean assaults on unchanging edifices but the last blows of a whole battery of innovations that went back decades. Major Catholic reforms had been conceded in 1778 and 1791, as additional toleration for Protestant Dissenters had been in 1779, with matching or more generous concessions in each case in Ireland. Unitarians, the most articulate and politically active of Dissenters, gained a major and long sought-for concession in 1813 when the repeal of the Blasphemy Act of 1797 made the advocacy of anti-trinitarian ideas considerably less hazardous. Reform of local authorities and poor relief regimes belonged in a continuous process of revision and reassessment that had proceeded throughout the eighteenth century.

Even church reform began in reality with the efforts of liberal-minded bishops, and evangelically inclined clergy and laity to put their house in order by a series of measures that commenced in the 1770s. Thomas Gilbert's Acts of 1777 and 1781 were designed to improve the incidence of clerical residence by financing adequate housing. The first legislative assaults on non-residence, pluralism, and curate poverty were made in 1796, 1803, 1804, and 1813. Repeated demands for measures to improve the church's provision for urban areas were eventually to produce the Church Buildings Act of 1818. These measures were not necessarily very effective. Moreover they sprang to a considerable extent from the need to confront the challenge of the Nonconformist churches. Initiatives such as the Church Missionary Society, projected in 1799, and the National Society for the Education of the Poor, founded in 1811, belonged in a pattern of revival that forms a long prehistory to the tumults of the 1830s. But whatever their origins and intentions, they are evidence of a long-standing concern with the need for reform. The ecclesiastical Whigs of the 1830s, far more than they ever admitted or perhaps appreciated, were the inheritors of a well-established reforming legacy. Significantly, it was the Anglican churches in Wales and Ireland, whose first steps on the path of reform were more hesitant and less effectual, that were to be overwhelmed by religious and political change and eventually disestablished.

The central thrust of Victorian culture is often described as one of self-conscious 'improvement', a powerful engine of concern with the enhancement of the individual's spiritual, moral, and material prospects and the social environment in which they could be grounded. This is precisely the thrust that has been seen at work in this volume as early as the 1740s when indeed the term 'improvement' came to have the meaning that it was so long to retain. The results were diverse and might be expressed through people as varied as Methodist and other evangelical revivalists, campaigning philanthropists, political reformers, and opinion-formers in all kinds of cultural or intellectual activity. Characteristic Victorian 'virtues' – self-help, voluntary association, and public campaigning for progressive causes – all belong in this thoroughly eighteenth-century mentality. The difference was more one of scale than substance. The values for which many fought in one century were accepted by almost all in the next.

The *Weltpolitik* of nineteenth-century Britain certainly reflected new powers and responsibilities as well as changing international contexts. But it also inherited much that would have been familiar to eighteenth-century statesmen. Naval mastery continued to be the key to home defence and overseas expansion. The balance of power in Europe remained essential to British interests even if Britons were less frequently called upon to take up arms to secure it. And while imperial attitudes and ambitions fluctuated as they always had, the American Revolution, which had seemingly disrupted the progress of the British imperial juggernaut, did not turn out to be the great caesura in the history of the empire that many had expected it to be. In the nineteenth century there were no wars of independence against

English settler colonies nor did the territorial extension of empire cease, though pace and policy varied considerably from one era to another.

Of course, the institutions, formal and informal, of the islands changed hugely, as did the daily life of their inhabitants. But much that occurred in the nineteenth century belonged in a pattern of development that can be traced back ultimately to the late decades of the seventeenth century. It was then that a stable pattern of political evolution had been made possible, and then that commercial expansion on a quite new scale had propelled the insular economies into an era of sustained capitalist growth. The pace and patterns of economic growth continue to be debated but what is undeniable is the massive urbanization, the new 'mineral economy', and the relative displacement of labour from agriculture to manufacturing that marked the late eighteenth-century experience especially in England itself and in parts of Scotland and Wales, if not Ireland. The social and cultural consequences that flowed had a degree of continuity about them that made the British Isles uniquely dynamic and yet also uniquely stable, at any rate by comparison with other parts of Europe. The increasingly unified politics of the three kingdoms both reflected and reinforced these underlying transformations.

That is not to say that the enormous increase of British power and influence was inevitable, let alone untroubled. But today, a quarter of a millennium after these tendencies towards growth and stability settled into a discernibly consistent pattern, around the 1750s, the distinctive nature of what occurred has become ever clearer. The twentieth century was to witness, on the one hand, the decline of the power and influence and, on the other, the gradual dissolution of the old unities. All the evidence suggests that those tendencies will continue, throwing into ever higher relief the distinct and original character of the eighteenth-century experience.

Further reading

Introductory and general

Bartlett, T., *The Fall and Rise of the Irish Nation: The Catholic Question 1690–1830* (Dublin, 1992).

Bayly, C. A., *Imperial Meridian: The British Empire and the World 1780–1830* (London, 1989).

Black, J., *A System of Ambition: British Foreign Policy 1660–1793* (London, 1991).

—— and Porter, R. (eds.), *The Penguin Dictionary of Eighteenth-Century History* (London, 1996).

Brewer, J., *The Sinews of Power: War, Money and the English State, 1688–1783* (London, 1989).

Cannon, J., *Parliamentary Reform 1640–1832* (Cambridge, 1973).

Clark, J. D. C., *English Society 1688–1832* (Cambridge, 1985).

Colley, L., *Britons: Forging the Nation 1707–1837* (New Haven, 1992).

Devine T. M., *Exploring the Scottish Past: Themes in the History of Scottish Society* (East Linton, 1995).

—— *The Scottish Nation, 1700–2000* (London, 2000).

Dickinson, H. T., *Liberty and Property: Political Ideology in Eighteenth Century Britain* (London, 1977).

—— *The Politics of the People in Eighteenth-Century Britain* (London, 1994).

Dickson, D., *New Foundations: Ireland, 1660–1800*, 2nd edn. (Dublin, 2000).

Duffy, M. (ed.), *The English Satirical Print, 1600–1832* (6 vols. of illustrated commentaries on diverse themes; Cambridge, 1986).

Foster, R. F., *Modern Ireland, 1600–1972* (London, 1988).

Harris, T. (ed.), *Popular Culture in England c.1500–1850* (Basingstoke, 1995).

Hay, D., and Rogers, N., *Eighteenth-Century English Society: Shuttles and Swords* (Oxford, 1997).

Hill, J., *From Patriots to Unionists: Dublin Civic Politics and Irish Protestant Patriotism, c.1660–1840* (Oxford, 1997).

Hoppit, J., *The New Oxford History of England: A Land of Liberty? England 1689–1727* (Oxford, 2000).

Jenkins, G. H., *The Foundations of Modern Wales 1642–1780* (Oxford, 1987).

Langford, P., *The New Oxford History of England: A Polite and Commercial People: England 1727–1783* (Oxford, 1989).

—— *Public Life and the Propertied Englishman 1689–1798* (Oxford, 1991).

McDowell, R. B., *Ireland in the Age of Imperialism and Revolution, 1760–1800* (Oxford, 1979).

Marshall, P. J. (ed.), *The Oxford History of the British Empire: The Eighteenth Century* (Oxford, 1998).

Moody, T. W., and Vaughan, W. E. (eds.), *A New History of Ireland* iv. *Eighteenth-Century Ireland 1691–1800* (Oxford, 1986).

Morgan, P., *A New History of Wales: The Eighteenth Century Renaissance* (Llandybie, 1981).

Porter, R., *English Society in the Eighteenth Century* (London, 1982).

Prest, W. R., *Albion Ascendant: English History, 1660–1815* (Oxford, 1998).

Rogers, N., *Crowds, Culture and Politics in Georgian Britain* (Oxford, 1998).

Rule, J., *Albion's People: English Society 1714–1815* (London, 1988).

Shaw, J. S., *The Political History of Eighteenth-Century Scotland* (Basingstoke, 1999).

Smout, T. C., *The History of the Scottish People 1560–1830* (London, 1969).

Stevenson, J., *Popular Disturbances in England 1700–1832* 2nd edn. (London, 1992).

Contested kingdoms, 1688–1756

Colley, L., *In Defiance of Oligarchy: The Tory Party 1714–60* (Cambridge, 1982).

Connolly, S. J., *Religion, Law and Power: The Making of Protestant Ireland 1660–1760* (Oxford, 1992).

Harris, T., *Politics under the Later Stuarts: Party Conflict in a Divided Society 1660–1715* (Harlow, 1993).

Hill, B.W., *Sir Robert Walpole* (London, 1989).

Holmes, G., *British Politics in the Age of Anne*, 2nd edn. (London, 1987).

Horwitz, H., *Parliament, Policy and Politics in the Reign of William III* (Manchester, 1977).

Jones, C. (ed.), *Britain in the First Age of Party 1680–1750: Essays Presented to Geoffrey Holmes* (London, 1987).

Kenyon, J. P., *Revolution Principles: The Politics of Party 1689–1720* (Cambridge, 1977).

Lenman, B., *The Jacobite Risings in Britain, 1689–1746* (London, 1980).

McNally, P., *Parties, Patriots and Undertakers: Parliamentary Politics in Early Hanoverian Ireland* (Dublin, 1997).

Murdoch, A., *The People Above: Politics and Administration in Mid-Eighteenth-Century Scotland* (Edinburgh, 1980).

Owen, J. B., *The Rise of the Pelhams* (London, 1957).

Riley, P. W. J., *The Union of England and Scotland* (Manchester, 1978).

Rogers, N., *Whigs and Cities: Popular Politics in the Age of Walpole and Pitt* (Oxford, 1989).

Shaw, J. S., *The Management of Scottish Society 1707–64: Power, Nobles, Lawyers, Edinburgh Agents and English Influences* (London, 1983).

Speck, W. A., *The Butcher: The Duke of Cumberland and the Suppression of the 45* (Oxford, 1982).

Thompson, E. P., *Whigs and Hunters: The Origin of the Black Act* (London, 1975)

Enlightenment and faith

Bossy, J., *The English Catholic Community 1570–1850* (Oxford, 1976).

Brown, C. G., *Religion and Society in Scotland since 1707* (Edinburgh, 1997).

Connolly, S. J., *Religion, Law and Power: The Making of Protestant Ireland 1660–1760* (Oxford, 1992).

Corish, P., *The Irish Catholic Experience* (Dublin, 1985).

Gilbert, A. D., *Religion and Society in Industrial England* (London, 1976).

Haakonssen, K. (ed.), *Enlightenment and Religion: Rational Dissent in Eighteenth-Century Britain* (Cambridge, 1996).

Hempton, D., *Religion and Political Culture in Britain and Ireland* (Cambridge, 1996).

Jacob, M. C., *The Radical Enlightenment: Pantheists, Freemasons and Republicans* (London, 1981).

Livingstone, D. N, and Withers, C. W. J. (eds.), *Geography and Enlightenment* (Chicago, 1999).

Outram, D., *The Enlightenment* (Cambridge, 1995).

Porter, R., *Enlightenment: Britain and the Creation of the Modern World* (London, 2000).

—— and Teich, M., *The Enlightenment in National Context* (Cambridge, 1981).

Rack, H. D., *Reasonable Enthusiast: John Wesley and the Rise of Methodism* (London, 1989).

Rudwick, M. J. S., *Scenes from Deep Time* (Chicago, 1992).

Sher, R. B., *Church and University in the Scottish Enlightenment* (Princeton, 1985).

Walsh, J., Haydon, C., and Taylor, S., *The Church of England c.1689–c.1833: From Toleration to Tractarianism* (Cambridge, 1993).

Ward, W. R., *Christianity under the Ancien Régime 1648–1789* (Cambridge, 1999).

Watts, M. R., *The Dissenters*, ii. *The Expansion of Evangelical Nonconformity* (Oxford, 1995).

Governing diverse societies

Andrew, D., *Philanthropy and Police: London Charity in the Eighteenth-Century* (Princeton, 1989).

Beattie, J. M., *Crime and the Courts in England 1660–1800* (Oxford, 1986).

Brewer, J., and Styles, J. (eds.), *An Ungovernable People: The English and their Law in the Seventeenth and Eighteenth Centuries* (London, 1980).

Charlesworth, A., (ed.), *An Atlas of Rural Protest in Britain 1548–1900* (London, 1983).

—— et al., *An Atlas of Industrial Protest in Britain 1750–1990* (Basingstoke, 1996).

Crossman, V., *Local Government in Nineteenth-Century Ireland* (Belfast, 1994).

Davison, L., et al., *Stilling the Grumbling Hive: The Response to Social and Economic Problems in England 1689–1750* (Stroud, 1992).

Devine, T., *Clanship to Crofters' War: The Social Transformation of the Scottish Highlands* (Manchester, 1994).

Eden, F. M., *The State of the Poor in England and Wales* (first pub. 1797).

Garnham, N., *The Courts, Crime and the Criminal Law in Ireland 1692–1760* (Blackrock, 1996).

Hay, D., et al., *Albion's Fatal Tree: Crime and Society in Eighteenth-Century England* (London, 1975).

Howard, John, *The State of the Prisons in England and Wales* (first pub. London, 1777).

Howell, D., *The Rural Poor in Eighteenth-Century Wales* (Cardiff, 2000).

Innes, J., 'The domestic face of the military-fiscal state', in L. Stone (ed.), *An Imperial State at War: Britain from 1689 to 1815* (London, 1994).

—— 'The state and the poor: Eighteenth-century England in European perspective', in J. Brewer and E. Hellmuth (eds.), *Rethinking Leviathan: The Eighteenth-Century State in Britain and Germany* (Oxford, 1999).

—— 'What would a "three kingdoms" approach to the study of eighteenth-century social policy entail?', in S. Connolly (ed.), *Kingdoms United? Great Britain and Ireland since 1500, Integration and Diversity* (Dublin, 1999).

Innes, J. and Rogers, N., 'Urban government 1700–1840', in P. Clark (ed.), *The Cambridge Urban History of Britain 1550–1840* (Cambridge, 2000).

Jenkins, P., *The Making of a Ruling Class: The Glamorgan Gentry 1640–1790* (Cambridge, 1983).

Jones, M. G., *The Charity School Movement: A Study of Eighteenth-Century Puritanism in Action* (Cambridge, 1938).

Macinnes, A., *Clanship, Commerce and the House of Stuart 1603–1789* (East Linton, 1996).

Malcolm, E., in Donnelly, J. S., and Miller, K. A. (eds.), *Irish Popular Culture 1650–1850* (Dublin, 1998).

Midgley, C., *Women against Slavery: The British Campaigns 1780–1870* (London, 1992).

Mitchison, R., *The Old Poor Law in Scotland: The Experience of Poverty 1574–1845* (Edinburgh, 2000).

Palmer, S., *Police and Protest in England and Ireland 1780–1850* (Cambridge, 1988).

Post, J. D., *Food Shortage, Climatic Variability and Epidemic Disease in Industrial Europe: The Mortality Peak in the Early 1740s* (Ithaca, NY, 1985).

Sinclair, Sir John, *Statistical Account of Scotland* (first pub. 1791–9).

Smith, A. E., *Colonists in Bondage: White Servitude and Convict Labour in America 1607–1776* (Chapel Hill, NC, 1947).

Thompson, E. P., 'The moral economy of the English crowd in the eighteenth century', in *Customs in Common* (London, 1991).

Walker, D. M., *A Legal History of Scotland* v. *The Eighteenth Century* (Edinburgh, 1998).

Webb, S., and Webb, B., *English Local Government from the Revolution to the Municipal Corporations Act* (9 vols.; London, 1906–29).

Whetstone, A., *Scottish County Government in the Eighteenth and Nineteenth Centuries* (Edinburgh, 1981).

The wealth of the nation

Albert, W., *The Turnpike Road System in England, 1663–1840* (Cambridge, 1972).

Berg, M., *The Age of Manufactures: Industry, Innovation and Work in Britain, 1700–1820*, 2nd edn. (London, 1994).

Brewer, J., and Porter, R. (eds.), *Consumption and the World of Goods* (London, 1993).

Crafts, N. F. R., *British Economic Growth during the Industrial Revolution* (Oxford, 1985).

Crouzet, F., *The First Industrialists* (Cambridge, 1985).

Daunton, M. J., *Poverty and Progress: An Economic and Social History of Britain, 1700–1850* (Oxford, 1995).

Dickson, P. G. M., *The Financial Revolution in England: A Study in the Development of Public Credit, 1688–1756* (London, 1967).

Hoppit, J., *Risk and Failure in English Business, 1700–1800* (Cambridge, 1987).

Hudson, P., *The Genesis of Industrial Capital: A Study of the West Riding Wool Textile Industry, c.1750–1850* (Cambridge, 1986).

—— *The Industrial Revolution* (Oxford, 1992).

Mathias, P., and O'Brien, P., 'Taxation in Britain and France, 1715–1810. A comparison of the social and economic incidence of taxes collected for the central governments', *Journal of European Economic History*, 5 (1976).

Muldrew, C., *The Economy of Obligation: The Culture of Credit and Social Relations in Early Modern England* (Basingstoke, 1998).

Neeson, J., *Commons: Common Right, Enclosure and Social Change in England, 1700–1820* (Cambridge, 1993).

O'Grada, C., *Ireland: A New Economic History, 1780–1939* (Oxford, 1994).

Overton, M., *Agricultural Revolution in England: The Transformation of the Agrarian Economy, 1500–1850* (Cambridge, 1996).

Pressnell, L. S., *Country Banking in the Industrial Revolution* (Oxford, 1956).

Richards, E., *A History of the Highland Clearances: Agrarian Transformation and the Evictions* (2 vols.; London, 1982–5).

Rule, J., *The Vital Century: England's Developing Economy 1714–1815* (London, 1992).

Snell, K. D. M., *Annals of the Labouring Poor: Social Change and Agrarian England, 1660–1900* (Cambridge, 1985).

Wrigley, E. A., *Continuity, Chance and Change: The Character of the Industrial Revolution in England* (Cambridge, 1988).

—— *People, Cities and Wealth: The Transformation of Traditional Society* (Oxford, 1987).

—— and Schofield, R., *The Population History of England, 1541–1871: A Reconstruction* (London, 1981).

The culture of improvement

Bindman, D., *Hogarth* (London, 1981).

Borsay, P., *The English Urban Renaissance: Culture and Society in the Provincial Town 1660–1770* (Oxford, 1989).

Brewer, J., *The Pleasures of the Imagination: English Culture in the Eighteenth Century* (London, 1997).

Cannon, J., *Aristocratic Century: The Peerage of Eighteenth-Century England* (Cambridge, 1984).

Carter, P., *Men and the Emergence of Polite Society, Britain 1660–1800* (Harlow, 2001).

Chitnis, A. C., *The Scottish Enlightenment: A Social History* (London, 1976).

Christie, C., *The British Country House in the Eighteenth Century* (Manchester, 2000).

Clark, P., *British Clubs and Societies 1580–1880: The Origins of an Associational World* (Oxford, 2000).

—— (ed.), *The Cambridge Urban History of Britain*, ii. *1540–1840* (Cambridge, 2000).

Corfield, P. J., *The Impact of English Towns, 1700–1800* (Oxford, 1982).

Hankins, T. L., *Science in the Enlightenment* (Cambridge, 1985).

Hutton, R., *The Stations of the Sun: A History of the Ritual Year in Britain* (Oxford, 1996).

Langford, P., *Englishness Identified: Manners and Character 1650–1850* (Oxford, 2000).

Malcolmson, R.W., *Popular Recreations in English Society 1700–1850* (Cambridge, 1973).

Murdoch, A., *British History 1660–1832: National Identity and Local Culture* (Basingstoke, 1998).

Pittock, M. G. H., *Inventing and Resisting Britain: Cultural Identities in Britain and Ireland 1685–1789* (Basingstoke, 1997).

Porter, R., and Roberts, M. M. (eds.), *Pleasure in the Eighteenth Century* (Basingstoke, 1996).

Shoemaker, R., *Gender in English Society 1650–1850: The Emergence of Separate Spheres?* (Harlow, 1998).

Spadafora, D., *The Idea of Progress in Eighteenth-Century Britain* (New Haven and London, 1990).

Sweet, R., *The English Town 1680–1840: Government, Society and Culture* (London, 1999).

Vickery, A., *The Gentleman's Daughter: Women's Lives in Georgian England* (New Haven, 1998).

Williamson, T., *Polite Landscapes: Gardens and Society in Eighteenth-Century England* (Stroud, 1995).

Wilson, R., and Mackley, A., *Creating Paradise: The Building of the English Country House 1660–1800* (London, 2000).

Contested empires, 1756–1815

Baugh, D. A., 'Maritime strength and Atlantic commerce: The uses of "a grand marine empire" ', in L. Stone (ed.), *An Imperial State at War: Britain from 1689 to 1815* (London, 1994).

Black, J., *America or Europe? British Foreign Policy, 1739–63* (London, 1998).

—— *British Foreign Policy in an Age of Revolutions 1783–1793* (Cambridge, 1994).

Bowen, H. V., *Revenue and Reform: The Indian Problem in British Politics, 1757–1773* (Cambridge, 1991).

Christie, I. R., *Stress and Stability in Late Eighteenth-Century Britain: Reflections on the British Avoidance of Revolution* (Oxford, 1984).

—— and Labaree, B. W., *Empire or Independence, 1760–1776* (Oxford, 1976).

Conway, S., *The War of American Independence 1775–1783* (London, 1995).

Cookson, J. E., *The British Armed Nation 1793–1815* (Oxford, 1997).

Dickinson, H. T. (ed.), *Britain and the American Revolution* (London, 1998).

—— (ed.), *Britain and the French Revolution 1789–1815* (London, 1989).

Duffy, M., *The Younger Pitt* (London, 2000).

Elliott, M., *Partners in Revolution: The United Irishmen and France* (Oxford, 1982).

Emsley, C., *British Society and the French Wars 1793–1815* (London, 1979).

Harling, P., *The Waning of 'Old Corruption': The Politics of Economical Reform in Britain, 1779–1846* (Oxford, 1996).

Mackesy, P., *The War for America, 1775–1783* (London, 1964).

Marshall, P. J., *Problems of Empire: Britain and India, 1757–1813* (London, 1968).

Middleton, R., *The Bells of Victory: The Pitt-Newcastle Ministry and the Conduct of the Seven Years War, 1757–1762* (Cambridge, 1985).

Peters, M., *The Elder Pitt* (London, 1998).

Philp, M. (ed.), *The French Revolution and British Popular Politics* (Cambridge, 1991).

Rodger, N. A. M., 'The continental commitment in the eighteenth century', in L. Freedman, P. Hayes, and R. O'Neill (eds.), *War, Strategy and International Politics: Essays in Honour of Sir Michael Howard,* (Oxford, 1992).

Scott, H. M., *British Foreign Policy in the Age of the American Revolution* (Oxford, 1990).

Sherwig, J. M., *Guineas and Gunpowder: British Foreign Aid in the Wars with France 1793–1815* (Cambridge, Mass., 1969).

Spence, P., *The Birth of Romantic Radicalism: War, Popular Politics and English Radical Reformism, 1800–1815* (Aldershot, 1996).

Thomas, P. D. G., *John Wilkes: A Friend to Liberty* (Oxford, 1996).

Wilson, K., *The Sense of the People: Politics, Culture and Imperialism in England, 1715–1785* (Cambridge, 1995).

Chronology

1703 Act of Security and Act anent Peace and War passed at Edinburgh

William King appointed archbishop of Dublin

1704 Battle of Blenheim; the 'Tack' controversy; Queensberry removed as result of 'Scotch Plot'; Squadrone experiment of political management in Scotland fails; sacramental test imposed in Ireland

1705 Whig influence in English ministry; Aliens Act passed at Westminster; restoration of Argyll and Queensberry in Scotland

Theatre built at Bath; Richard Nash arrives at Bath, soon to become Master of Ceremonies

1706 Act for Protection of Honest Bankrupts

1707 Union of England and Scotland

Edward Lhuyd, *Archaeologia Britannica*, first volume

1708 Whig ministry; Jacobite invasion of Scotland attempted; Scottish privy council abolished

United East India Company formed

1709 Wharton, Viceroy of Ireland, fails to repeal sacramental test in Dublin

Richard Steele, *The Tatler* (to 1711)

Harrison's Assembly Rooms and Walks, Bath

Abraham Darby smelts iron with coke

Naturalisation Act passed at Westminster; patent for SPCK in Scotland

1710 Impeachment of Henry Sacheverell; fall of Godolphin; Tory landslide at general election leads to Harley ministry

George Frederick Handel's first visit to London

Sun Fire formed

1711 MPs Qualifications Act

Joseph Addison and Richard Steele, *The Spectator* (to 1712)

Handel's *Rinaldo*, first Italian opera composed for London

Occasional Conformity Act

1712 Marlborough replaced as Captain General by Ormond

Samuel Clarke, *The Scripture Doctrine of the Trinity*; Jonathan Swift, *Conduct of the Allies*

Thomas Newcomen's steam engine

Patronage Act; repeal of Naturalisation Act; last witchcraft trial

1713 Peace of Utrecht ending War of Spanish Succession; failure of motion to repeal Act of Union; Irish parliament of 1713 ends in failure

1714 Death of Queen Anne and succession of George I

Whig purge of government and local offices

Schism Act

1715 General elections in Britain and Ireland: Tory defeat; Riot Act; Jacobite rising in Scotland; Whig split in Ireland between Brodrick and Conolly factions

Jonathan Richardson, *An Essay on the Theory of Painting*

Society of Ancient Britons founded

First enclosed dock at Liverpool

1716 Whig Schism in England: Walpole and Townshend in opposition; Septennial Act; Argyll loses office in Scotland

Hanover Square, London, begun

Grand Lodge of Freemasons, London; Convocation ceases to meet; Bangorian controversy in Church of England

1717 Dispute between British and Irish House of Lords over appellate jurisdiction

Isaac Newton, *Opticks*

1718 Isaac Carter establishes Welsh language press at Trerhedyn (Ceredigion)

Inoculation for smallpox introduced

1719 War with Spain; Jacobite invasion in Scotland; repeal of Occasional Conformity and Schism Acts; Peerage Bill defeated; Bolton in Ireland fails to repeal sacramental test

1720 Declaratory Act affirming parliamentary supremacy over Ireland; Walpole and Townshend resume office; death of Stanhope

Westminster Hospital (first subscription hospital) founded

Cavendish Square, London, begun

South Sea Bubble; Royal Exchange Insurance for marine insurance

1721 Nicholas Thomas establishes Welsh language press at Carmarthen

Calico Act banning wearing of calico; The Honourable Society for Improvement in the Knowledge of Agriculture

1722 Whig majority at general election; death of Sunderland; Walpole prime minister; exposure of Atterbury Plot

1723 Prosecution and exile of Bishop Atterbury; Wood's Halfpence controversy in Ireland

English Act for construction of parish workhouses

1724 Daniel Defoe, *A Tour through the Whole Island of Great Britain* (to 1726); Jonathan Swift, *Drapier's Letters*

'Levellers revolt' against enclosure in south-west Scotland

1725   Carteret Lord-Lieutenant of Ireland; Walpole has Pulteney dismissed; Conolly installed as sole 'undertaker' in Ireland; Roxburgh replaced by Argyll as principal Scottish manager

Henry Bourne, *Antiquitates Vulgares*

Grosvenor Square, London, begun

First improvement commission in London; Malt Tax riots in Scotland

1726   Jonathan Swift, *Gulliver's Travels*; *Craftsman* commences

1727   Death of George I and accession of George II; Walpole briefly gives way to Wilmington before being restored to power

Royal Bank of Scotland formed

Indemnity Act

1728   Alexander Pope, *The Dunciad*; John Gay, *Beggar's Opera*

Queen Square, Bath, begun

1729   Parliament House (Edward Lovett Pearce), Dublin, begun

Wesley's Holy Club begins meeting

1730   Carteret retires as Irish Viceroy; fall of Townshend

Matthew Tindal, *Christianity as Old as the Creation*

Lindsey's Assembly Rooms (John Wood, elder), Bath, opened

1731   Treaty of Vienna with Austria; Dorset, Lord-Lieutenant of Ireland, fails to repeal sacramental test

Griffith Jones launches circulating school scheme, Wales

Dublin Society founded

1732   Act requiring property qualification for English and Welsh county JPs

Burlington's Assembly Rooms, York, opened; Vauxhall Gardens, London, opened

Kay's Flying Shuttle

Protestant Dissenting Deputies formed

1733   Excise crisis resulting in Walpole's withdrawal of bill; Henry Boyle elected Speaker of Irish House of Commons

George Cheyne, *The English Malady*

Secession Church in Scotland formed; first Charter Schools in Ireland

1734   Walpole's majority reduced at general election

Society of Dilettanti founded

1735   Dorset again fails to repeal sacramental test in Ireland; Boyle firmly established as 'undertaker' in Ireland

William Hogarth, *Rake's Progress*

Evangelical conversion of Howel Harris and Daniel Rowland

1736   Porteous riots in Edinburgh

William Warburton, *Alliance between Church and State*

Witchcraft Act abolishing offence

1737   Frederick Prince of Wales forms Leicester House Opposition; in Ireland Brabazon Ponsonby threatens dominance of Boyle

Theatre Licensing Act

Salisbury, first provincial improvement commission

1738   George Frederick Handel, *Saul*

John Wesley's 'heart-warming' experience at Aldersgate Street in London

1739   Convention of Pardo; War of 'Jenkins's Ear' with Spain; Admiral Vernon's victory at Porto Bello; Argyll breaks with Walpole ministry

David Hume, *A Treatise of Human Nature*

Foundling Hospital, London, founded; Gaming Act

1740   War of the Austrian Succession

Samuel Richardson, *Pamela*; Richard Challoner, *Garden of the Soul*; Thomas Arne, *Rule Britannia*

Inverary laid out; Hogarth's portrait of Thomas Coram

London Hospital founded

Horse-Racing Act

Hard winter of 1740–1

1741   Failure of attack on Cartagena

George Frederick Handel, *Messiah*

Music Hall (Richard Castle), Fishamble Street Dublin, opened

Harvest shortages: famine in Ireland, grain riots in England and Scotland; new legislation against sheep stealing

1742   Fall of Walpole; Carteret, Secretary of State, sends army to assist Austria

Henry Fielding, *Joseph Andrews*; Batty Langley, *Ancient Architecture Restored and Improved*

Cambuslang revival

1743   Battle of Dettingen; Treaty of Worms; Henry Pelham First Lord of the Treasury; Pitt's attack on 'Hanoverian' policy; death of Argyll, succeeded by his brother Islay

1744   Battle of Toulon and declaration of war with France; Carteret (now Granville) forced to resign

1745   'Young Pretender' lands in Scotland, takes Edinburgh, wins Battle of Prestonpans

Lying-in Hospital (Bartholomew Mosse), Dublin, founded

1746   Jacobites retreat from Derby, defeated at Culloden

1747 Anson and Hawke naval victories; Peace of Aix-la-Chapelle; George Stone, archbishop of Armagh, begins to undermine Boyle
Samuel Richardson, *Clarissa*; William Hogarth, *Industry and Idleness*; Samuel Johnson, *Plan of a Dictionary of the English Language*
Horace Walpole acquires Strawberry Hill
Scottish heritable jurisdictions abolished

1748 David Hume, *Enquiry Concerning Human Understanding*

1749 Henry Fielding, *Tom Jones*
Embezzlement criminalized

1750 Orchard Street Theatre (George Dance), Bath, opened

1751 Death of Frederick Prince of Wales
William Hogarth, *Beer Street, Gin Lane*
Lancelot Brown sets up in London as independent garden designer; Adam Smith appointed Professor of Logic, and William Cullen Professor of Medicine, Glasgow; Honourable Society of Cymmrodorion founded
Calendar Act; Gin Act; death of Philip Doddridge

1752 Murder Act; Bawdy House Act

1753 'Money Bill' dispute in Dublin; Boyle joins 'patriot' opposition and appeals to public opinion
William Hogarth, *The Analysis of Beauty*
Jewish Naturalisation Act; Marriage Act; Apostolicum Ministerium of Benedict XIV organizing Catholic Church in England

1754 Franco-British hostilities in Ohio valley; death of Henry Pelham; duke of Newcastle prime minister
David Hume, *History of England*
King's Circus, Bath, begun; Select Society, Edinburgh, founded; Society for the Encouragement of Arts, Manufactures, and Commerce founded; Sankey Navigation begun
Repeal of Jewish Naturalisation Act

1755 Samuel Johnson, *Dictionary of the English Language*

1756 Seven Years War with France; loss of Minorca leads to resignation of Newcastle and Pitt-Devonshire ministry
Joseph Black expounds existence of 'fixed air', appointed Professor of Anatomy, Glasgow
Scottish magistrates given same liquor licensing powers as English

1757 Pitt–Newcastle ministry; Militia Act riots; East India Company victory at battle of Plassey
Wide Street Commission, Dublin; Rotunda Hospital (Richard Castle), Dublin, opened

1758 Aberdeen Philosophical Society founded
Bridgewater's canal begun

1759 'Year of Victories': Guadeloupe, Minden, Goree, Quebec, Lagos, Quiberon Bay
Laurence Sterne, *Tristram Shandy*
Josiah Wedgwood's Burslem pottery

1760 Conquest of Canada completed; Battle of Wandewash and capture of Pondicherry, destroying French power in India; death of George II and accession of George III
Society of Artists of Great Britain founded
Magistracy opened to Tory families again

1761 Resignation of Elder Pitt
Jean-Jacques Rousseau, *Julie, ou La Nouvelle Héloise*
Bridgewater Canal opened
Relief Church in Scotland formed

1762 War with Spain; capture of Havana and Manila; Newcastle replaced by earl of Bute as prime minister
James Macpherson (Ossian), *Fingal*
The Poker Club, Edinburgh, founded; Merrion Square, Dublin, begun
Westminster Paving Commission

1763 Peace of Paris; Bute gives way to George Grenville as prime minister; John Wilkes and general warrants case; cider tax

1764 Wilkes expelled from parliament
Horace Walpole, *The Castle of Otranto*
Rotunda (John Ensor), Dublin, begun

1765 Grant of 'diwanni' of Bengal to East India Company; Grenville replaced by marquess of Rockingham; Stamp Act and American non-importation campaign
'Whiteboy' disturbances in Ireland

1766 Repeal of Stamp Act; Rockingham replaced by earl of Chatham (formerly Pitt); grain shortages and riots
Irish legislation for county infirmaries

1767 Townshend duties provoke American protests
James Craig's plan for New Town, Edinburgh, chosen; Royal Crescent, Bath, begun

1768 Chatham succeeded by duke of Grafton; Middlesex election controversy
Laurence Sterne, *A Sentimental Journey*
Royal Academy founded; Adelphi (Robert Adam), London, begun
Lady Huntingdon's seminary at Trefeca in Wales

1769   Wilkesite petitioning movement for reform

Joshua Reynolds, *Discourses*

Cook's first voyage to Pacific

Patents for Hargreave's spinning jenny, Watt's separate condenser, Arkwright's water frame; Wedgwood's Etruria factory

1770   Grafton succeeded by Lord North; Falklands Islands crisis; Grenville's Elections Act

Edmund Burke, *Thoughts on the Cause of the Present Discontents*; Oliver Goldsmith, *The Deserted Village*

Feathers Tavern petition

1771   Wilkesite challenge to parliamentary control of publication of debates; New Shoreham Disfranchisement Act

Henry Mackenzie, *The Man of Feeling*; Tobias Smollett, *Humphry Clinker*

Gwyneddigion founded; Upper Assembly Rooms (John Wood younger), Bath, opened

1772   Pantheon (James Wyatt), London, opened

Grain shortage and riots: legislation against forestalling repealed; Staffordshire and Worcestershire canals linked

1773   East India Regulating Act; Tea Act and Boston Tea Party in protest

Oliver Goldsmith, *She Stoops to Conquer*

New Stock Exchange; Spitalfields Act regulating silkweavers' employment

Society of Jesus dissolved by Clement XIV

1774   Coercive or 'Intolerable' Acts and Quebec Act

Letters Written by the Earl of Chesterfield to His Son

Hanover Square Rooms, London, opened; Joseph Priestley discovers 'dephlogisticated air'

A. M. Toplady's hymn 'Rock of Ages, Cleft for Me'

1775   Hostilities in America: Lexington and Concord

Richard Brinsley Sheridan, *The Rivals*

Matthew Boulton and James Watt partnership

1776   American Declaration of Independence

Edward Gibbon, *Decline and Fall of the Roman Empire*; Oliver Goldsmith, *The Vicar of Wakefield*; Adam Smith, *Wealth of Nations*; Tom Paine, *Common Sense*

1777   Philadelphia captured but surrender of Burgoyne at Saratoga

Richard Brinsley Sheridan, *The School for Scandal*; John Howard, *State of the Prisons in England and Wales*

1778   War with France
Highland Society founded in London (1784 in Edinburgh)
Roman Catholic Relief Act; Societas Evangelica formed

1779   War with Spain; invasion threat in Channel; Wyvill's reform movement; Irish agitation for commercial reform and legislative independence
Dissenters' Relief Act

1780   Dunning's Resolution against crown influence; Gordon riots; war with Holland
Collection of Hymns for Methodist use
Westport (Co. Mayo), laid out
Samuel Compton's mule for spinning cotton

1781   Cornwallis's surrender at Yorktown
Henry Cavendish discovers water is a compound, not an element
Watt's patent for sun and planet gear

1782   Fall of North ministry; Rockingham ministry March–July, succeeded by earl of Shelburne; Battle of the Saints saves Jamaica; Irish legislative autonomy granted; creation of distinct Home Office and Foreign Office; economical reform legislation
Joseph Priestley, *History of the Corruptions of Christianity*

1783   Peace of Versailles and American independence; Fox–North Coalition replaces Shelburne but is dismissed by the king and replaced by the Younger Pitt
Royal Society of Edinburgh founded
Henry Cort's patent for puddling iron
First Sunday school opened by Robert Raikes in Gloucester; hard winter and grain shortages: dearth in Highlands relieved from government stores

1784   Pitt's India Act
Arthur Young commences *Annals of Agriculture*
New Assembly Rooms (Richard Johnston), Dublin, begun
First mail coach London to Bristol; Watt's patent for parallel motion
John Wesley ordains bishops for American Methodism

1785   Pitt's parliamentary reform proposals defeated
Royal Irish Academy founded
Pitt's Irish Commercial Propositions fail

1786   Sinking Fund to pay off National Debt established
Richard Payne Knight, *An Account of the Remains of the Worship of Priapus*
Cartwright's power loom patented
First Sabbath school in Scotland at Aberdeen

1787   Eden Commercial Treaty with France; Anglo-French confrontation over Holland; impeachment of Warren Hastings

Sarah Trimmer, *Oeconomy of Charity*

Proclamation against Vice Society founded; Irish Act to provide county police forces; public anti-slavery campaign gets underway

Dissenting campaigns for repeal of Test and Corporation Acts (to 1790)

1788   George III's illness and resulting regency crisis

Attempts to suppress Stamford bull-running begin

1789   William Blake, *Songs of Innocence*; Iolo Morganwg, first publication of fabricated Welsh medieval poems; modern form of eisteddfod emerges

1790   Nootka Sound crisis with Spain

Edmund Burke, *Reflections on the Revolution in France;* William Blake, *Marriage of Heaven and Hell*

1791   Canada Act; Church and King riots in Birmingham; Society of United Irishmen, Belfast

Tom Paine, *Rights of Man;* John Sinclair, *Statistical Account of Scotland*

Catholic Relief Act

1792   Catholic Relief Act, Ireland

Mary Wollstonecraft, *Vindication of the Rights of Women*

Cisalpine Club formed; Baptist Missionary Society formed

1793   War with Revolutionary France; Irish militia established despite protests; Irish Catholics enfranchised

Board of Agriculture founded, first president Sir John Sinclair

1794   First call for home defence volunteers; treason trials; Portland Whigs join government

William Blake, *Songs of Experience;* Richard Payne Knight, *The Landscape, A Didactic Poem*

New Drury Lane Theatre (Henry Holland), opened

1795   War with Holland; Rebellion in West Indian colonies; Orange Order founded

Thomas Paine, *Age of Reason*

Harvest shortages and riots

London Missionary Society formed; Methodist Plan of Pacification

1796   War with Spain; militia expansion in England results in riots; French invasion of Ireland attempted

Society for Bettering the Condition of the Poor founded in London

1797   Mutiny at Spithead and the Nore; Scottish militia established despite riots; victories of St Vincent (against Spain) and Camperdown (against Holland)

William Wilberforce, *Practical View*

Bank of England cash payments suspended

Methodist New Connexion founded

1798   Irish Rebellion; Home defence volunteers raised; Nelson's victory at the Nile

T. R. Malthus, *Essay on Population*; William Wordsworth and Samuel Coleridge, *Lyrical Ballads*

1799   Income tax introduced; British defeat of Mysore and control of southern India

West India Dock Act; Combination Act

Church Missionary Society formed

1800   Malta captured; Act for Union of Britain and Ireland

Food riots; Richard Trevithick's high-pressure steam engine

1801   Union of Britain and Ireland implemented; resignation of Pitt over Catholic Emancipation; Henry Addington's ministry; Battle of Copenhagen

First census

1802   Peace of Amiens

1803   War with Napoleonic France; new volunteer forces raised; Maratha War 1803–5 extends British power in central India

Warehousing Act; East India Dock Act

John Milner appointed Vicar Apostolic of Midland District

1804   Pitt returns as prime minister; war with Spain

William Parkinson, *Organic Remains of a Former World*

British and Foreign Bible Society formed

1805   Battle of Trafalgar

William Wordsworth, *The Prelude*

Beaufort Square Theatre, Bath, opened

Irish legislation for establishing dispensaries

1806   Death of Pitt; Ministry of 'All the Talents'; conquest of Cape of Good Hope; Continental System embargo on British exports

1807   Slave trade abolished; fall of 'Talents' over Catholic Emancipation; duke of Portland's ministry; British defeat at Buenos Aires

Geological Society of London

1808   British troops in Iberian Peninsula

Catholic Board formed

1809   Walcheren expedition fails; collapse of Portland ministry; Spencer Perceval prime minister; Curwen's Act against sale of seats in parliament

1810   London riots in support of Sir Francis Burdett; George III's illness

First Scottish joint-stock bank

1811   Regency of Prince of Wales

Drury Lane Theatre destroyed by fire and rebuilt

Luddite machine-breaking riots in Midlands and North begin; Glasgow weavers' riots

National Society for Education of the Poor formed; Primitive Methodist Connexion formed

1812   Perceval assassinated, succeeded by earl of Liverpool; war with USA

Gas Light and Coke Company formed in London

Act of Toleration

1813   American invasion of Canada repulsed; Wellington's victory at Vittoria

East India Company monopoly in Indian trade abolished

First Methodist Missionary Society formed

1814   Defeat of Napoleon; British burn Washington but reverses elsewhere lead to Peace Treaty of Ghent with USA

Apprenticeship clauses of Elizabethan Statute of Artificers repealed

Thomas Chalmers begins urban parochial experiment in Glasgow

1815   Return of Napoleon: 'Hundred Days' war; Battle of Waterloo; Peace Treaty of Vienna

Maps

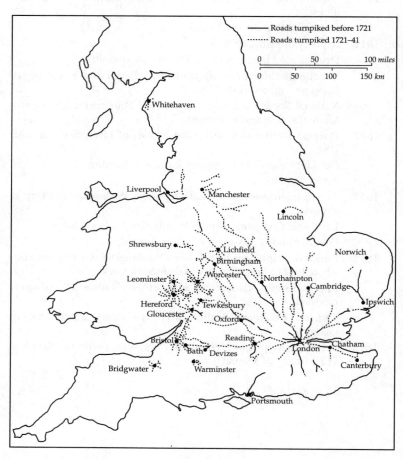

Map 1 The turnpike road network in 1741

Map 2 The turnpike road network in 1770

Map 3 The canal system in the early nineteenth century

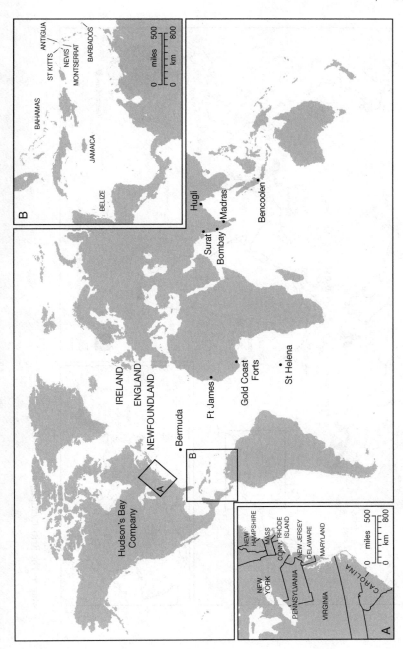

Map 4 England's empire in 1689

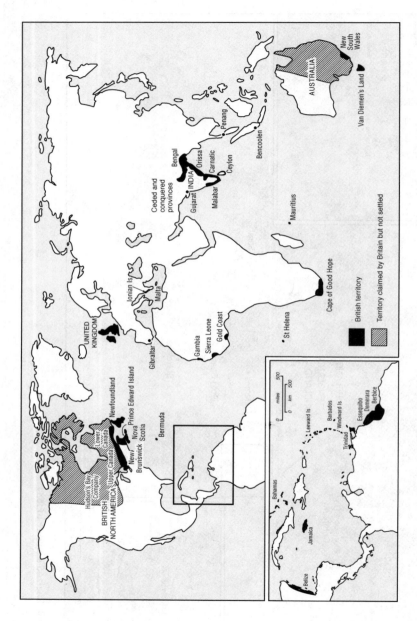

Map 5 The British empire in 1815

Index